THE PARISH CHURCHES
OF LEICESTERSHIRE
Volume 2
Le - W

THE PARISH CHURCHES OF LEICESTERSHIRE

Volume 2
Le - W

ANDREW SWIFT

First published 2013 by Velox Books
208 Milligan Road, Aylestone. Leicester LE2 8FD

Copyright © Andrew Swift 2013

Text, design, photographs and illustrations © Andrew Swift 2013

Photographs: Cover, Saltby St Peter
Frontispiece, Melton Mowbray St Mary
This page, Twycross St James

ISBN 978-0-9575701-1-5

Printed and bound in Great Britain by Digital Print Media Limited, St Ives, Cambridgeshire

INTRODUCTION TO VOLUME TWO

In an ideal world this work on Leicestershire's parish churches would have appeared in a single volume, but the constraints of printing practicalities dictated that a split into two volumes was desirable. The two volumes are designed to run straight on alphabetically by settlement name, the first volume covering churches A – La and the second, Le – W. Thus, those who preferred to obtain volume two before volume one, will need to refer to volume one for the customary foreword, preface and introduction. However, they will find at the end of this volume the usual bibliography and references.

One thought that has arisen in my mind since penning the introduction in volume one is the rapidly changing internal appearance of our parish churches, particularly the older and medieval buildings. Now that we are well on into a new millennium it has become increasingly unacceptable to congregations, particularly newcomers to the church family, to sit on hard benches in draughty, cold buildings that lack even basic amenities like toilets and some form of kitchen facility. An area where people can circulate, sit in comfort and have a drink before or after services is also deemed, quite rightly, desirable. Thus a majority of the churches I have visited have already taken steps to upgrade their church or are drawing up plans. The main constraint, unsurprisingly, is finance in most cases, but the will is clearly there to make churches more comfortable. The upshot of all that of course, is that many older fittings like pews, bulky Victorian organs and the like are being superceded and replaced, and the face of our churches is being irrevocably changed. Many churches have seen the advantages of holding social events, particularly musical presentations, in their buildings and have modified their interiors to accommodate them. Audio-visual advances have made it desirable to install screens, projectors, microphones and hearing loops. There hasn't been anything like it since the Victorian reformers and restorers put their stamp onto and into medieval churches, and I believe that what is happening today will have almost as great an impact over the next 20 or 30 years as that great upheaval in the 19th century.

Whilst all the foregoing is entirely understandable and laudable, I see the same potential problems as did the last generation when contemplating the wholesale disposal and vandalising of medieval features and fittings that undoubtedly took place at the hands of Victorian restorers. Yet, this need not happen, it is perfectly possible to upgrade a church interior with all the modernisation required without losing the best of the medieval, and nowadays Victorian, aspects. I have seen it in churches like Evington St Denys and Shepshed St Botolph, whose interiors are models of how it should be done.

Tilton on the Hill St Peter

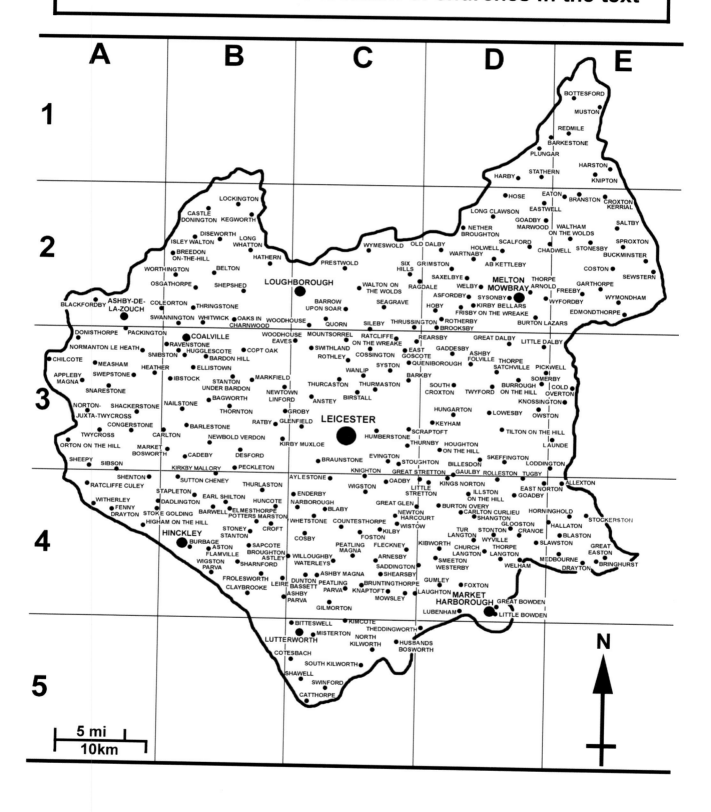

Leicestershire and the location of churches in the text

All churches are located by a letter/number reference on this map and also by an Ordnance Survey grid reference.

THE CHURCHES

SHACKERSTONE ST PETER

THE ANGLICAN CHURCHES OF LEICESTER

In order to cover all of the numerous and very varied Anglican churches in regular use in the city of Leicester, certain amendments to the plan of this book are necessary. It is not possible or desirable to allocate the same space to the 19th - 21th century City of Leicester churches as has been given to the largely one settlement/one church arrangement in the rest of the county. The main reason is that the information available about these establishments is substantially less than that for the other churches, their history is short and also, regrettably, they have in most cases less to offer in terms of interest. However, they certainly deserve description and illustration, but it is on a reduced scale. Nearly all inner city and suburban churches of Leicester are kept firmly locked and in some cases gaining access is problemmatical, this factor has certainly not helped in obtaining data. Yet the threat to these buildings from vandalism and theft is considerably greater than in most of the rest of the county, and the case for locking is easier to accept. I must give grateful acknowledgement here to the comprehensive and admirable book by Geoff Brandwood on the Anglican churches of Leicester (1984), from which some of the data used in this section regarding 19th and 20th century Leicester churches has been gleaned.

As has been explained elsewhere, the churches of the old medieval villages now subsumed in Leicester have been given their own separate entries, and because of their demonstrably greater importance and interest, the five medieval churches of Leicester city are accorded equal coverage to those of the county. Firstly in this section we will look at the fine medieval churches of the City of Leicester, then move on to the post-medieval buildings.

A sad byline on the state of the Anglican church in certain areas of Leicester is the steady loss of churches through 'redundancy' i.e their small congregations can no longer generate enough income to keep the church open. Since I began writing this book, at least four have succumbed. The most alarming closure was St Peter in Belgrave in mid-2010, one of the most important medieval parish churches in the city, with nationally recognised Romanesque features including a marvellous Norman doorway. It seems unthinkable that such buildings should be abandoned, but the church has to balance its books. The real tragedy is not the abandonment by the Church of England, but that no other organisation, civic, conservation or otherwise, has come forward to take over the care of the building. Other casualties recently have been the fantastic neo-Gothic St Saviour, which since its closure has been seriously vandalised. St Barnabas and St Gabriel were also closed in 2011.

One of Leicester's finest medieval churches, St Margaret

All Saints

St Martin

Holy Trinity

The Martyrs

St Mary de Castro

St Nicholas

St Aidan

St Anne
A Leicester churches scrapbook

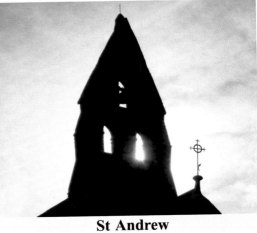

St Andrew

9

LEICESTER'S MEDIEVAL CHURCHES

ALL SAINTS, Highcross Street

C3, SK 583 048

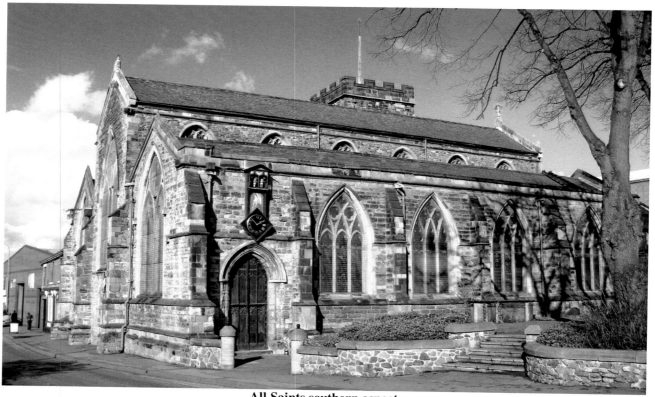

All Saints southern aspect

All five of Leicester's medieval churches have demonstrably Norman or earlier origins. All Saints has some excellent Norman details, but the building on the whole is not a pretty one, the plan we see today is too irregular and lacks balance. That's not to say that All Saints is without interest, quite the opposite, it is a fascinating building, largely of the early 1300's. It has enjoyed a very chequered history, from being at the heart of medieval Leicester, to finding itself marginalised, almost cut off by modern road and city development schemes. At a dark time in the early 1980's its very existence was under threat, poorly patronised and forgotten by all but a handful of dedicated supporters. But All Saints pulled through, rescued by the Churches Conservation Trust, and today sees occasional services, and is often visited by historians and others interested in ancient Leicester. It gives its name to a Conservation Area, and the future now seems secure. The elements of the building are conventional, consisting of tower, aisled nave and chancel, but the details are decidedly odd. The tower lies almost detached to the north, joined to the rest of the church via a tall narrow archway into the eastern end of the north aisle. That wasn't the original arrangement, and the consensus is that the tower was detached when first built in Norman times (only the basal section is of that age). Then there is the marked skew on the nave and aisles, created by the line of the west end of the building being dictated by the course of the road, which runs north west/south east. The chancel is a drab utilitarian red brick construction which replaced its medieval predecessor in 1830. It is now sealed off and used for non-ecclesiastical purposes; the east end of the nave now houses the altar. The most prominent feature from the outside is the fine west doorway, which is classic round-arched Norman, with chevron ornament, roll moulding and scalloped capitals to the shafts. Care is needed when viewing this doorway, it sits perilously close to the very busy road. A nice restored clock of 1620 can be seen above the doorway on the south west of the building. Inside are many excellent things, including a very fine 13th century font, two high openings to the vanished rood loft, rare 15th century wooden pulpit, 18th century 'mayor's chair', lots of mural tablets (some good, some bad), a stone coffin, characterful corbels and old woodwork including a 17th century sideboard, stall backs, tables and an old bench, also a little old glass and some battered medieval tiles.

All Saints from the east

The Norman west door

South door and clock of 1620

The nave and altar

Tower arch and Norman buttress

C13th font

Mayor's chair

Medieval tiles

?Fish head corbel

Sideboard of 1661

Old stall back

C15th pulpit

Rood loft openings

St Margaret seen from across St Margaret's Way

One of Leicester's finest buildings, St Margaret is many church lover's favourite of the five medieval city churches. Much of that affection is generated by the magnificent Perpendicular tower, a landmark throughout the centre and north of the city, a point of reference for many Leicester natives throughout their lives. Lesser buildings come and go, road and development schemes are initiated, abandoned and begun again, but St Margaret stands serene, untroubled by the passing years notwithstanding the requirement that people continue to love it and keep it in good repair. The overwhelming impression of the church is of a Perpendicular building, thanks to the tower and impressive south porch, with parvise (upper room), but like all Leicester's old churches, the story goes back much further. Excavations in the nave and north aisle undertaken many years ago revealed footings, stonework and a well which suggested at least a Norman age for the foundation, although some authorities suggest Anglo-Saxon beginnings. However, nothing above ground of that age survives, it is not until the 1200's that structural evidence in the details of the arcades (supported by dogtooth and leaf carving) becomes available. The greatest period of activity in medieval times was in the mid-15th century when money became available for an ambitious building and rebuilding phase, when the tower, south porch and chancel were constructed. The tower and porch have been mentioned, but the chancel is also a tour-de-force, with almost more glass than stonework, a typical Perpendicular trait. As is usual, the Victorians made several sallies at St Margaret, led by three of the big names in 19th century church architecture - R. C. Carpenter (1840's), G. Gilbert Scott (1860's) and G. E. Street (1880's). Between them they thoroughly rejigged the interior, remodelled some exterior features and probably replaced all the windows, leaving the unmistakeable Victorian stamp which pervades the church today. Look inside for the Bishop Penny (d. 1520) tomb in the sanctuary, a great number of mural tablets of mixed quality, 13th century ironwork on the inside of the west door, 15th century font, sedilia in the chancel, the excavated well shaft near the chancel arch and the stylish Victorian décor, stained glass and stone carving in the chancel.

From the west

From the south east

The very fine sanctuary

Looking along the nave to the chancel

Paired trefoil openings above chancel arch

Quality stained glass

Bishop Penny's tomb (d. 1520)

Detail of chancel screen

The area around the font

C13th ironwork, west door

Major tablet of 1649

The soul ascending, behind the altar

St Martin's tower and spire are an inspiring presence in Leicester's city centre

Leicester's largest church, St Martin was designated as the cathedral for the reinstated Diocese of Leicester in 1927. Opinions are divided on its merits but it is certainly a powerful presence in the heart of Leicester, and has always enjoyed the closest relationship of all Leicester's churches with the city's people and workers. The reservations that are expressed centre on the overriding Victorian aspect of the cathedral, which was created by wide-ranging refitting and restoration in the 19th century which left the building with little to suggest it was founded in Norman times. To some, the St Martin of today might appear a little staid and formal. Yet it undoubtedly has a stately and impressive interior, and the Victorian work, chiefly effected under the direction of Brandon over a long period in the middle years of the 19th century, is of excellent quality. The plan is ambitious, with a spacious nave and chancel, chancel chapels, double south aisle, north aisle, two porches and lots of other nooks and crannies. But the piece de resistance is the tower and spire combination, in a classic Early English style, massive and attractive, which are adjectives that rarely go together. If you didn't know where to look, the only evidence of the building's Norman foundation would be missed, a single small length of billet moulding high up in the south wall of the north aisle. The Norman church was cruciform, and that plan provided the template for today's building, although later aisles and chapels have masked the cross-shaped outline. The interior is fitted out with high quality and lavishly designed furniture, features and fittings, but almost everything is 19th or 20th century in origin. However, it is worth seeking out the older items, which can be found all over the building; these are mostly memorials of various kinds, some dating back to the 15th century. In fact the highlight of St Martins is its multiplicity of memorials, some are of admirable ambition and quality. Several hours could easily be spent in their study. One of the best is the fabulous Whatton memorial of 1656 which can be found on the north aisle north wall. Soon St Martin will have another very special feature, when the body of King Richard III, recently discovered in Leicester, is formally interred in the chancel. The beautifully preserved 17th century pulpit with tester and the 13th century arcades should not be overlooked, but the modern wood and metal chairs that constitute the cathedral's seating certainly should be!

Ornate south porch

Statue of St Dunstan in niche

Nave and beautiful screen

St Dunstan's Chapel

South arcades

Modern glass

Victorian font (1849)

C17th pulpit with tester

Whatton memorial (1656)

Other excellent memorials

Phipps memorial tablet (1768)

Nave roof angel

Organ, west gallery

15

ST MARY DE CASTRO, Castle Street

St Mary's fine tower and spire dominate the old castle area

For sheer interest and allure, St Mary de Castro stands supreme in Leicester. There is no other church remotely like it, its history and evolution are complex and difficult to unravel; even the experts can only get so far. That means that visitors with even basic knowledge of church architecture have an opportunity to exercise their observational skills and add their opinions. What is known is that the foundation of a church here in the heart of medieval Leicester is tied up directly with the Castle, which stood just a few metres from St Mary's doors. In fact some of it still does although no-one coming here for the first time would know that, as the scanty remains lie hidden behind a much later exterior. A castle has to have its chapel and St Mary was founded shortly after the Norman castle was established here in the late 11th to early 12th century. At first it was simply a long narrow building without aisles or tower, but as the centuries passed more and more was added, each phase of building leaving a signature in the fabric. There is still much Norman work distributed around the church, some in unexpected positions with regard to the present layout. The very oldest fabric is probably the short length of low blind arcading at the west end of the nave, and then there are several windows with typical round arches with chevron and other patterning, some hidden away high in the old Norman nave external south wall, now internal. The undoubted star in this Norman firmament is the fabulous set of sedilia in the chancel with orders of chevron carving in the round heads and intricate carving on the capitals. There is a significant Early English component including the south aisle, which originally formed a separate parochial church until absorbed into the greater church as a south aisle. The tower is an oddity and was constructed within the west end of the south aisle as an internal tower, until it bursts clear of the roofline and surges skywards with an eye-catching tall needle spire. There is lots more information about St Mary out there, no more can be done here but list a few things not already mentioned that must be seen on any visit. These include external restored Norman doorways and windows (some original), a fancy 13th century font, some medieval tiles nearby, lots of mural tablets, exceptional late Victorian reredos, quirky stone figures, piscinae, a fine set of Early English sedilia in the south aisle and rood loft stairs. Outside is an atmospheric churchyard filled with fine old Swithland Slate headstones.

Original and renewed Norman details on the exterior

Looking from the chancel to the nave   **The chancel**

C12th and C13th sedilia

C13th font   **Norman arcading**   **Springer figure**   **Poppyhead with face**

St Nicholas from the south

Three out of the four medieval churches in Leicester have some material indications of foundation in at least Norman times, but only St Nicholas retains significant evidence of its long and complex evolution in the form of substantial extant masonry. And what a history it has, quite the most fascinating of all Leicester's churches. It probably began shortly after the Romans abandoned Britain, leaving their buildings in Leicester to crumble, as elsewhere in the country. Clearly the present St Nicholas Circle was at the heart of Roman Ratae Coritaneum, as excavations have proved, and the largest piece of standing masonry is the Jewry Wall, just yards from St Nicholas. It is believed that in the period 700-800 AD an open area immediately to the east of the Wall was chosen for the building of the first church. The proximity of available building stone from the derelict Roman buildings was probably a factor because in all St Nicholas's early fabric, there is Roman tile and brick; there are also some Roman columns in the churchyard. That first Anglo-Saxon church was probably rebuilt around 900 AD, because that is the date assigned to two marvellous late Saxon windows which can be seen in the nave north wall. These have Roman tiles formed into rounded heads. There is also significant Saxon fabric in the rest of the nave, including large quoin stones in the south west corner. The shape of the church in Saxon times is uncertain, but the Normans introduced (or followed) a cruciform plan and built (or rebuilt) the tower to their own unmistakeable pattern and as a next step created north and south arcades to aisles. All that was early in the Norman story because the round arches are basic and unchamfered. Other important Norman features are the embellished south doorway and a lancet window to the west of it. The Early English contribution is the south chapel and the lovely arcade from that into the chancel, plus some other modifications. Much later, there were the inevitable 19th century changes, including the replacement of the north aisle, building of a north transept and the much-mourned destruction of the Norman south arcade. This description is a mere snapshot, but St Nicholas retains elements of all the chapters in its story, a visit is essential in order to read this gripping tale.

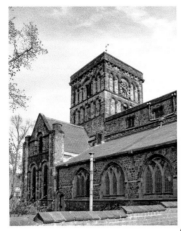

St Nicholas from the north west, south and north east

Roman columns in the churchyard

Norman arcade and Saxon windows

The Saxon windows in the nave wall

Norman detail on the tower

Nave and chancel arch

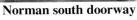

Norman south doorway

Wall memorials

?Jacobean chair

The Perpendicular font

19

POST-MEDIEVAL CHURCHES OF LEICESTER

CHRIST CHURCH, THURNBY LODGE

C3, SK 638 049

Christ Church's simple, clean lines

Thurnby Lodge is a large, specially designated dormitory region to the east of Leicester, almost all the housing is post-1950. A church was clearly needed to service the new population and in 1957, Christ Church was the result. It was remodelled in 1977. The building has no pretensions to grandeur and is a plain, brick-built edifice, but has some distinction thanks to the tall brick stack surmounted by a cross, and a good doorway. The interior is similarly functional but is comfortable and attractive, with some fittings brought from the closed Christ Church in Bow Street.

CHRIST THE KING, BEAUMONT LEYS

C3, SK 564 080

The eye-catching modern design of Christ the King

Like so many recently built churches in areas of new housing, Christ the King, constructed of brick in 1985, is required to fill an important role in the local community, and is used for many secular activities as well as offering the full facilities of a church. It is strategically situated in the midst of the retailing and social heart of Beaumont Leys. The design is confidently modern but manages to retain the look of a church through the tower-like projection and prominent cross that surmounts it. The church celebrated its silver jubilee with a programme of events in late 2010.

CORNERSTONE COMMUNITY CHURCH

C3, SK 574 063

No dedicated building, but a church just the same

In common with a few other churches in Leicester, Cornerstone Community Church began as a plant from a larger church, in this case Holy Trinity, which supported it until it was able to assume full independence in 2008. Also like other churches, it has no building of its own, instead it currently meets in a room in the John O' Gaunt pub on Somerset Avenue, which is in an area to the north west of the city centre. Groups also meet in the houses of members of the congregation.

HOLY APOSTLES, Imperial Avenue/Fosse Road South   C3, SK 571 031

Holy Apostles enjoys a prominent position facing Fosse Road South

Holy Apostles has a foot in two camps, being built at an interesting time for architecture, in 1923. Victorian principles still exerted an influence, yet many styles are freely used. Thus we see hints of Renaissance influence in the chancel, a Classical broken pediment and some obvious Gothic details such as the prominent west window. Yet modern practises were also introduced, such as the use of reinforced concrete in the construction. The Baptistry contains nice William Morris glass of 1952.

HOLY TRINITY, Regent Road   C3, SK 589 037

| Leicester's most flamboyant tower | East window glass | The sanctuary and its fine arch |

Holy Trinity is a real confection, some love it, probably more dislike it. It may be the most 'Victorian' of Leicester's church exteriors, with much overwrought Gothic styling, especially the very fussy tower and spire, which bristle with dormers, pillars, soundholes, etc. The inspired/notorious architect S. S. Teulon is responsible, he completely remodelled the church in 1871-2, from an original building of 1838 by Smirke. Late 20th century changes removed almost all the Victorian detail inside, except in the sanctuary area. The church previously boasted side galleries and a full set of pews but all that has been swept away. However, beneath the east window in the sanctuary the mosaic of the Last Supper remains, as does the tiling, and most of the rest of the original fittings.

ST AIDAN, NEW PARKS

C3, SK 556 056

St Aidan's design is thoroughly modern, but inside there is a more traditional feel

Modernism truly came to Leicester in 1959 with the completion of St Aidan and its contemporary, St Hugh in Eyres Monsell. Designed by Basil Spence, both churches embrace the architecture and materials of the 20th century, and dispense with many elements of the traditional church plan. The most obvious manifestations of that are the skeletal tower, standing away from the main building, and the partly abstract mural on the external west wall. Fine, polished, fossiliferous limestone font.

ST ALBAN, BELGRAVE

C3, SK 597 060

St Alban was built in 1905-6

The Parish of the Resurrection in Belgrave was badly hit in the round of church closures of 2010-11, losing both the important medieval church of St Peter, and also the relatively recent St Gabriel, leaving just one church, the Edwardian St Alban on Harrison Road. This is a big, barn-like, brick building with little pretension to beauty. There are nods in the direction of Early English styling, e.g. the west window, but generally the church appears to have been designed for quantity (i.e. capacity) rather than quality. Its continued existence is supported by its use as a community centre as well as a church.

ST ANDREW, Jarrom Street

C3, SK 584 037

St Andrew is impressively designed, but ultimately a little forbidding

One of Leicester's more impressive Victorian churches, built in 1860-2, the authentically cruciform St Andrew illustrates well the desire of the founders and the designer Sir Gilbert Scott to make a big powerful statement. In no sense can the building be thought of as beautiful, but as pure design, it has its admirers. The basic premise is a simplified, loosely Early English church, but the use of brick and its sheer size gives St Andrew an institutional air, despite the use of various coloured materials, contrasting diapering, and pleasing touches such as the attractive apse with its Romanesque arcading. There is no tower, and the three bell bellcote (only one bell remains) is situated on the nave gable west of the apse. The effect of St Andrew can be almost intimidating from the outside, but internally things soften a little. The church also hosts the Church of the Good Shepherd, Leicester's church for the deaf.

ST ANDREW, LEICESTER FOREST EAST   C3, SK 531 033

St Andrew was built in 1966

It must be said that St Andrew possesses one of the least inspiring church designs in Leicestershire. It has all the modern amenities of space, light, comfort and heat, but architecturally it sits with the worst of utilitarian 20th century buildings, of a type with school halls and warehouses. It isn't ugly, it simply lacks individuality. It has a large adjoining church hall, widely used by the community, so performs an admirable service to the surrounding area, both spiritually (it hosts a joint congregation of Anglicans and Methodists) and socially.

ST ANNE, Letchworth Road/Westfield Road   C3, SK 563 045

St Anne is one of Leicester's best C20th churches

St Anne restores the reputation of 20th century church architecture in Leicester. Built in 1933-4 it makes an assertive statement, tall and individual; its very boldness, compactness and power puts one in mind of Romanesque/Norman churches. Architecturally it cannot be compared at all with such churches, it is simply the feeling it conveys, helped considerably by its elevated setting. The style, if anything, is a kind of chunky modernism, but the layout is mostly conventional, with nave, chancel, passage aisles, etc. A larger building was planned, but never completed through lack of funds.

ST CHAD, Broad Avenue/Coleman Road

Some imaginative touches take St Chad above the mundane

At first sight St Chad is a rather uninspiring modern construction, built in 1968, but it possesses features which take it out of the ordinary. The roof is a steep long monopitch, which creates the interesting contrast of a high wall to the west and a low one to the east. The high wall permits the mounting of a large stylised figure of St Chad, complimented by an adjacent long window. The picture is further enhanced by a good representation of the crucifixion set in a pleasant lawned area. At the north west corner a narrow, high feature wall carries a bell and the church's name, and is surmounted by a crucifix. Next to the wall is a large window which permits plenty of light to enter the church. Along the low east wall is a row of simple slit windows, and the main entrance.

ST CHRISTOPHER AT THE SAMWORTH ACADEMY, Trenant Road

A large new school, but the church is very much part of the enterprise

St Christopher has undergone many changes since its foundation in 1927 in a converted barn. Three buildings have followed, each more ambitious than the preceding one. For many years a building on Marriott Road was used, from which the church decamped to its present location. Like so many church buildings of the last 40 or so years, its present base, built as recently as 2007, is not primarily a church and has several other functions, the main one being that of a school. However, the presence of a church community is clearly announced by the crucifix and church title mounted by the entrance.

ST HUGH, EYRES MONSELL

The 'fire station' tower dominates St Hugh

St Hugh can be considered alongside St Aidan at New Parks, with which it shares many characteristics. Both were designed by the Basil Spence Partnership and have ugly, skeletal towers, although St Hugh's is more substantial. Thankfully the enthusiasm for such constructions was of brief duration. The original ambitious project of 1957-8 at St Hugh for church, hall and cloister was never completed, so much so that the actual church building was never started. Since then, the originally planned church hall has fulfilled the function of the church, and has been gradually improved over the years by the committed congregation.

ST JAMES THE GREATER, London Road   C3, SK 600 033

St James impressive Renaissance frontage

St James is a little bit special, and possesses one of Leicesters finest post-medieval interiors. It was built in the main in 1899-1901, but not completed at the west end until 1914. Externally all that can be seen easily is the west frontage, which is a bold attempt to create originality around a loosely Renaissance style, complete with pediments on the central block, flanked by cupola-topped towers. Much elaboration was added, and the doorways at ground level are impressive. The interior draws universal admiration, and is a lovely basilica-like space, based on the Renaissance interior of Torcello Cathedral near Venice. Many fine things can be seen, including magnificent arcades, friezes below the clerestory, carved terracotta angels, marble pillars and beautifully realised decorative motifs everywhere. The apsidal sanctuary is particularly fine. There is some interesting glass, including windows by Theodora Salusbury. As others have noted, the stiff gothicised interiors so beloved of the Victorians are a distant memory here.

ST JOHN THE BAPTIST, Clarendon Park Road   C3, SK 602 026

As seen from Clarendon Park Road   **Main north door**   **Plate tracery and a French style fleche**

St John, built in 1884-5, is a fine, confident church, boldly designed and realised. Stylistically an Early English template is carried successfully around the whole church. It is a shame that, like St James the Greater, not all the church can be appreciated, as the plainer south side is all but unviewable. But fine though the exterior is, the grandeur is most pronounced inside where the arcades are taken up to the roof, and are demarcated into low passage aisles below and a continuous gallery above. The baptistry is done in quite a different style, with low powerful pillars linked by arches, giving a crypt-like feel. The marble font is large and stylish. The sanctuary is beautifully balanced with the high tri-partite reredos echoed in the three tall lancets forming the east window.

ST LUKE, STOCKING FARM
C3, SK 582 075

Three views of St Luke and its elevated setting

Though completed in 1966, the largely brick-built St Luke still presents a strikingly modern appearance, with its six-sided central block flanked by aisles, and a tall and most imposing tower to the east. On the face of the tower is a large stylised figure of St Luke. Inside, the altar is central with a suspended representation of a crown of thorns above, while the pulpit is sited against the east wall. The south west side has a concave wall and entrance, through which the church hall is reached.

ST PAUL & ST AUGUSTINE WORSHIP CENTRE, Kirby Road
C3, SK 574 044

The 'new' church building　　　　　**And the old**

The Victorian church of St Paul, built in 1870-1 by Ordish and Traylen, was another of Leicester's church casualties when it closed in the early 2000's. It remains in situ and for sale. It was sad to note the loss of the religious function of such an individualistic building, with its amazing apse and five bold gabled windows, but the church didn't die. Instead the congregation decamped about 20 metres to an undistinguished building, not the least church-like in its appearance, formerly used as a college and Sunday School, where the mission continues alongside numerous other community activities.

ST PETER, St Peters Road
C3, SK 599 039

As no overall view is possible of St Peter, here are four snapshots from around the church

St Peter resides in an area inhabited by a largely non-Christian population. That lack of potential members of the Anglican community recently resulted in the demise of sister churches St Saviour and St Barnabas, and St Peter is now the only church in the benefice. The church is traditionally designed in stone, with conventional tower at the west end and two aisles, but the designer G. E. Street, wishing to express Victorian predilictions and Leicester's aspirations, embellished the design with an apsidal chancel with transepts (the southern one with an apse of its own) and a big porch off the south face of the tower. All that created an overwrought feel, to the detriment of the building.

ST PHILIP, Evington Road   C3, SK 608 033

St Philip is still a major feature on Evington Road

The gradual overhaul of Victorian taste, and the development of a simpler, more functional style after 1900 is well shown by St Philip of 1909, which shows little of the stiff Gothic detail so beloved of designers in the preceding century. Nevertheless, it retains a Gothic ethic, but the lines are cleaner and less fussy, designed to fulfill the basic requirement of a church, that of efficiently seating a large congregation. The most eye-catching feature are the three pedimented gables around the building. Inside, the design is satisfying if rather dull, with a large nave, brick arches and passage aisles.

ST STEPHEN, East Park Road/St Saviours Road   C3, SK 607 044

St Stephen is another of Leicester's considerable Victorian piles

St Stephen's most arresting feature is its capacious overall roof, steeply pitched and extending well down towards the ground, somewhat reminiscent of that of a chalet, but on a grander scale. Otherwise this is not an exceptional design and like many red brick late Victorian/Edwardian churches it is rather dull and institutional. A couple of conjoined transepts at the north east corner give it some individuality, together with an unusual arrangement at the east end of five lancets between two stepped buttresses, with a higher bellcote in the gable above. The theme of lancet windows is continued all around the church, in the form of pairs between buttresses in the north and south walls. As at St Chad's, a prominent crucifix is set in front of the east wall.

ST THEODORE OF CANTERBURY, Sandfield Close

The light grey thermalite structure of St Theodore stands out in a predominantly red brick area

Thermalite, used in the construction of St Theodore in 1980, is very much a modern material, and St Theodore is very much a modern church. The layout is modular, essentially four 'boxes', but these are distinguished by differently directed roofs. It might be passed over as just another functional 20th century utilitarian building, but a few key features make it quite clear that this is a religious building. The name board is an obvious feature, but it is the tall 'tower' surmounted by a cross at the front of the building that makes the most effective statement. Yet at the same time, St Theodore performs a number of other functions for its community and only the western 'box' is used as the church. Other parts of the building have support, retail, administrative and non-religious community functions.

THE MARTYRS, Westcotes Drive

Tower, nave and eastern apse

The Martyrs was built following an initiative from St Mary de Castro church in the city. It is a severe, no-nonsense Victorian preaching box of 1889-90 situated off the leafy Westcotes Drive, built with plain lines and simple lancet windows. Ornamentation is kept to a minimum; however, designer Ewan Christian enlivened the building with an apse at each end, at the west end for a baptistry and a larger one at the east end for the sanctuary. Without them and the oddly sited south east tower with its elongate pyramidal roof (or low spire), this would be a very dull building. Two aisles were planned but only the southern one was completed, the northern one remains as a shallow extension to the north wall. The reredos and panelling around the sanctuary were put in place as 1st World War memorials.

RECENT CHURCH CLOSURES IN LEICESTER

St Barnabas

St Gabriel

St Peter, Belgrave

St Saviour

St Peter enjoys a key position in the heart of its village

St Peter is a hybrid church. At first glance the weathered old sandstone tower and attractive short recessed spire indicate a medieval church of around the early to mid-1300's, but then a reassessment is required when the rest of the building comes into view. That, clearly, is not 14th century although the style is inspired by churches of that time. Once again, we see a familiar pattern in Leicestershire, a complete Victorian rebuilding but with the retention of the tower and spire. The odd thing here is that the new building was undertaken with quite a different type of stone from the sedimentary rock used for the tower, a pinkish igneous granite from nearby quarries. There appears to have been little thought about blending the two parts aesthetically. Nevertheless the 'new' parts have clean uncluttered lines and certainly don't jar stylistically. On the other hand, their design is rather mundane and uninspired. It seems that at the time of the rebuilding, 1867-8, St Peter was certainly in need of renovation, a report from the late 18th century indicates that the fabric was in very poor order and crumbling, so this may have been a case of the Victorians rescuing a church rather than simply reordering it. The plan is standard in detail, with apart from the tower and spire, nave with north aisle, chancel with vestry running off to the north, and south porch. The nice thing inside is that very little has changed since 1868, and that affords a fairly rare opportunity to inspect a complete Victorian ecclesiastical vision. However, some modernisation is planned to provide new amenities. Particularly good is the duotone stonework on the arcade and chancel arches, a gentle blend of yellow and grey. The font sits proudly at the west end of the nave central walkway, and is an attractive carved design featuring various motifs including the symbols of the evangelists. It predates the rebuilding, and is from 1851. Several either 18th or 19th century mural tablets were also inherited from the earlier church, the best of these are located on the tower east wall, and commemorate the Cart family and Susannah Smith (south and north sides of tower arch respectively). The Smith tablet has a stylish scene of Death mowing down Ionic columns. The stained glass should also be inspected, with several windows being of very good quality.

St Peter from the south

Chancel and vestry

The medieval tower

Looking from the tower eastwards

Nave and tower arch

Duotone stonework in the arcade

Sanctuary and altar

Sumptuous Victorian Gothic details on the chancel piers

Death wields his scythe

Ornate font

St Peter and St John in stained glass

31

LITTLE BOWDEN ST NICHOLAS

St Nicholas enjoys an attractive approach

The village of Little Bowden is very much physically and politically a part of Market Harborough these days, but retains something of its original small settlement atmosphere. That a church should be established at a site where nearby flows the River Jordan should come as no surprise, although Little Bowden's tiny stream scarcely merits such a grand name. St Nicholas is a tidy, attractive ironstone building which seems never to have had a tower. The present two-bell bellcote dates from 1900 and succeeded a wooden structure which itself replaced an original stone construction on which the design of the present day bellcote may have been based. Apart from the lack of a tower, St Nicholas is otherwise a medieval church dating from the 13th century with a standard range of features, namely nave with north aisle, chancel, an unusually sited vestry of 1928 at the south west end of the nave with porch attached, and another porch on the north. A post-13th century extension to the north aisle reaches to the end of the chancel and houses a chapel. The nave roof is pitched at a very low angle, and appears flat-roofed from the ground. That was the layout until 2008, when a substantial new western extension was built to house a meeting room and an ambitious range of other features. The extension, while bringing much-needed improvements in facilities and access, and benefitting the community, might be considered out of scale with the rest of the church. It has also disrupted its traditional form, and therefore may not please those concerned about the aesthetics of church buildings. However, the sympathetic ironstone fabric should blend well with a few seasons weathering. The windows in the rest of the church are a mixture of styles but none appear to be original, most probably date from Bodley's restoration of 1900-1. The chancel is dated 1776 in its gable, but this may refer to a phase of repair rather than a new chancel built from scratch. The interior is neat but unexceptional, the aisle arcade is 13th century with low quatrefoil piers and there is also an arcade from the chancel to the north chapel. The pulpit is a good 18th century example and the font with its simple Maltese Cross motif appears to be old. There are a few mural tablets, the best can be found in the chancel. A good show of headstones enhances the churchyard.

The view from the south west is dominated by the new extension

The north porch

Window head stops of 1900-1

St Nicholas from the south

North chapel window

33

St James enjoys a splendid setting

St James is one of Leicestershire's secret gems, little known or visited, but one of the best churches of its type in the county. It enjoys a lovely hilltop setting above the hamlet of Little Dalby, amongst fine hill scenery with a panoramic view north over the flatlands towards Melton Mowbray. It can be reached by car via a rough track, but far better to park in the village and take the steep path that winds up the hill across a field with increasingly fine retrospective views as one climbs. What greets the visitor as they arrive at the top is a classic Victorian Gothic church with a particularly impressive tower and spire. All shades of Gothic seem to get a look in, from Early English through Decorated to Perpendicular, but the whole holds together very well. However, St James isn't quite what it seems, because despite the overwhelming Victorian aspect, its foundation was much older, in medieval times, and what we see is a comprehensive rebuilding by Brandon in 1851. He added the transepts as new builds and rebuilt the rest from scratch, to produce a building that consists of tower with broach spire, clerestoried aisled nave with transepts north and south, chancel and south porch. Around the building is a cornucopia of imaginative gargoyles, head stops, ball flower and other ornamentation, a terrific display of early- to mid-Victorian exuberance in decoration. The interior was completely refitted in 1851 and, to our great fortune, almost the full layout and fittings have been retained, offering a rare opportunity to appreciate a genuine Victorian ecclesiastical setting. And it was one that didn't stint on cost, the fittings are all of high quality, the carving, both in stone and wood, is excellent. An angel theme runs throughout the church, from roof corbels, to wall plate bosses, to pier responds on the chancel arch. The pulpit is a tour-de-force, simply bursting with vivacious carving. The font has fine quality high relief carving. On a smaller scale many arm rests on the benches are carved into the figures of men and beasts, some fantastical, and great fun to hunt out. However, all is not so positive, a palpable atmosphere of melancholy envelops the church. It is simply not used enough, and its isolation and relative obscurity make it a rather mournful place. This is a church that should be visited and used far more, the door is usually open.

From the south east

Early English details on the tower

Lovely example of the stonecarver's art

Looking from the nave to chancel, and vice-versa

Sedilia and piscina in the sanctuary

The font

Chancel pier respond

Angel corbel

North transept wall plate with angel boss

Wonderful pulpit

More fine carving

LITTLE STRETTON ST JOHN THE BAPTIST   D4, SK 668 003

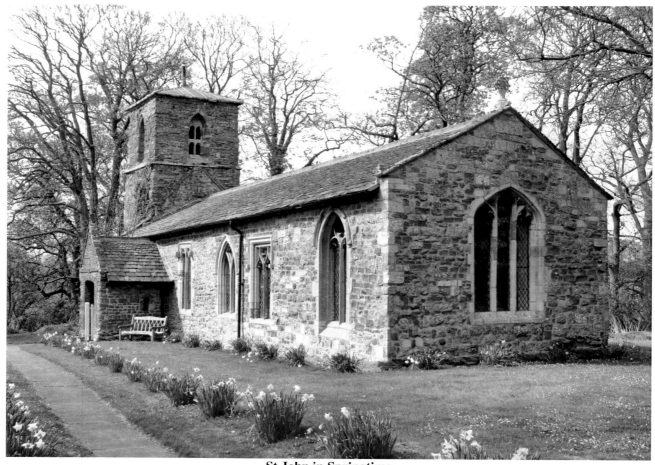

St John in Springtime

Picture the fictitious England of P. G. Wodehouse, where tiny villages have age-old churches where whiskered incumbents deliver two hour sermons to a scattered congregation of bored locals and toffs down for the weekend. The old woodwork creaks, dust drifts through shafts of sunlight coming through ancient glass, bees drone and long hot August afternoons fade gently into mellow warm twilight. Fictitious? Well, of course, but here in Little Stretton the imagination can be let loose for a while, for this indeed is a charming rustic church set in a tiny sleepy village surrounded by lovely countryside. Standing in St John's peaceful churchyard, surrounded by trees, the 21st century seems a long way away. The ironstone fabric is mellow and age-worn, the tower with its quaint low pyramid roof is just as it should be, and the nave and chancel, under one roof, have five windows on the south side which are all different. In contrast the north side has no windows at all, just a blocked Norman doorway. The main south doorway, very much still in use, is also Norman and good. The porch is a patchwork of brick, stone and slate. Quirky, individual and altogether irresistible, that's St John the Baptist. However, an ancient building like this one, without a large congregation to support it, is also subject to the ravages of time and decay, and all has not been well with St John of late. But it was cheering to see on a recent visit that repairs and a clean up inside and out have revitalised the building. Always there's more to do, but the sight of a large christening party waiting in bright sunshine to enter was most encouraging for the future. Inside there's nothing that will stop the visitor in his or her tracks, but the simplicity is entirely appropriate, and though modest, there are good fittings here. The font dates from around 1300 and has a design of arches around the bowl. There is some nice woodwork to admire including 17th century altar rails and similar rails fronting the choir stalls, possibly from an old screen. The pulpit of dark wood is 18th century, and some battered medieval bench ends have been built into later benches at the west end. Another old bench near the font still has poppyheads, but is no longer used for seating. A scattering of interesting mural tablets adorn the walls. A visit to St John is a must for any church lover.

The rustic tower

Norman doorways, used and disused

The chancel

The nave

C17th balustered rails

C18th pulpit

Medieval bench end

The font c.1300

Narrow tower doorway

Memorial tablets

C17th aumbry (3 locks!)

Afternoon sunshine

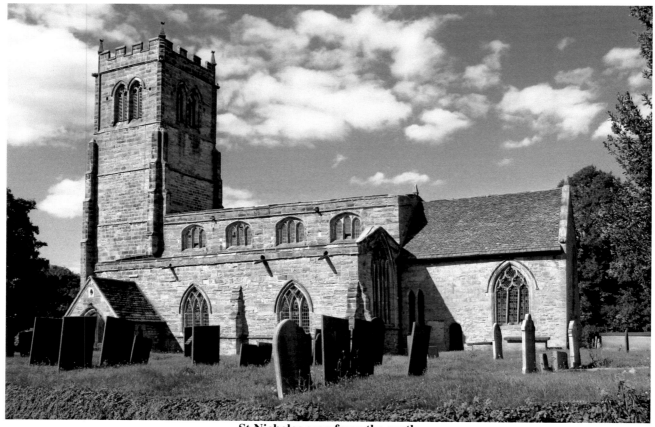

St Nicholas seen from the south

St Nicholas is a veritable treasure-house, one of the finest collections of medieval to 18th century fabric, fixtures and fittings in the county. Anywhere else in the country and it would be far better known, but there is no concession to commercial exploition or overt tourism here. However, there is a downside to this relative obscurity, because St Nicholas is set in a tiny village and has to manage its assets on the income from a small congregation, and that has led to inevitable neglect in certain quarters and it is sad to see a few of its treasures disappearing behind dust, cobwebs and general clutter. That's not to say the church is not looked after, generally it is and the main features are cared for and maintained. The foundations of the building were laid down in Norman times and there is evidence for that in a nice blocked round-arched northern doorway and another into the chancel to the south. Other remnants of Norman fabric are dotted around, the best being part of an arch which is kept at the west end of the north aisle. Even older is a fragment of a, probably, Saxon cross which is built into the inner west wall of the porch. Most of the building is 13th to 14th century and the layout is a familiar one, with imposing Perpendicular west tower, aisled nave, chancel and south porch. There are several excellent windows from various periods, especially the impressive east windows of the aisles. Also, see the skewed Decorated south window of the chancel, a victim of settlement. Inside, the attractions start as soon as the church is entered. Here are two fonts, one Norman, the other a dainty 18th century model. Near to the second of these is a very well preserved 16th century incised grave slab, another resides nearby on the south wall. Two others elsewhere are badly worn. Above the chancel arch is a dazzling royal arms of Anne and texts in panels. Below these is a 15th century screen in excellent order, another parclose screen of similar age divides off the south aisle chapel. The west gallery still survives. In the north aisle are 18th century box pews and a two-decker pulpit. The chancel has a wonderful array of mural memorials for members of the Bainbrigge family, one dated 1614 is especially grand and elaborate; a painted alabaster tomb of 1501 for Lady Elizabeth Ferrers in the south chapel is very fine. 15th century benches can be found in the nave, and a relatively abundant collection of medieval glass fragments adorns several windows. The altar rails are 17th century. There is much more, Lockington is not to be missed.

Intersecting tracery, south aisle

Norman north doorway

Saxon fragment in the porch

Nave and west gallery

Altar and C15th screen

The sanctuary

Royal arms and text panels

South chapel with parclose screen

Two-decker pulpit

Norman font

Medieval roof boss

Elizabeth Ferrer's tomb, 1501

Incised slab

Bainbrigge memorials, 1614 and 1779

Very fine medieval glass survivals

LODDINGTON ST MICHAEL & ALL ANGELS

St Michael enjoys one of the most picturesque settings in Leicestershire

That Loddington St Michael survives as a working church is a small miracle. The tiny village of 80 or so souls it serves lies some distance away and most visits have to be made on foot over rough pasture land. Further, St Michael stands completely alone, no other building is anywhere near. That should add up to a recipe for closure, yet the church continues and thankfully is still there for us to enjoy. Its very isolation and setting are amongst its greatest assets from an aesthetic point of view. This part of east Leicestershire is very scenic yet little visited, the view of the church from the south is very fine and one approach through a belt of trees leaves the sight of the church until the last moment and is worthy of a visit purely on its own merits. Once there, the building doesn't disappoint, although the fact that services are sparse and very little other use seems to be made of the church (hardly surprising in view of its isolation and difficult access) embues a melancholy and lonely air, especially inside, where the church is left to dream wistfully to itself. The building is mostly of mellow ironstone and the layout is standard and symmetrical, with tower with plain parapet, aisled nave, chancel and south porch. Much of the fabric dates from the 'golden age' of church building in Leicestershire, i.e. 13th to 14th century, but the south doorway has a round arch and may be earlier. Alternatively it may be a survival of a design more characteristic of earlier times. Above the doorway is an unusual quatrefoil window. The clerestory and certain windows are later Perpendicular additions. The porch with its flattened arch was probably added sometime after 1500. The church received the customary Victorian restoration in 1859 which left the interior with a predominantly 19th century appearance thanks to the replacement of most of the woodwork, which introduced the seating, the nicely carved screen, and details around the altar such as the altar rails and reredos. A royal arms of Victoria in the north aisle was probably added around the same time. Yet there are older items still to be found, including an old deep font with lancet design which may be early 13th century. The nave roof looks old, perhaps mostly 15th or 16th century, but one beam is dated 1777, so some repairs have evidently been effected. The pulpit is a good Jacobean example, and the windows contain some pieces of medieval glass.

St Michael north side

The porch

Chancel south side with its large windows

Round-arched south doorway

Age-worn path to the south door

The lovely approach through the woods

LONG CLAWSON ST REMIGIUS

St Remigius's cruciform shape is well shown from the south

You will have to travel many miles before you come across another church dedicated to the obscure St Remigius, and that's just one of this church's distinctive features. Another is that St Remigius is a cruciform church, and Leicestershire doesn't have too many of those. Add to all that a spacious and attractive churchyard and mellow ironstone fabric, and the end result is one very appealing and characterful church. But it very nearly wasn't here for us to enjoy, its fate seemed to be sealed in the early 1890's when it was very nearly demolished and replaced with a new building. That was a result of the awful state into which St Remigius had descended. However, in stepped the Bishop of Peterborough, who forbade the destruction and ordered restoration. That restoration was very far-reaching, and much of the fabric was refurbished, rebuilt or replaced. Nevertheless, the basic outline of the church remained unchanged and many fittings were retained. That outline is of central tower with transepts, aisled nave and chancel which itself has a north aisle. Substantial porches stand to north and south off the nave aisles. There can be little doubt that the basic core of that design was laid down in Norman times. Very little remains of that original building, but a small Norman window has survived, reset into the south transept east wall. Inside, the eye is immediately drawn to the central tower and crossing, such an arrangement invariably impresses, with the massive supporting piers reinforcing the powerful effect on the senses and the void of the tower itself opening out above the onlooker. The arcades of three bays with their octagonal piers are quite similar and are probably 14th century, another possible Norman survival is the resused circular abacus on one of the north arcade piers. The font with its ornament of blank tracery on the stem, bowl with shields and leaves on the underside is hard to date but appears to be pre-1600 at least. Arguably the most worn effigy in Leicestershire resides at the entrance to the chancel north aisle, it must have spent a good proportion of its life outside. A hidden gem is a small stone altar of 1737 with latin inscription that has been concealed underneath the present altar and behind its cloth. A nice royal arms of 1799 sits above the north doorway, but has become very much darkened with age. There are three interesting mural tablets, one in the chancel and two on the south chapel south wall.

St Remigius from the north

North porch, tower, transept

Reset Norman window

Looking along the nave to the crossing and chancel

Through the tower arches

Garton brothers memorial

Very worn C13th or C14th effigy, perhaps of Ralph de Bozon

Characterful heads

The font

C18th stone altar, beneath the communion table

George III royal arms

43

All Saints unusual plan is apparent in this view from the south east

There is no other church like All Saints in Leicestershire, its plan is unique for the county. Although most of the fabric is post-1300 and much was restored in the 19th century, it seems that the church's layout was established before 1066 and was based on an old concept of how a church should be laid out. The main element is the unusual position of the tower, which stands at the east end of the south aisle. Originally it would have stood free on three sides and would only have connected with the rest of the church via an opening into the south east corner of the nave. It is largely Norman apart from the topmost stages, and retains Norman windows on three sides, the west one blocked and partly obscured by the south aisle. Later, in the 14th century, the north and south aisles were added (the north is the older), and because there was no tower at the west end, it allowed the three west gables of nave and aisles to be modelled into a distinctive feature, more typical of older cathedrals and much larger churches, with high-pitched roofs and tight gable angles. It makes for a very impressive western frontage as seen from the main road. A western entrance into the nave was retained, also more characterstic of large early medieval and older churches. The chancel is probably medieval but has seen alteration since, including being shortened in the early 19th century. A more conventional south doorway was created and typical porch added after all the other main elements were in place. Finally the Victorians gave All Saints a new vestry tacked onto the south wall of the chancel and a vigorous refit and restoration, which resulted in the still very Victorian appearance of the interior and the replacement of all the windows, which were, it appears, inspired by authentic Decorated sensibilities. The interior holds few surprises, but it is interesting to see two lancet windows still in place in the west wall of the tower, which now forms the east wall of the south aisle. Features to look for include some fine woodwork including a 15th or 16th century chancel screen, pulpit of 1613, a chair of 1655 and two contemporary chests. The font with three rows of incised crosses is Norman, but is recut. There are few memorials, but those that remain include some good 17th and 18th century mural tablets, the showiest being a marble urn on pedestal with flame finial and inscriptions behind draped curtains, of 1779. The oldest, a very plain tablet for Abigail Smith, is dated 1695.

All Saints most distinctive west end

From the south west

Lancets, now internal

Looking west down the nave

The late medieval screen

The font

Pulpit of 1613

Mural tablets for William Wilde (L) and Abigail Smith (R)

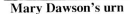

Mary Dawson's urn

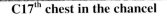

C17ᵗʰ chest in the chancel

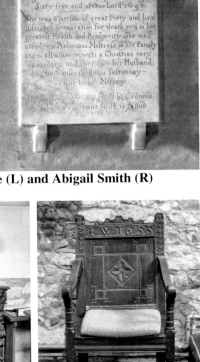

Cromwellian chair

THE CHURCHES OF LOUGHBOROUGH

ALL SAINTS, Steeple Row   **C2, SK 538 199**

All Saints is perfectly situated on raised ground at the confluence of several roads

All Saints is Loughborough's main parish church and, fittingly, is a fine large town church. At first sight it looks entirely Victorian, and indeed Sir George Gilbert Scott undertook a rigorous and extensive restoration between 1859 and 1862 which left an overwhelming fingerprint on the appearance of today's church. But the church is really much older, and historians claim that Saxon and Norman churches stood on the site. That may well be so, as this site is at the highest point in the older part of Loughborough and is the obvious place to establish a place of worship (and influence). Nothing remains of those early churches, but Loughborough's medieval prosperity meant that when a new church was constructed in around 1330 in Decorated times, there was no shortage of money, and a grand building resulted. That ambitious Decorated building must have been a sight to behold, yet more embellishment was to come in the 1400's when the tower was modified and beautified into the imposing structure we see today. It stands comparison with the spectacular Perpendicular towers of Somerset, which it resembles. But beyond that, the present day church explorer will find few medieval features in today's church, apart from the beautiful 14th century arcades and tower and chancel arches. Once that is accepted, the church can be inspected on its own terms as a marvellous example of Victorian opulence and ambition. As with so many Victorianised buildings All Saints interior follows a Gothic template, but imbued with the Victorians own values of quality and workmanship. As befits the chief church of the second town of Leicestershire, the plan of the church is expansive, consisting of tower, aisled nave with further outer south aisle, transepts, long chancel and two-stage south porch that stands flush with the outer south aisle. Inside all is space and restrained grandeur. All Saints memorials are splendid and the best of these reside in the chancel, the most ostentatious being that to Joanna Walter, who died in 1673, and two of her children. Two very Amazonian looking angels flank a badly deteriorated inscription. Another fine memorial is to members of the Tate family and features a kneeling angel scything corn, and the one in latin for George Bright who died in 1696 is good too. The nave roof is splendid with gilded bosses and angels on the wall posts, and the strange font may be 16th century. There is a great deal more inside and out, and an exploration of All Saints is most rewarding.

The splendid tower

Tower west window

From the south east

View west along the nave

…. and looking east

The curious font

Ornate C17th chair

The graceful north arcade

The Burton Chapel in the outer south aisle

Jonah and the whale

Three wall memorials L to R: Joanna Walter, Tate family, George Bright

Ancient headstone

ALL SAINTS, Thorpe Acre

Revamped 'front' (west) of All Saints   **The north side shows more of the old church**   **The bellcote**

All Saints in Thorpe Acre is a largely modern building on the north side of Loughborough, but at its core lies an original Victorian church. An ever increasing catchment area has resulted in the original small, simple Victorian building (which was built to replace the medieval church at Dishley, now a picturesque ruin) being swamped by successive overhauls, extensions and refits so that little can be seen from the west, or remains internally, of the 1845 building as erected by William Railton. This original building was in the Decorated style, and some windows remain. The east window is by Kempe and Co., and dates from 1892. The western bellcote is still in place and a curious minaret type 'chimney' on the north side may also be original.

EMMANUEL CHURCH, Forest Road

Views around Emmanuel

For many hundreds of years All Saints was adequate for Loughborough's spiritual needs, but in the early 1800's with a burgeoning population it was realised that another church was needed for the people moving to new housing that was extending to the west of the town. That turned out to be Emmanuel, on Forest Road, which was built between 1835-37 by Thomas Rickman. Nothing was stinted on the building, which is a fine, traditionally-styled, neo-Gothic church with tall slender tower, nave, two aisles and chancel, and was erected using both Decorated and Perpendicular principles. The battlemented nave is tall and elegant and as well as the two aisles also has a clerestory. Inside, the arcades have slim octagonal piers. In 1909 the chancel was lengthened and other alterations took place, and since then many other changes have taken place. In recent years the interior has been completely reordered, so that while the church is now comfortable and welcoming to its large congregation, it has very little internally that would interest a church historian, and the old churchyard is now a lawn. Emmanuel church sponsors a wide range of activities and there are many sub-groups within its congregation. It also hosts a football team, which was quite common for churches many years ago but which, these days, is rather rare.

ST MARY-IN-CHARNWOOD, Nanpantan

C2, SK 503 171

Views from the north and south east　　　　**Interior view**

St Mary can be found just as the Charnwood hills begin to rise on the outskirts of Loughborough. It was constructed in 1888 as a mission hall and the look is vaguely neo-Gothic, but that style was then beginning to show much simplified lines. St Mary is an unpretentious yet quietly attractive building consisting of nave and chancel under one roof, with porch and a western bellcote. Local igneous rock is the main building stone. In recent years the old vestry was replaced by a chapter house for church and community use. The church has further internal changes planned and also has an ambitious project to restore the woodland at the back of the building.

THE GOOD SHEPHERD, Park Road

C2, SK 535 180

The west frontage　　　　**Church and church hall**

Like St Mary, Good Shepherd began as an Emmanuel Church sponsored project, as a Mission Hall, and was opened in 1938. Subsequently it has been steadily modernised and improved and achieved the status of Parish Church in 1979, serving the people of the Shelthorpe estate. It is brick built and very plain, with nave and chancel under one roof, and western entrance porch above which is a bellcote. An adjoining church hall was built in 1959.

More wall memorials in Loughborough All Saints

All Saints is a beautifully balanced building

Few settings can rival that of All Saints at Lowesby. The church is perfectly situated on the slope of a hill that ascends towards the tiny village, and looks out over some of the finest east Leicestershire countryside. In the season there are not many more attractive places to stretch out on the grass and tune into the atmosphere of tranquillity, broken only by natural sounds (and the odd tractor). If you like your natural history (and you should!) there are butterflies and a myriad of insects in the summer, and wild flowers if the mowing hasn't been too severe. Many birds frequent the spacious churchyard, and can live in peace. The church is a lovely sight too, beautifully proportioned and built of honey-coloured ironstone, with limestone facings and parapets. In addition, the tower and west face of the south aisle are ornamented with an attractive banding pattern, created by alternating ironstone and limestone. When the sun shines on the stone, the colours come alive. The layout is standard, with western tower with battlements, aisled nave and battlemented chancel, plus south porch. A spire was in place until it was removed in the 18th century. There are indications of a 13th century origin for the church, including some stiff leaf carving in the south arcade and blocked doorways on the north side. However, most of what can be seen today is Perpendicular work and the windows are especially harmonious, although most if not all are 19th century replacements. The east window has an inventive pattern of typical Perpendicular type. A delightful frieze or corbel table runs below the chancel battlements and continues onto the north aisle, and features an eclectic variety of heads and fleurons, the heads carved with wry humour. At intervals amongst the heads are gargoyles, some of which incorporate human motifs. The interior has nothing of great historical importance to offer, and received the customary 19th century restoration, but there is one nice ornate wall memorial originating in the late 17th century to members of the Wollaston family, in the style of a cartouche with a framework of scrolls and a rather ominous-looking skull at the base. The octagonal font is thought to be 13th century and is of rather crude workmanship. The east window of the chancel south wall is a memorial to a member of the Fowke family who died in 1897.

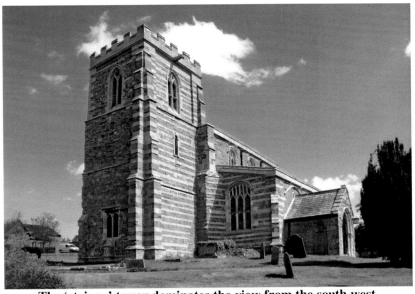
The 'stripey' tower dominates the view from the south west

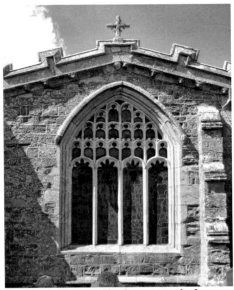
Fancy Perpendicular east window

All Saints looks good from any angle

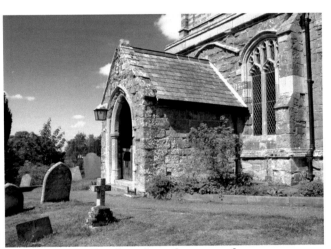
Porch and south approach

External memorial tablet, a gargoyle and figures from the corbel table

North side blocked doorways – tower, aisle and chancel

51

All Saints bathes in early evening sunshine

Lubenham has one of the most interesting churches in Leicestershire, full of mysterious corners and rare survivals, with a genuine antique and unrestored atmosphere. A list of its treasures and fittings would probably take up the whole of this entry, without any further description. The church has a tower, aisled nave, chancel and south porch. The story begins, as far as material evidence goes, in the 12th century with a Norman church. Of that church the north arcade piers remain, low, round and sturdy, with one original square abacus with foliate carving and faces at the corners. A round arch which might be latest Norman or somewhat later leads from the chancel to a north chapel which dates from the early 1200's. The doorway into the north aisle also has a round arch and may be Norman, also some walling at the east end of the south arcade. The east end of the north aisle was a chapel and much later a schoolroom, and is now used as a meeting room. It contains several interesting items, including some old panelling, 13th century piscina and sedile, a squint, a charities board of 1810 and a ?Jacobean chest, plus a lively ancient stone head. The north aisle stretches the full length of the nave, but the south has had a much more chequered history, having been built, partly taken down and rebuilt all before the 15th century. Today it is little more than a transept, having lost its west bay and chapel at the east end. Part of a blocked arch which led into the chapel still exists in the chancel and also the blocked arch to the west bay. For some reason the Victorian restorers laid only the lightest hands on Lubenham, and the last people to leave a significant mark on the interior were the Georgians in 1810-12, who installed the box pews and two-decker pulpit. The box pews retain their original numbers and are altogether a fine set. An even older Jacobean box pew still resides in the south aisle, behind a distressed door with balusters, and was probably used by the owners of Thorpe Lubenham Hall. In the sanctuary is a very fine carved oak communion table, which dates from the 1600's, accompanying it is a chair of similar vintage. Dotted around the church are other odd survivals, such as medieval bench ends, fragments of medieval wall paintings, mural tablets and much more. All Saints is an absolute must on any tour of Leicestershire churches.

Views around All Saints

From the west end   **From the east end**   **North arcade with Norman piers**

Detail of the east window   **Donations board**

Recess in sanctuary   **The squint**   **2-decker pulpit**   **Rood door, painting**   **Wall painting**

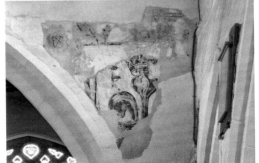

Wall painting beside the chancel arch   **Round arch to chapel**   **Hanoverian Royal Arms**

53

St Mary from the end of Church Street as storm clouds gather

Lutterworth is the chief town of south Leicestershire, yet its population is only around 9,000, much less than many other of Leicestershire's market towns. That small town/large village demographic is reflected in the Grade 1 listed medieval church of St Mary, which is large and spacious yet retains an intimate atmosphere. The building has an expansive plan with a stylish tower with huge disproportionate pinnacles added in the 18th century as part of a new upper stage, nave, aisles and chancel. There are also vestries, an organ chamber, south porch, clerestory, and a chapel in the north aisle. The west end of the south aisle today houses a café area. Much of the look of the interior is the result of the restoration by Gilbert Scott in 1866-9, when many new furnishings and fittings were installed, such as the seating, the grand font and reredos. However, the origins of the church go back much further into the 13th century, as there are still extant lancet windows and a piscina of that date. All that long history has resulted in the accummulation of many items guaranteed to delight the church lover, but St Mary's greatest claim to fame is its association with the religious reformer and dissident John Wycliffe (c. 1328-1384), who preached and died here. Many items have Wycliffe associations, although it must be said that attribution directly to Wycliffe's time is not certain in most cases. One particularly treasured survival is an ancient faded cope, said to belong to Wycliffe. The pulpit in the chancel incorporates many parts of a medieval forerunner which may possibly have been used by Wycliffe. A fine old portrait of the man resides in a vestry and has been the source of uncountable reproductions in books, etc, over the years. A Wiclif (sic.) memorial of 1837 is mounted on the east wall of the south aisle, incongruously surrounded by modern day electric instruments and other trappings of the 21st century church. Also not to be missed are a fine 15th century alabaster tomb in the north aisle chapel, wall paintings of which the most interesting is a representation of the 'three living and three dead' allegory on the north wall of the north aisle, 15th century brasses in the north aisle and nave floors, gilded bosses in the nave roof, a squint from north aisle to the sanctuary, old parish chest, good communion rails (C18th) and altar table (C16th), the original medieval wooden font and a fine array of mural tablets.

St Mary from the west

Looking from chancel to nave

Nave and 'doom' painting

'Three living and three dead'

The unidentified C15th tomb

..... and detail of the figures

Old chest

C14th nave roof and bosses

Mural tablet

Brass eagle lectern

North aisle brass

Wycliffe portrait

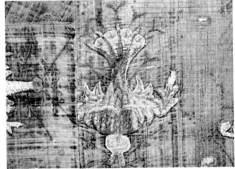
Detail of the ancient cope

'Wycliffe's pulpit'

Wycliffe memorial of 1837

The squint

Screen in the chancel

The C19th font

St Peter from the south

West Leicestershire is peaceful and little visited, except for one area. That is the site of the great history-changing battle in 1485 known as the Battle of Bosworth. There is no doubt that without that taking place the little town of Market Bosworth would be almost unknown outside of Leicestershire. It was the town's 'lucky break' to have its name assigned to the battle, and since then its historical importance has been assured. Yet, it seems that it was indeed a lucky break for Bosworth, because recent, and dare it be said, definitive, research, has revealed that the battle actually took place some miles south west of Bosworth, far nearer the villages of Stoke Golding and Dadlington. Be that as it may, Bosworth is worth a visit in its own right, because it is indeed a fine little town, blessed with a stately hall, now a hotel but once the seat of the Dixie dynasty. And that brings us to the church of St Peter, because its affinities clearly lie with the nearby hall, and several Dixies, both marked and possibly unmarked, lie in the church. Their memorials form one of the best features of the mainly 14th century Decorated building, two in particular, in the chancel to Reverend John Dixie (d. 1719) and in the north aisle to the notorious bully and ignoramus (if historical accounts are to be believed) Sir Wolstan Dixie (d. 1767), are notable. The former features the white marble figure of a prostrate mourning woman, with large cartouche above. As for the rest of the church, its basic configuration follows the familiar tower with spire, aisled nave, chancel, south porch arrangement. The tower is battlemented, as are the nave and aisles. An external stair turret to the former rood loft protrudes from the angle of nave and chancel on the north. Nothing is dramatic or unusual, but taken with the pleasant churchyard, the whole effect is balanced and satisfying. Inside, the Victorian hand is quickly apparent and the whole atmosphere belongs to that era. Except for the lovely 14th century arcades and fabric, most of the interior is 19th century in origin and the fittings are of very good quality, including the excellent screen, carved wood fittings in the chancel and the saints carved in stone in the niches either side of the altar. The vaulted stone sedilia are impressive. One good medieval survivor is the ornate 14th century font with its shields and tracery patterns. Two windows, including the main east window, have stained glass by Kempe.

From the north east **Chancel arch and screen** **The font and nave**

The north arcade and clerestory **The font** **Sir Wolstan Dixie memorial**

Wright family memorial **Owl on the screen** **The beautifully furnished sanctuary** **Detail of reredos**

Detail of the Rev'd Dixie monument **Details from the Kempe stained glass windows**

St Dionysius sits in the heart of Market Harborough   **Tower details**

Few churches in Leicestershire, or indeed England, enjoy such a marvellous position as St Dionysius, which dominates Market Harborough from all points of the compass and sits right by the main road through the town. And just in case anyone might miss it, the church possesses one of the finest spires to be seen anywhere in a small English town. It is the spire that gives the church its fame and that has drawn many fine words from church historians, a perfect broach atop a lovely tower. The lower parts of the tower are the oldest parts of the building, the west door is typical of a time around 1300, also the window above it with intersecting tracery. The basal parts of the chancel arch are also of around 1300, but in the main the building is later 14th or 15th century in date. The porches, north and south, are both two-storey, a sign of medieval prosperity, and indeed Market Harborough is still a thriving town. The rest of the church is of standard appearance, with nave, two aisles and a long chancel. There is a sharp contrast between the limestone of the tower and spire and the ironstone of the rest. Everything on the outside might lead to the expectation of similarly good things inside, but the interior is rather uninspiring and lacking in eye-catching features, while still an impressive space. On entering, the font greets the visitor, but instead of a medieval model, this one is Victorian and that is a clue to the overall appearance of the interior. The restorer was E. F. Law in 1857 and little escaped his attentions. Unfortunately the fittings he introduced have no special qualities, although the reredos has some merit. More restoration took place in 1887, yet oddly the north and south galleries which were built during an interval from the 17th to the 19th centuries, survived these upheavals and are still in place today. The box pews had to go of course, but instead of being replaced, they were reworked to form the pews we see today. Throughout the changes of the 19th century, the excellent Perpendicular arcades with their unusual piers, also the tower and chancel arches, have come though unscathed. Since 1660 they have been joined by the excellent Restoration royal arms, which was originally above the chancel arch but now reside over the tower arch, below the old roofline of the nave. 14th century sedilia in the chancel were discovered behind plaster in 1857 and reinstated. There are several windows with good 19th century and later glass.

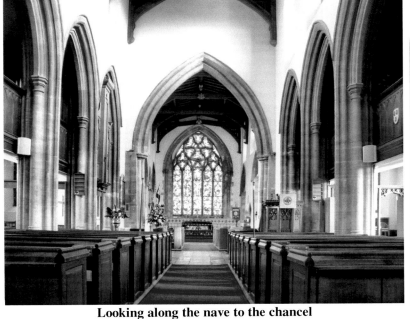

Looking along the nave to the chancel   The chancel

The C19th font   Modern and Victorian stained glass   Arcade pier

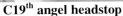

C19th angel headstop   Tower stairway   Charles II royal arms

MARKET HARBOROUGH ST HUGH   D4, SP 737 866

The building is of brick, and was opened in 1940 to replace a 'tin tabernacle'. The nave and chancel are housed under one long roof, but planned aisles were only partly built. A transept comes off the north wall, and accessory buildings have been added over the years. To the south east is a slim, short tower with bellcote. Windows are simple lancets.

Church and St Hugh statue

Two views of Markfield's igneous stone tower and sandstone battlements and spire

Markfield church is not quite what it seems to the visitor approaching from the south. From there it appears to have a conventional configuration of medieval western tower with spire, nave, and south porch. Around 14th century one might surmise, and that at least is correct, except that the porch is of around 1830. One might just note that there isn't the usual chancel at the east end, but nothing looks particularly out of the ordinary. However, while what we see is certainly how the church used to look a couple of centuries ago, a series of later rebuildings to the north has created a quite different building. The old nave is now the south aisle and north of it is a 'new' nave and chancel, continued northwards by a north aisle. Thus, the tower is now a south west tower. The rearrangement began in 1826 when the old lean-to north aisle was rebuilt and changes were made to the chancel arch, by Daniel Knight. However, that was not the answer to St Michael's problems, because in 1865 along came Millican and Smith to completely remodel everything north of the old nave, in the course of which a new nave and chancel were created and a north aisle built. The end result was that to all intents and purposes, except for the basic fabric of the south aisle and the tower, St Michael is a Victorian church, completely fitted out as such. Those seeking medieval artifacts and features will be disappointed. Yet, right at the other end of the time scale, there is some evidence that a church stood here at least in Norman times, and possibly earlier. The evidence is several stones incorporated into the south aisle external wall which are carved with unmistakeable Norman chevrons. On entering, little of the remodelling applied to the building can be detected, although it might be thought odd to see a tower arch at the west end of the south aisle. Apart from that, the interior is a typical 19th century one, with a familiar 20th century overprint by way of carpets and improved lighting. However, the south arcade is medieval with octagonal piers and double chamfered arches, while the north arcade has rounded piers and is Victorian Gothic. The white ashlar stone pulpit is attractive and has a built-in eagle lectern. The font is contemporary and similarly styled, with a dish-type bowl with raised inscription, a central stem and four surrounding pillars. The church has a few mural tablets, but overall St Michael's interior lacks features of interest. Several windows have stained glass, of differing styles, mostly late Victorian.

Top of tower and spire

Blocked window, south aisle

Norman stonework in the south aisle wall

Views looking west and east along the nave

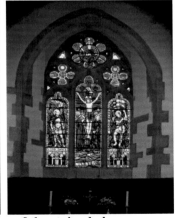
Three examples of the stained glass

South arcade

The pulpit

The font

St Laurence's multi-hued west end faces Measham's High Street

St Laurence is rather uncomfortably marooned in a sea of tarmac, with the only remaining area of green churchyard out of sight to the east. However, this green area is a pleasant spot to sit and relax, although it is a pity that nearly all the gravestones have been removed. A church never looks its best when sited in a car park, and is denuded of gravestones. The removal of the tree enthusiastically obscuring the west end of the south aisle would also help. Yet, this is an interesting building with some rare and attractive features. First of all the fabric consists of multi-toned sandstone which has weathered to a delightful range of hues from red to grey to black (the latter due to industrial pollution), sculpted by wind and rain into pretty contours. Externally, the layout appears to be unexceptional – tower with battlements and pinnacles, nave with two aisles, south porch – but there is no chancel. Inside, it is confirmed that there is just a single large space, the arcades of the nave simply run straight on to the east wall. However, a chancel area has been created by use of furnishings. Then there is the tower itself, at first glance it seems medieval and of a piece with the rest, which is mostly 14th century, but in fact it was built in the late 1730's and has tell-tale signs of that period in the round arched west door and belfry windows, with their keystones and imposts. It's a shame that some of the repair work was undertaken using quite unsympathetic stone, especially over the west door. The whole church is battlemented and nicely symmetrical, the east end being especially satisfying. There are two other odd aspects of the design, one is the unusual west end of the north aisle, which features a blocked doorway over which is a renewed round window. The other oddity is the arch standing off the north aisle at its eastern end, which may be the last remnants of a chapel, or a gateway into the eastern churchyard. The interior is spacious and well appointed, with box pews and a west gallery, also a good display of stained glass.

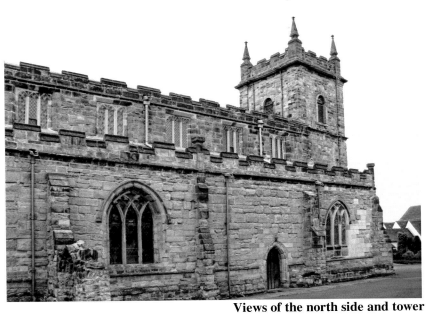

Views of the north side and tower

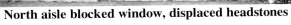

North aisle blocked window, displaced headstones

The enigmatic arch

Ancient headstone

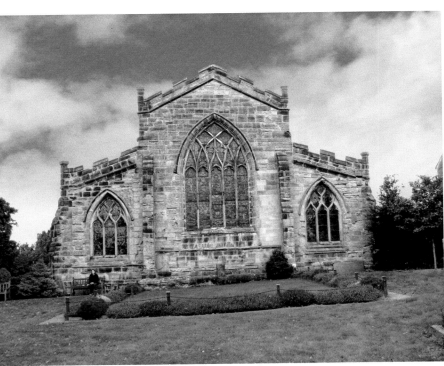

The eastern elevation

MEDBOURNE ST GILES

E4, SP 799 931

The southern aspect

A fine village and lovely English countryside all around make Medbourne an enticing prospect for a visit. Add to that a fascinating (open) church in a beautiful setting on an ancient site and a great day out is assured. How ancient the site is will probably never be established for sure, but it is roughly circular and slightly raised, often signs that it was established in pre-Christian times for ritual purposes or worship. The deliberate placing of Christian churches on such locations is probably commoner than available hard evidence suggests, and may have happened here. The plan of the church is unusual. Tower, nave and chancel are more or less as expected, but the south aisle is no more than a stub which is rapidly curtailed by a large south transept, itself with an eastern aisle, and on the north side there is a corresponding transept but no aisle. The consensus seems to be that more expansion and embellishment on the lines of the southern half of the church was planned but never executed. Whatever the reasons for the plan, it makes for a fascinating interior. The south transept is a rather splendid area, considerably enhanced by the east aisle which is equipped with an altar and piscina, and some very posh 13th century sedilia, which, however, were relocated from elsewhere to their present position. Near the sedilia is a 13th or 14th century grave slab, broken into three pieces, and a little further west in the transept is a nice recess which contains a sadly mutilated effigy, lacking legs, probably 14th century. The responds of the south transept arcade both have carved human figures, the northern one shows two men apparently hugging each other, and the southern a crouching man; both carvings are of considerable antiquity. There is more evidence of a 13th century origin for St Giles in the chancel arch, which has a bold string of nailhead along its hood. Compared to the south transept and its aisle, the nave and chancel are regulation Victorian in appearance, with little to catch the eye. At the west end of the nave is a plain 13th century font on later legs, capped with a 17th century wooden cover rather like a cowl. In the space below the tower a large pendulum of the church clock still solemnly marks the hours with an audible and oddly reassuring tick tock. The pulpit is 18th century on a later base, and a royal arms of 1778 hangs above the south door.

St Giles from the south west

Bridge and tower

The south door

Looking east and west along the church

South transept

Sedilia in south transept

Battered effigy in its recess

Pulpit, wall tablet, grave cover

What are they looking at?

The font

St Mary from Burton Street, and the magnificent tower

Very few Leicestershire churches can be considered to be amongst the best in the country, but the magnificent St Mary at Melton Mowbray is certainly one. It has a large, cathedral-like conception and plan, and indeed was considered in 1926 for the honour of being the cathedral of the newly reconstituted Diocese of Leicester. Only the fact that it wasn't in the county town could have led to that not happening, because it is by far the finest church in the county. Work of all periods can be discovered, some of it obvious, some not. Few would suspect that at the base of the tower is Norman work, because the overall look is that of a Perpendicular church. That earliest work dates from around 1170, the next significant contribution came in Early English times when the beautiful central section of the tower was commissioned, with its lovely harmonious windows. There followed a long interval between 1280 and about 1350 when the main fabric of the nave, chancel, aisles and transepts was completed. The transepts themselves have aisles, a very rare feature in a parish church. The west or Galilee porch is a fine ornate construction of around 1325. The tower was probably completed sometime late in the 15th century. That was also the time when the amazing clerestory was put in, which runs all around the church, except for the chancel. Its exuberance is breathtaking, there is barely any wall to be seen, just identical windows. Needless to say, the church inside is flooded with light. The interior has a great sense of space and grandeur and on entering via the west porch one is struck by the delicious feeling that fine things are there to discover, and indeed there are. There are several tombs and memorials, the first one seen if a counter-clockwise route is taken, is earliest 14th century, and is an effigy of a knight in a recess, with crossed legs. In the south transept are several good features, including two tomb chests, the best one being of an unidentified lady in alabaster from the 14th century. On the walls are several memorials, some very lively, particularly the large wall memorial to Sir John Bennett of 1738. An incised slab from the late 16th century lies in the floor. A window in the south aisle contains collected fragments of medieval glass, some of the motifs still fairly complete. The chancel is quintessentially Victorian, but very fine with super woodwork and a splendid screen. There are many more agreeable items to discover.

From the north west

The nave

Charles II arms

Chancel and sanctuary

Looking towards the nave from the chancel

The crossing

C14th effigy and recess

Two fine tomb chests in the south transept east aisle

Detail of the C14th effigy of a lady

Piscina in chancel

Incised slab, 1597

Memorial, 1738

Memorial, 1759

Mural tablet, 1661

One of very few corbels

Shuckburgh Ashby grave

St Leonard from the north

Misterton is a much shrunken hamlet, little more these days than the church, the Hall, the old vicarage and a few houses, but the church is fairly large with a good-sized churchyard. Clearly it benefitted from the sponsorship of the powerful Poultney family, who ruled the roost in this area from the Hall for a long period in medieval and later times. St Leonard has a bold broach spire atop its substantial 14th century tower and due to the trees that obscure the lower parts of the church, the tower and spire are the overriding impression that registers with visitors. The tower is constructed of grey sandstone, but many other shades of sandstone are apparent in the rest of the church, especially the north aisle whose stones have a lot of red tonation. This results in a pleasing appearance and adds interest, quite apart from the satisfying symmetrical lines of the building. The plan of the church is tower and spire, nave with two aisles, chancel, and a splendid two-storey south porch with vaulted roof and internal access stairway to the top floor. The north aisle has an unusual parapet of blank quatrefoils. The interior is a good mix of medieval survivals and the elements of a comprehensive Victorian refit of 1863, with a keen antique atmosphere and lots of corners to explore. Amongst the best features are two post-medieval alabaster tomb chests, one from the 16th and one from the 17th centuries. Both contain scions of the Poultney dynasty. The older one has a very fine effigy of Michael Poultney (d. 1567), in full armour. The other for John Poultney (d. 1637) has a simple black top without effigy, but has shields on the sides. Several 19th century memorial mural tablets can be found on the walls. Most of the fittings are from the 1863 restoration, including the substantial octagonal drum font, pulpit and attractive altar rails. Also the nicely realised Last Supper marble reredos. Medieval features include the sedilia and piscina in the chancel, a recess or sepulcre in the south aisle, another piscina and window sill sedile in the same aisle and the pointed tower arch. The chancel arch with duochrome stonework on the inner chamfer is 19th century. The arcades unusually have no capitals and the arches sweep down to merge seamlessly into the polygonal piers. Although the nave pews are Victorian, some intricately carved 16th century bench ends were incorporated. Some south aisle pews also have 16th century elements built in.

Two-storey south porch

The north aisle

Looking along the nave to the chancel

The south chapel

Late C19th marble reredos

C19th font

C16th bench end

Tomb chests of Michael Poultney (left and centre) and John Poultney (right)

Christ Church from the south, new extension to the right

Christ Church has a pleasant setting on the side of Castle Hill and faces an attractive green that climbs up from the main road through Mountsorrel. It was built in 1844, using the granite which crops out in the immediate area. The chancel was extended in 1899. It is a tall, but fairly simple building and consists of tower with chamfer spire, nave and chancel. An Early English style with long lancets was adopted, with west door through the tower. In the late C20th an extension was constructed and subsequently enlarged on the south side to house church and community rooms, but unfortunately the construction obscures much of the eastern side of the church, and appears rather incongruous. On the other hand it considerably increases the church's appeal within its community.

Christ Church from The Green

Weathercock

Belfry openings

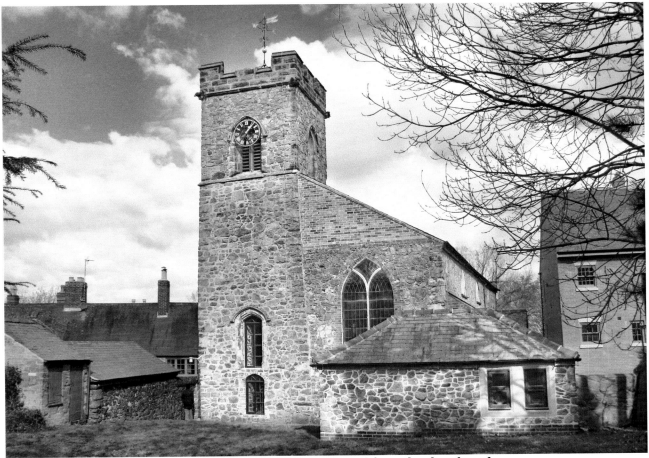

The west, in reality more south, end from the churchyard

One hesitates to call any church ugly, but, externally at least, there is a temptation with St Peter. Let's just say odd. Even the orientation is more north-south then east-west. It looks as if elements of many churches of many periods and many fabrics were thrown together and made to fit. The plan is north-west tower, nave and chancel under one roof, north porch, Victorian extension to the south, modern organ chamber and a further modern extension in the small west churchyard. A south aisle has lost its arcade and is now integral to the rest of the interior. No one style dominates, but the history began with the tower, the lower two thirds of which may be 13th century. The top stage is 14th century and so is some of the rest of the core of the church. But perhaps the greatest input was in the late 18th century when the church was expanded and many changes were implemented. The obvious external manifestations of that phase are the large, typical Georgian window in the west elevation and the clock on the east gable. The Victorians also made major changes to St Peter in 1870, including replacing almost all the windows, and the much more conventional (and pleasant) interior is almost entirely Victorian in concept.

Seen from Leicester Road

St Peter with its extensions

Tower top stage

St Nicholas from its churchyard to the south

Not at all your standard Leicestershire church, St Nicholas is well worthy of a visit. The building dates from the late 13th century, and saw little change until Pearson's extensive restoration of 1882. The church is prettily set in the heart of its village and has a pleasant churchyard. The building itself is unusual, there are no aisles, yet there are two transepts, resulting in a cruciform shape. The nave and chancel are not differentiated and are under one roof, instead of a tower we have a bellcote. Those factors should pique interest, and the interior doesn't disappoint. The immediate impression, although not borne out in detail, is of a priory or monastic church. This effect is brought about by the wide, continuous nave and chancel, the two transepts disappearing off mysteriously to left and right, the stripped walls and the pious gloom that envelops the church. Lights can easily be activated, but in some ways it is more atmospheric to leave them off. The first thing that presents itself on entering via the south door is the font, not a particularly distinctive one, but it is old, probably Early English and wears the battle scars to prove it. Looking towards the chancel the excellent wooden screen with its half doors is a prominent feature, and that too appears old. In a way it is, because although it was made in the 19th century, the wood used for it is much older and came from Kibworth Grammar School. The chancel houses good things, including a very old altar stone that was reinstated during the 1882 restoration. There are three wall tablets, not especially distinguished except for a classic High Victorian Gothick one of 1852 for the Reverend Tindall, but the piscina is nice and the painted panelling to either side of the altar is charmingly sentimental. Exploring the transepts it is quickly appreciated that both were formerly chapels, as each has a piscina, the one in the north transept is particularly good and has head stops. The south transept is still set up as a chapel, and has a communion table, plus some venerable 17th century panelling, said to be from the manor house at nearby Knaptoft. The main south door has interesting head stops, one has suffered badly over the years but the other is better preserved and bears an odd appendage on the top of its head. The remains of a holy water stoop can be seen by this door.

Views around St Nicholas

Looking east and west along the nave   **Oak screen and chancel**

Panelling by the altar   **The font**   **Chancel piscina**

North transept piscina and old parish chest   **The head by the door**   **Rev'd Tindall mural tablet**

MUSTON ST JOHN THE BAPTIST

St John from Church Lane

The scattered village of Muston lies in the far north of Leicestershire, in the little north east 'horn' that projects into Nottinghamshire and Lincolnshire. Unlike neighbouring Bottesford, St John has no illusions of grandeur, being fairly small, but it does have a complete church plan of tower with fine broach spire, aisled nave, chancel and two substantial porches north and south. The 15th century clerestory has three flat-headed windows each side. St John stands in a good churchyard and looks well in the uninterrupted view from Church Lane. Weathering over the centuries has sculpted an appealing rustic appearance. The basic fabric is ironstone, but liberal use is made of limestone, particularly in the spire and buttresses. The nave and tower are 13th century and the tower, aisles and chancel are 14th century. The broach spire is perhaps contemporary with the tower, or a little later. The top of the tower features tall corner pinnacles and a corbel table with small, quirky heads. The spire has three sets of lucarnes that diminish in size markedly up the spire, the topmost set appearing tiny from the ground. The gabled porches almost certainly post-date the rest of the church and may be 15th or 16th century, the northern one has two rather oversized pinnacles and a battlemented gable. Inevitably there was a major restoration in the 19th century by Charles Kirk when much furniture was replaced and fabric and windows remodelled. However, several medieval features survived the refit, particularly a nice set of around 20 bench ends with poppyheads. These are thought to be 15th century, as is the font, whose pristine carving nevertheless suggests it has been recut, possibly during the 19th century restoration. The four heads at the base of the font are a striking feature. The wooden screen and handsome pulpit are also attributed a medieval origin, but are so much remodelled and renewed as to appear Victorian, certainly the small rood figures and improving texts on the former are 19th century. What are undoubtedly medieval are the two arcades, with the south being the older, with stiff leaf, masks and other carving on the capitals which indicates a 13th century age. Medieval glass fragments survive in the chancel south windows.

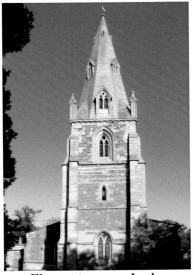
Elegant tower and spire

Memorial set into the south porch

The rather ungainly north porch

Looking east along the nave to the screen

Looking west from the sanctuary

The pulpit

C15th font

Medieval poppyhead

Medieval glass

The rector and churchwarden of 1685 left their mark on beams in the south aisle

 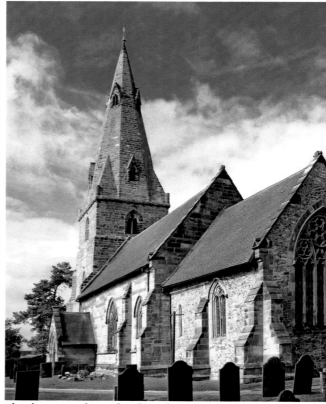

Nailstone's splendid broach spire is a prominent landmark

All Saints is certainly a powerful presence externally, due mainly to the large, bold tower/broach spire combination, but the other parts of the church are just the right proportions to complete the picture harmoniously. Added impact is provided by the large north aisle, which matches the nave in proportions. The use of building materials is interesting and highlights the different phases of construction. The oldest part of the present church is probably the cobblestone chancel, which retains two dissimilar blocked lancet windows, one to the north and one to the south, thereby a date sometime in the late 1200's is indicated. By the time the nave was built (or almost certainly rebuilt) in the 14th century the builders chose to use smartly cut sandstone ashlar. The tower is also made of sandstone ashlar but here the blocks are somewhat rougher cut, suggesting that the nave and tower were built at different times, although probably both in the 14th century. The broach spire is a little more difficult to interpret, because though the ashlar blocks appear to be smaller that those of the tower, that is probably because the use of small blocks is more appropriate for spire construction. The top of the tower previously boasted pinnacles, but in recent years these were removed as a safety measure. However, the worn corbel table is still in place. Some remains of the pinnacles can be inspected at the foot of the tower, north side. The tower has two oddities, one is a rather fancy round window or occulus in the west wall which looks 18th century, the other is a very narrow, low south doorway. West doorways in towers are quite common but southern ones, especially so near the main entrance to a church, as here, are somewhat rarer. It has to be said that the commodious interior of All Saints is an austere, seemingly little-used space with few focal points, and is one of the less inspiring experiences in a Leicestershire churches tour. In mitigation, at the time of my visit certain items including the fittings of the north chapel had been stripped out for wall painting, which will undoubtedly have brightened things up. What there is to see includes two fonts, a Victorian one dating from a major restoration in 1853, and the bowl of a much older one which sits on a log. A 16th century incised slab is located near the chapel table, but having been used as a base for a stove at one time, it is in poor shape. The original medieval tower arch is unusually flamboyant, with four orders of chamfers. The Victorian fittings are generally utilitarian rather than beautiful, but the stone pulpit is attractive, and the angels on the chancel arch responds are cheery.

Round window in the tower

Blocked lancet in the chancel

Looking west from the chancel

All Saints austere interior

Chancel and sanctuary

Tower arch

Charles II table of 1664

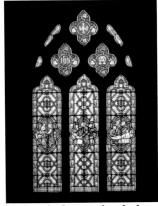

Fonts old and new

The stone pulpit

Incised slab

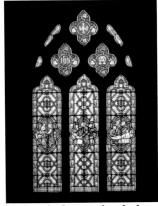

Nave window stained glass

Poppyheads

All Saints bristles with battlements

Narborough can hardly be called a village these days, it expanded in the mid – late 20th century to become a satellite suburb of Leicester, with around 7000 inhabitants. As usual, that growth has been at the expense of the village's character, yet around All Saints a little enclave of older housing has survived and the atmosphere there is less frenetic. The church too is an oasis of calm and is a fine building, if the unfortunate recipient of overly vigorous Victorian makeovers. Today's church would be immediately recognised by its 19th and early 20th century congregations, so much do the Victorian and, to a lesser extent, Edwardian fittings and atmosphere still dominate the interior. The plan is familiar and very 'Leicestershire', with a typical tower, attached to an aisled nave and chancel, plus south porch. The Victorians added an organ chamber off the chancel to the south, with a more substantial vestry to the north. The vestry has a very fine Swithland Slate roof, which shows off very well the classic pattern of slating with the Swithland type, with little 'uns at the top, grading down to big 'uns at the eaves. Accurate dating of the building is difficult due to the relatively few clues available, but certainly the tower and basic fabric is at least 14th century in origin. The chancel was rebuilt by Bacon in 1883 to an Early English template, and it is an excellent example of the Victorian version of that distinctive philosophy, with several stylish flourishes like the plate tracery windows and the archways and doors into the organ chamber and vestry. The wrought iron screen is quite excellent, with very delicate tracery complimented by neat low stone walls. The reredos is also very smart, with two gilded angels standing guard on either side. As for the fabric internally, the lovely medieval arcades immediately draw admiration, with their shafted piers, and the tower arch is tall and slender. The chancel arch dates from the 19th century restorations. The font may be 15th century yet has a crispness that suggests later recutting. Surviving in the south aisle are medieval sedilia and piscina, associated with a former chapel in that area. Almost all the other fittings are 19th century, but all are of good quality, such as the pulpit on its marble shafts. Amongst the collection of mural tablets there are a few 18th century examples, and another written in Greek. There is window glass of 1929 by Theodora Salusbury in the north aisle.

From the south east

Tower from Church Lane

Approach to main entrance and south porch

Stately nave and arcades, from west and east

The font

Shaw brass of 1870

Chancel details, and aumbry

Sedilia and piscina in the south aisle

Mural tablets in the chancel

NETHER BROUGHTON ST MARY

St Mary is a classic ironstone church, in a lovely setting

The peaceful village of Nether Broughton is less than a kilometre from the Nottinghamshire boundary in the north of the county. Its neighbour, the 'other' Broughton, Upper, is only a kilometre away, yet is in Nottinghamshire. St Mary is beautifully situated on the northern edge of the village in a large verdant churchyard, where a pleasant hour can be spent taking in the surroundings and searching for 'Belvoir angel' headstones. These are a distinctive type of slate or, more rarely, limestone headstone popular in eastern and north eastern areas of Leicestershire in the 17th and 18th centuries, which feature a carving at the top depicting the soul in the form of a radiant face flying heavenwards on angel wings. Nether Broughton has one of the best collections anywhere of these early headstones, several of them loose and stacked by the church walls. The church is a classic ironstone building with the usual limestone dressings and additions, including the overlarge set of battlements and pinnacles on the tower. Its history is a familiar one from 13th century beginnings to the customary 19th century refit, during which time the aisles and clerestory were added. The wide-ranging restoration of 1881 saw most of the windows and internal fittings replaced. The south aisle is 13th century, but the north aisle was rebuilt in 1903. One oddity is the lack of entrances to the north and south, the church is accessed through a west door in the tower. There seems never to have been any other public entrances, or porches, just a priest's door (now blocked) in the chancel north wall. Above the west entrance is a curious half window which may have been truncated to accommodate the doorway below, or may have been relocated here from elsewhere. The chancel has no windows to the north, also a little odd. The interior is rather sparse and lacks major items of interest, but an exploration will reveal a few treasures. One of these must be sought out in the vestry, it is a stone with Saxon interlace work, probably from a cross. Another single carved stone is set into the south wall of the south aisle, and depicts an Agnus Dei, or Lamb and Flag. That one is later, possibly 13th century. The chancel arch respond capitals show nailhead decoration, also the west respond in the south arcade. The communion table is a good 17th century example.

St Mary seen from the north　　　　　　Entrance is through the tower

Niche and statue, east window　　　Looking towards the chancel　　　The north arcade

Saxon interlace fragment (?from cross)　　Agnus Dei, possibly C13th　　'Belvoir angel' headstone

St James has a very un-Leicestershire like appearance

St James at Newbold Verdon brings a touch of the Arts and Crafts movement to Leicestershire, and has an appearance that is unusual in this part of the world. However, on closer study it will be appreciated that only the tower and spire support this assertion, the rest of the church is quite standard in style. The curious fact is that the top stage of the tower and the shingled Home Counties spire were erected only in 1960, long after the Arts and Crafts movement had passed its acme. The rest of the church isn't old either, although rather older than the spire, and was built in 1899 by local stalwarts Goddard and Company, to a generally Perpendicular model. The plan is of tower and spire, nave, north aisle, chancel, transeptual south vestry running off the chancel, and south porch. That layout may well correspond to the plan of the medieval church that preceded this one, although the vestry was probably a new addition. The stonework looks so pristine that it is hard to believe that the base of the tower may be Norman; like many Leicestershire churches it seems that the medieval tower was not taken down at the time of Victorian rebuilding. However, in the years leading up to the addition of the top stage and spire, old photographs show that only the bottom two stages of the old tower were still standing. Whilst it is true that the 1899 church was new, some older fabric was incorporated in the present building. The medieval three-light lancet window in the west wall of the north aisle is an example of this. The three-light window in the east wall of the aisle is also medieval and may have been retained from the old church. With the exception of the tower and spire, St James is not exceptional, but is a tidy, harmonious building with some nice touches. The south front of the vestry has imaginative decoration which includes an attractive doorway and a sundial, and the south porch is a pleasing construction, complete with niche and statue of St James. In contrast to the rather more decorative south frontage, the north side of the church is very dull. Inside, everything is spruce and well-cared for, but the fittings are essentially conservative. The arcade is slightly unusual, in that the piers lack capitals. The fleurons here are a pretty touch. The five-light east window is a strong feature, with some good glass. The font bowl may be 13th century.

The distinctive tower and spire dominate these views

The south porch

The vestry

Vestry door

Sundial and spire

C13th lancet

From the shady churchyard of 1876

St Luke is one of those churches that hides away from its village, lying as it does about half a mile to the south beyond the main Leicester to London railway line and the Grand Union Canal. There is a small cluster of buildings nearby, but the surroundings seem remote and very rural. Standing next to the small church it is hard to realise that the southern edges of Leicester's sprawl are only a few miles to the north. St Luke has almost no frontage to the south and the tower sits right on the road, but to the rear (north) is a fairly commodious churchyard which was inaugurated for burials in 1876, when parent church Wistow closed for interments. One grave marker that always catches the eye is a white painted miniature church, not at all like St Luke, which marks the resting place of a young boy. The building is very unpretentious and modest, and only the 13th century pyramid roofed, low tower remains from the medieval church. The rest was thoroughly rebuilt in 1834 with the nave and chancel under one roof, and no aisles. To the north are brick-built transeptual extensions to house the organ and vestry. There is a doorway incorporated into the vestry extension. The main entrance is through a 16th century west doorway in the tower. The application of stucco to the nave/chancel was unfortunate, even the red bricks beneath would have been preferable. Despite its 13th century date, the tower has a very Norman look and two phases of building can be clearly seen, with cobbles for the bottom half and rough ironstone blocks for the upper. A west lancet window in the cobbled bottom section is probably original. The interior is very modest, with simple furniture and fittings, but entering from the west through the tower is always diverting and offers a different perspective on the interior. All is tidy and uncluttered, but ultimately rather uninspiring. Nothing is very old, but the plain font with its long stem dates from 1777 and other fittings may also be from around the same date. It is known from church records that a western gallery was erected at the time of the 1834 rebuilding, but as was very frequently the case, that had a short life and succumbed during further refitting in 1874.

St Luke from the south east, and west

The C13th/14th tower

St Luke has a charming setting

The east end and churchyard

The extensions to the north

The little white church

All Saints from the west

Leicestershire is not high on most tourist's itineraries, but if there is one area that does draw the crowds, it is Charnwood Forest, that most scenic expanse of rough hill country. Of all the areas of Charnwood, Bradgate Park attracts the most visitors, and Newtown Linford has for long enjoyed the unofficial title of capital of Bradgate, for the main entrance to the Park is in the village. Furthermore, the medieval church of All Saints is situated immediately adjacent to that main entrance and car park. The custodians of the church have long been aware of that fact, and have always taken pains to welcome visitors, both to services and for sightseeing tours inside. The church can also boast connections with the Grey family and thereby its most famous member, Lady Jane Grey, the nine day queen, who lived in Bradgate House in the Park. The Greys were patrons of All Saints for a long period in the Middle Ages. With all that pulling power, the village wisely opens All Saints doors to visitors on weekend afternoons in the season. What the visitor finds is an immaculately kept church and churchyard, well worthy of its position in the tourist limelight. On the other hand All Saints is not a building that boasts a great number of old fittings and features, having been heavily modified by Victorian restorers in the years 1894-5, and again even more so in the year 1915 when the vestry and organ chamber were added and the chancel was refurbished in the Arts and Crafts style. These remodellings left the church with a present-day plan of west tower with recessed spire, nave, chancel and north aisle which incorporates a 16th century north transept. There is also a Victorian south porch of 1860. A highlight of the exterior is the Perpendicular window in the nave south wall, which has a transom and flattened 'Tudor' arch. Despite the lack of medieval items, there are several interior features of interest, including a chancel beam or tympanum on which is mounted a George III arms and two shields, some nice glass in the east window which includes a representation of Lady Jane Grey, a screen near the tower door which contains pieces of old oak from 1633 and the 17th century, an old grave marker used for calligraphy practise and a good 18th century mural tablet.

Views of All Saints from the south and south east

Features of the south frontage

Tower and porch   **The east end and window**   **Sundial of 1706**

Headstops   **The clock**   **Cast iron grave marker**

NORMANTON LE HEATH HOLY TRINITY   A3, SK 377 127

From the south

Normanton le Heath is a small village in the west of the county, standing independent and alone some distance away from neighbouring settlements. For a small village it boasts a fairly substantial and impressive church, with a plan of tower and recessed spire of excellent proportions, nave and chancel under one roof with no chancel arch, and a north aisle that runs almost the full length of the building. Within the aisle is a north chapel, and the overall dimensions of the aisle are not far off those of the nave, giving rise to an almost two-nave configuration, a not unfamiliar phenomenon in Leicestershire (see Broughton Astley and nearby Nailstone). Like most churches in the west of the county, the building stone is local sandstone, pale in hue. One notable feature is that the church is orientated exactly E-W, which is unusual for a medieval church, most diverge slightly or more so from that preferred line. The building except the tower was constructed over an interval in the 14th century within the Decorated period of architecture and all the windows are in that style, and very fine they are too, although it seems that all the tracery has been renewed, probably during Victorian restoration. The tower and spire are somewhat later than the body of the church and show Perpendicular stylings. The south porch appears to be much later altogether. The inevitable 19th century restoration took place under G. E. Street in 1854, but it seems likely that there were other spells of remodelling in that century. The church is very prettily set off Main Street in Normanton and the almost square churchyard is also attractive and quite large. Inside there is a good feel of an old church, and several items demand attention. The screen across the north chapel used to run across the entrance to the chancel, and is largely 15th century, with some skilful foliate carving. The probably 13th century font (?from an earlier church) is of a specialist local type, with thick ribs running up the bowl. Examples of very similar fonts can be seen at neighbouring Ibstock and Nailstone. Sadly, Holy Trinity has recently been placed on the English Heritage 'at risk' register, due to problems with damp, but the community are rallying round to overcome the threat.

Views from the west and south east

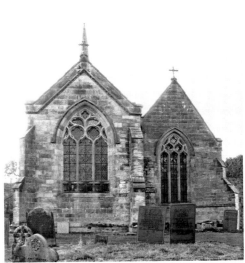

The east end

Fine tower and spire

Ogee-headed doorway, north aisle

A battery of gargoyles protects the tower

89

A splendid Leicestershire church – North Kilworth St Andrew

The largely 14th century St Andrew has a satisfying symmetrical outline, due to the similar dimensions of the two aisles. However, they are not contemporary, the north aisle is 14th century while the south is 19th century. The oldest part of the building is the 13th century chancel, although this has renewed tracery externally and was restored during Victorian times, a restoration that included a fancy priest's doorway to the north. However, inside, the chancel north and south windows retain their Early English details, including detached shafts on the jambs. The east window is entirely Victorian, but also has shafts. The north wall of the clerestory has its original 14th century quatrefoil windows, enclosed in square frames. The south wall has matching Victorian versions. The tower and spire were begun in Decorated times in the early 14th century but by the time the upper parts were built, some Perpendicular detail was included, pointing to a lengthy period of construction. The north porch and shallow organ chamber off the chancel south wall are both 19th century. The interior has several points of interest, not least the completely dissimilar arcades. The 14th century north arcade by itself is unusual, as it lacks capitals and the arches sweep down uninterrupted into the piers, but the south arcade is a Victorian confection of clustered shafts and very bold foliate capitals. For the architect of the restoration of 1855-6 Joseph Clarke to deliberately create such a clashing style was perverse to say the least. Many of the other interior features and fittings also date to that restoration of 1855-6, including the substantial square font with its pretty red marble legs, the seating, reredos, communion table, altar rails and lectern. The roof painting in the chancel is also Victorian. Of the older survivals, the tower arch is 14th century and there is a medieval rood loft opening above the pulpit. The attractive 16th century polygonal pulpit itself is interesting and rare for Leicestershire, and has a pleasing wine-glass shape. Several memorial tablets adorn the walls, none of any great age, but those to Admiral Man Dobson and his son Hyde tell fascinating stories, which can be expanded upon by information available on the internet.

The north side of St Andrew

The tower

The nave, chancel and south arcade

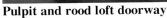

Pulpit and rood loft doorway

Victorian font

Stained glass detail

Mural tablets to Admiral Man Dobson, his son Hyde, Jane Belgrave and Elizabeth Pochin

The pretty chancel built of reddish sandstone is prominent in this view from the north east

Norton-juxta-Twycross is a small settlement way over in the west of the county, very close to the Warwickshire border. It may well be one of those villages that has migrated over the centuries, because the early 14th century church of Holy Trinity is situated right on the northern edge of Norton with only open country to the north of it. The church has no great claim to fame and is a modest building, consisting of just tower, nave and chancel, with a later vestry added on the north of the chancel in 1850, but it has that charm that comes from a pleasant situation in a homely English village and hundreds of years of love and care from its villagers. The tower is a typical one for Leicestershire, with battlements. There was a spire until 1890, but like many others it became unsafe, and was taken down. The same fate befell a south porch sometime after 1790. The west side of the tower has some interest and atmosphere, with a much eroded figure in a niche (was it once Christ in Glory?) and a beguiling old doorway above which is a window with early 14th century intersecting tracery. The rest of the building has evidence of rebuilding, much of it done during a sweeping restoration in the 19th century. It is clear that the nave is constructed of different sandstone blocks from those of the chancel, and judging by the condition of the stonework, much of the chancel's fabric is original and therefore older, while the nave has been rebuilt or refaced. All the window tracery appears to have been renewed but may echo the Decorated stylings of the originals, or at least is in the same spirit. A particular favourite of the author's are sunken churchyard paths, worn by the tread of innumerable feet over the centuries, and Holy Trinity has a fine example, which leads to the priests door in the chancel south side and no doubt was worn mostly by successive incumbents. The interior has much of interest and retains a lot of the fittings and furniture installed during an early Victorian restoration of around 1841. Very unusually these include an excellent set of box pews with poppyheads and a west gallery, which were beginning to become unpopular by that time. The pulpit, ornate font, stained glass and chancel furniture also date from 1841.

The south frontage of Holy Trinity

Looking from the east

Sunken path to the chancel

Niche and worn statue

Victorian main south doorway

Unusual table tomb of 1808

OADBY ST PAUL

C4, SK 635 006

Views around St Paul

The tentacles of greater Leicester are forever extending into the surrounding countryside, and Oadby forms the 'south eastern front' of this advance. Much new housing in that area led to a call for an Anglican presence here, and St Paul was built in 1982 to meet that need. The one storey building has a modern and undistinguished plan, and is made of pale artificial stone blocks with many windows. The building is also used for community activities. The interior is bland and featureless, yet clearly offers a welcoming and comfortable environment for worshippers, and the church is very popular.

OADBY ST PETER

C4, SK 623 003

From the north east

Oadby was sacrificed to greater Leicester many years ago and has settled down into being an undistinguished dormitory town which mistakenly disposed of many of its more interesting central buildings thinking that modernisation was the way forward. But St Peter survived and has benefitted from the expanded population to be a successful and pleasant church. It forms an oasis of calm, and the admirable medieval outline no doubt uplifts passers-by as they rush to their appointments or the shops. The plan of tower with imposing broach spire, aisled nave, chancel, north and south porches and vestry is mostly 14th century, but the latter is Victorian, built as part of a very vigorous and far-reaching restoration. The fabric is very mixed, and limestone, ironstone, sandstone, miscellaneous rubble and local igneous rocks are all represented. The interior strongly reflects the 1887 restoration, and little remains of the medieval church except the lovely arcades, chancel and tower arches, font and some south aisle features. The Victorian fittings are excellent, especially the reredos, pulpit and some fine stained glass. 20th and 21st century improvements have seen the introduction of modern facilities and seating, which have helped to create a welcoming ambience.

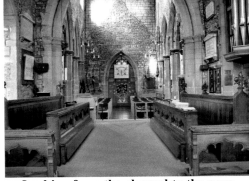

Two views of St Peter from the south **Looking from the chancel to the nave**

Looking from the nave to the chancel **Lovely south arcade** **Medieval piscina and sedilia in south aisle**

The pulpit and surrounding area **C14th font** **Fine stained glass, east window**

OAKS IN CHARNWOOD ST JAMES THE GREATER B2, SK 473 164

St James has a peerless setting in the heart of Charnwood Forest

St James is situated deep in Charnwood Forest in as pretty a location as almost any Leicestershire church. Yet it being here as a fully functioning church is a wonder, as it is miles from any significant settlement, and the name Oaks in Charnwood is simply that, there is no village here. Yet the church benefits from its lovely setting, and the congregation comes in from a wide area to enjoy it. It also shares a benefice with the much larger, almost urban, church of St Botolph in nearby Shepshed and no doubt can call for help from its big brother should it be needed. In addition, good relations are maintained with the neighbouring Mount St Bernards Abbey. Not surprisingly the church is also very popular for weddings, and the adjacent church hall is kept busy too. The building stone, inevitably, is the local Charnwood igneous rock, so local that it was quarried from right next to the church. The dressings and battlements are sandstone. The present building was built new in 1883 and replaced a very modest predecesor of 1815. The architect was Ewan Christian, who was responsible for several church projects in Leicestershire and elsewhere. The plan is simple and consists of tower, nave, chancel, south porch and vestry. The best feature of St James is the bold tower with its quaint pyramid roof, which imparts a slightly French air. The battlements are adorned at the corners with lively gargoyles. The interior is decent enough but rather mundane, however it has to be said that the chancel and sanctuary are very nicely presented. Almost all the fittings date from the building of the church in 1883, and include a good pulpit and two fonts. It seems reasonable to conclude that the much plainer disused font nearest the south door is the older of the two, and probably was retained from the 1815 church. An unusual feature on the nave north wall is a set of six lances, which are reliably authenticated as originating from the Battle of Waterloo, fought in 1815, and there is a claim that the original church of that time was actually consecrated on the day of the battle. The churchyard is most pleasant and has a good number and variety of gravestones, and is a beautiful sight in Spring when hundreds of daffodils come into flower.

The porch

Tower gargoyle

Looking east along the nave

The sanctuary

The excellent C19th pulpit

C19th fonts, the one on the right is the older

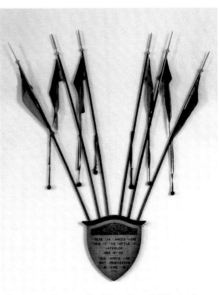

Lances from the Battle of Waterloo

OLD DALBY ST JOHN THE BAPTIST

St John from the north east

St John's setting, on a low hill in a churchyard of rounded outline, suggests that the site has been used for religious purposes for a very long time. An ancient medieval church did indeed stand on the site, but presumably fell into considerable disrepair, as it was demolished and swept away in the 1830's and a brand new building replaced it in 1835. That period just before the accession of Queen Victoria was an interesting one for church-building, as the ecclesiological movement (not yet known as such, the word ecclesiology was not coined until 1837) was gathering momentum but was not yet a major influence, together with various Oxbridge groups, on church design. So what we see at Old Dalby is a building with Gothic, Perpendicular-influenced architecture but of a plain stamp without the exaggerated neo-medieval stylings of the later 19th century. By 1894 when the church was restored, the tide of gothicism was receding, so even that event did little to elaborate the exterior or enrich the interior. St John consists of a slim battlemented tower, nave with short south aisle, chancel, battlemented north porch and vestry. The fabric is of sandstone ashlar blocks throughout, and the outline is regular and rather austere. Inside, the nave is also rather stark and spartan, and has few items of interest. However, the south arcade is enlivened with ornate pier capitals with leaf carvings, and the stone pulpit and complimentary low screen are distinctive. The church's highlight is undoubtedly the small collection of memorials and monuments to members of the Noel family, who were noted landowners and authority figures in the area since the time of Henry VIII. What the collection lacks in numbers it more than makes up for in quality and size, and there are three large monuments, unfortunately hidden away out of sight in an area behind the altar. The oldest, an alabaster chest tomb for Sir Andrew Noel who died in 1562, features himself and his two wives in effigy on the top. There is another alabaster chest tomb, an odd, almost miniature example from around 1580, featuring a threesome in effigy on top, this one for an unidentified lady and her two husbands. The last big monument is a bold, expresssive wall memorial with chest tomb for another Andrew Noel and his wife; he died in 1603.

From the south west

North porch and tomb

From the west end looking east

Monument for Andrew Noel (d. 1603) and wife, and tomb chest of Sir Andrew Noel (d. 1562) and his two wives

Small chest tomb for a lady and her two husbands from around 1580   **C14ᵗʰ stone coffin lid**

Headstone of 1693

Early headstones of 'Belvoir Angel' type

ORTON ON THE HILL ST EDITH

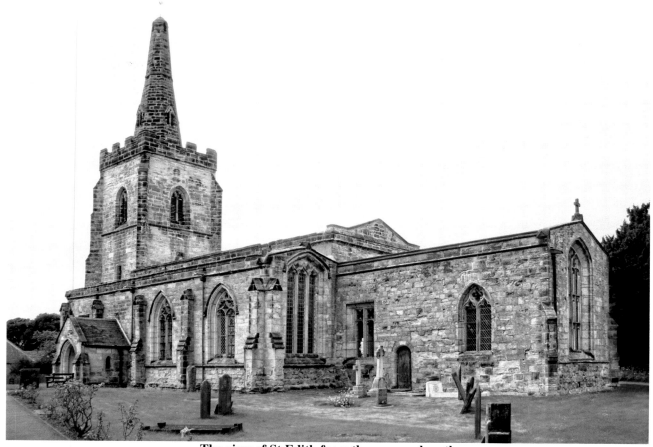

The view of St Edith from the approach path

St Edith is a terrific church for the ecclesiastical enthusiast and those who would indulge in a palpable sense of the past. It is one of Leicestershire's finest, but perhaps its regular congregation would prefer a little more comfort and modern facilities. St Edith really is a barn of a place where the cold must find its way in during the winter and the hard box pews take their toll during long services. However, for the historian, it is an essential church to see, as the features and fittings are of great interest. That interest begins even before the door is opened, because St Edith is a fine looking 14th century church with an array of varied windows, some of them originals from that century. The Decorated south doorway is worn with age and the weather (it has only been protected from the elements by a porch since the 19th century) but is also a lovely feature. The outline is given an added twist by the strange spire which once stood 35m high, but had to be reduced in height for safety reasons in 1950, leaving a mini-spire. The plan is of tower with aforesaid spire, nave, south aisle, chancel and south porch. Once there was a north aisle but it was reduced to a single bay in 1763, that portion was left to form a mausoleum for the Steele-Perkins family who lived at the now demolished Orton Hall. The interior is fascinating and is redolent of the past. It largely retains its pre-19th century appearance, which was only lightly brushed over by the customary Victorian restoration. There are 18th century box pews, a triple-decker pulpit still in its original position halfway down the nave, brick flooring and a 15th or 16th century nave roof. Another 18th century pulpit sits in the more usual position in front of the chancel. The Steel-Perkins mausoleum is an odd place which requires agility or a ladder to reach, as the bottom half is sealed and contains the tombs while the higher top half has memorials. A long list of intriguing fittings further beguiles the visitor, including a 13th century stone coffin lid serving as a bench in the south aisle, another large coffin lid with carvings at both ends, two 14th century piscinas, wall paintings, a delicate 18th century font, a squint from aisle to chancel, a marvellous effigy of a 14th century priest in the mausoleum, a tomb recess, 16th century incised slab and much more. A visit is highly recommended.

St Edith in winter

The south doorway

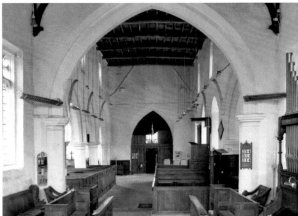
Looking west from the chancel

Box pews and triple-decker pulpit in the nave

C18th font

The squint

Old royal arms

Medieval painting

C16th incised slab

Tomb lid/bench

One of the Steele tablets

C14th effigy of a priest

Carved coffin lid, and niche

101

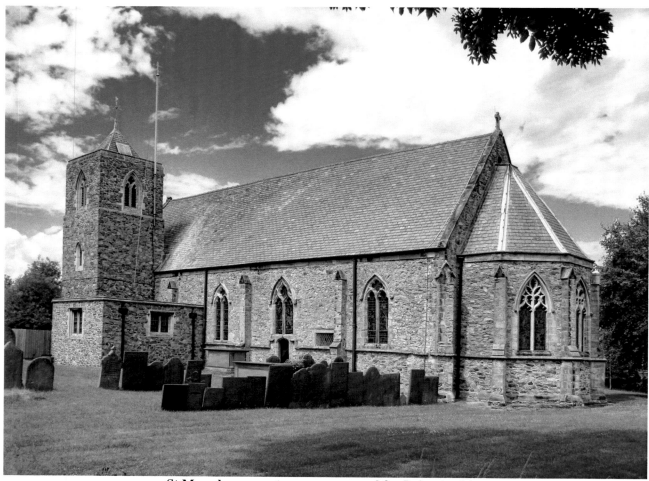

St Mary has an eastern apse, unusual for Leicestershire

St Mary's origins are rather murky, but there is enough evidence to suggest a 14th century foundation, at least. There are two ancient doorways, north and south, with ogee heads, or the remains of them, and these point to a date around that time. In addition, the north doorway is flanked by worn, but clearly medieval, heads. For several hundreds of years since that time the church consisted solely of a simple one cell building which housed a nave and chancel, without extensions or tower. Then during the Victorian restoration of 1861, someone, presumably the architect Joseph Mitchell, had the bright idea to add an apse to the east end to form an intimate chancel/sanctuary. It certainly added an air of distinction to what otherwise would be a very mundane building. As part of the necessary alterations for that project, the previously existing east window was removed and a big chancel arch inserted. This arch occupies a large area of the pre-existing east wall and must be much larger than the preceding window. Also in 1861 Mitchell, who restored several churches hereabouts, added a north porch. More major changes occurred in 1931 when a modest tower was erected; this had to be built onto on the south west wall of the nave due to lack of space in the traditional position beyond the west wall. The tower has a pyramid roof and exaggeratedly high flagpole. Also in 1931 the adjacent flat-roofed vestry was built. Time is gradually blending the Charnwood stone fabrics of these disparate elements into a pleasing harmony. The church is entered through the northern doorway which is patched and age-worn, but full of character. The interior lacks any immediately arresting features, but the eye is soon drawn to the apsidal sanctuary due to its finely structured roof. Closer inspection reveals some modest gems, one of which is a large squint in the south wall which allowed persons outside the church to view procedings at the altar. There are two piscinas, probably 14th century, which is odd for a church without aisles or obvious chapel areas. The stained glass in the south wall windows is excellent and shows marked pre-Raphaelite influence. The font is rather nondescript and hard to date. There are two decent mural tablets.

View from the north

The north and south doorways

Interior views of St Mary

The south wall of the nave, and squint

The two mural tablets

One of the two piscinas

Excellent late Victorian glass

OWSTON ST ANDREW

St Andrew from the north

Owston is a very small, remote village in the eastern Leicestershire uplands, and on a wet day, a bleak and rather forlorn one. Much the same applies to its church, little used now, it has plenty of time for contemplation of its more active and important past. That past was when it was part of an Augustinian abbey, witnessing every day the chant of monks and the whispering of prayers. The foundation of that abbey is thought to have been in the mid-12th century but little if any of the current church dates from then. The ground plan is decidedly odd, with a large high nave, north aisle that adjoins the nave for almost its full length, and a strangely sited tower with short spire which abuts the north west corner of the aisle. The reason for the tower's situation is probably the steep lie of the land immediately west of the nave, which would preclude the erection of buildings there. Entrance to the church is through a north door in the tower. Other buildings once abutted the present one, it is thought that a cloister may have run off the nave, for there is an ornate buttress on the south west corner. A chancel must once have run off the nave east end, its absence lends a truncated appearance to the church. Nearby are the sub-surface remains of other abbey buildings, including a gatehouse, fishponds have also been recognised. Of the older fabric of the church, the internal north doorway may date from the turn of the 11th/12th centuries, and the blocked south doorway perhaps even earlier. Internally, the walls are scraped bare and all is one great space, the absence of a custom-built chancel means that the east end of the nave performs that function. The sense of space is accentuated by the arcade which has very wide and high archways, with only two bays to span the length of the aisle. There are few medieval survivals apart from the basic fabric and the doorways, but a very early 14th century tomb recess is present in the north wall. Some fair quality 18th century mural tablets can be seen in the aisle, and two more are on the external east wall. A restoration took place in 1860-1 during which most windows were renewed and a new font, seating and altar rails were provided. The best Victorian feature is the stained glass, the west window in particular is excellent, with scenes from the life of John the Baptist done in a medieval style.

The top of the tower and spire

Tower and main entrance

Long uphill approach path

Aisle east wall

North doorway

The high nave south wall

South west buttress

Holy Rood from the north west

Holy Rood is another church that has found itself on the edge of its village, as later buildings have migrated further west and left it marooned on the eastern edge of Packington. In many ways it is a church rewarding of study despite the rather run-of-the-mill outer appearance. For a start the plan is a little bit unusual in that the nave is quite short while the chancel is relatively long; then there are the aisles which both exceed the nave in length but otherwise are quite dissimilar. The battlemented tower is quite conventional and of typical Leicestershire type, but then what is the purpose of the stone steps that lead up to a window on the west wall? Could there have been a door there once? A drawing from the 1790's clearly shows that there was indeed a door, probably used to access a ringing floor. The church is constructed of sandstone ashlar, which has worn well and seems in good order, which is noteworthy considering that the oldest parts like the tower arch and the south aisle are late 12th to early 13th century. The reason may be that a remit for structural work was issued in the 1760's and the stonework may have been partly renewed at that date. Also, the chancel was largely reconstructed as part of an early 20th century restoration. The medieval south porch is still going strong and is the main entrance, but the north one succumbed sometime after the aforesaid drawing of the 1790's figured it. The interior is not outstanding by any means, but there are some interesting features. Chief amongst these are three incised slabs, in widely varying states of preservation. They were found below the present floor level during the installation of the organ in 1894. One is all but illegible, another only retains detail of the wife of the couple originally illustrated, but the third is a fine piece in very good order. It dates from the 1580's and shows Raphe Leeson and his two wives. For some perverse reason this slab, one of the highlights of Holy Rood, is partly obscured behind a screen and a piano, and only the left hand side can be seen clearly. There are some spirited bench ends, probably 14th century, one showing a ?soul ascending in a particularly vivid carving. Holy Rood also has an excellent churchyard.

From the west

From the south east

The mysterious steps

Looking along the nave to the chancel

The north arcade

Details from two of the incised slabs

Medieval bench end

107

All Saints southern elevation

All Saints is a church for the connoiseur, full of interest and features. It is beautifully set and inside and out there is a marvellous array of medieval and other antique treasures. The atmosphere is just as evocative, the church came through the Victorian period relatively unscathed apart from light repairs and was only given major restoration in 1905-6, and that was very sensitively done to effect essential repairs and remove 'clutter'. Throughout it seems that the authorities' main aim was to return the church to the 'feel' of its 13th century heyday, and in that they succeeded. The interior today, after a further hundred years of mellowing, is superbly redolent of the past. The building, which consists of tower with spire, nave, chancel and north porch, is mostly 13th century and the oldest part may be the nave, which could have originally stood alone as a single cell building. The outline is odd and at some stage when its roof was lowered the nave fell out of balance with the chancel, which today sits many metres higher. The windows are a delightful mixture of original Early English (tower lancets, plate and intersecting tracery), Decorated and Perpendicular, plus later sympathetic replacements. Some of the doorways are early, particularly the disused south and the present north doorways. As for the interior, little more can be given here than an edited list of the most important features, there is a wealth of things to enjoy. Three stunning memorials can be found in the chancel, all for members of the Jervis family and dating from the late 16th to early 17th centuries. Two are heavily carved and worked tomb chests with incised lids, the youngest one is a wall memorial of a quite different style, but equally impressive. One chest sits under a superb 13th century recess. The stately pulpit and simple reredos are of 1685. A lovely set of benches from 1604 can be found in the nave, other even older examples reside at the back. The nave roof is not original but probably dates from the 16th century, and has some nice bosses. The medieval screen was discarded during the early 20th century restoration, but a section of it can be found in the tower. The font is a plain 13th century piece. A little medieval glass survives in a chancel window.

Three views of All Saints from the west, south west and north

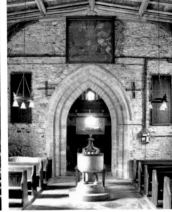

From the west end looking east   **The west end**   **Nave roof boss**

Easter sepulcre, Jervis tomb chests and hanging wall monument

Early C17th benches and late C17th pulpit

PEATLING PARVA ST ANDREW

The south approach to St Andrew is very picturesque

Peatling Parva might be perceived to dwell slightly in the shadow of its larger namesake, although the difference in population is a mere thirteen in Magna's favour according to the 2001 census. More it is the churches that differ in scale and importance, despite the fact that Parva actually has a more ambitious plan of tower, nave with two aisles, chancel, vestry and south porch. Yet its medieval survivals are few and the Victorians were nothing if not robust in their restorations, led by R. Kinle in 1876-7. His is not a well-known name amongst restorers, and I'm not aware of other work in Leicestershire by him. His efforts left St Andrew with an overwhelming Victorian stamp, especially the interior. However, the medieval origins of the building show through in several places, the tower is Perpendicular and has the characteristic battlements with corner gargoyles of that period. It also has a nice frieze of plain shields, and angle buttresses. The fabric of the chancel and south aisle is roughly coursed rubblestone and that suggests an even earlier foundation for those elements. In addition, the south aisle is short and narrow, a usually reliable medieval indicator, and its arcade internally supports a 14th century origin for both. It has an east lancet, and there is another in the chancel south wall, also early indicators. The north aisle is of 1877, as is its arcade, which mirrors exactly the southern one. Kinle's piece de resistance inside is the beautifully executed tripartite chancel arch, highly unusual and original. It imparts an air of religious mystery to the chancel beyond to the congregation seated in the nave. The font, as so often happens even in heavily Victorianised churches, has survived from the churches early days. Its deep, roughly hewn bowl, though unadorned, is clearly old and may be 13th century. The nave roof with its nice foliate bosses has undoubtedly been repaired, but seems not to have been renewed for a very long time; a 15th century age has been ascribed to it. Some of the stained glass is interesting, although none is of great quality. There are several pretty corners, such as the small altar area in the south aisle. Mural tablets are few, but a couple of decent 19th century ones can be found in the chancel.

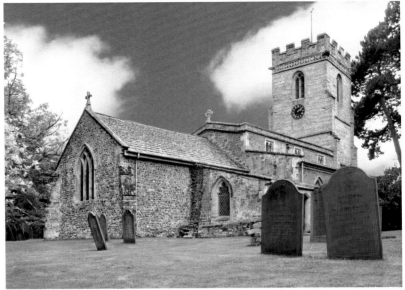

St Andrew from the north east and west

The nave and tripartite chancel arch　　　　**The south arcade**

The sanctuary　　**South aisle and altar**　　　　**Mural tablets**

Plain C13th font　　**Stained glass detail**　　**Openwork pulpit**　　**A pretty corner**

PECKLETON ST MARY MAGDALENE

A grand sight – St Mary from the south west

St Mary Magdalene is sited some way to the south of Peckleton, which might seem odd until it is realised that for its close neighbours it has Peckleton Hall and Peckleton Manor, both very old establishments despite the fact that the present buildings date largely from the 18th century. It seems very likely that the church was placed where it is primarily for the benefit of the inhabitants of the two 'big houses', who probably were main benefactors and sponsors during the church's medieval days. St Mary is beautifully sited on a little rise, clearly seen and prominent from all directions, and the building itself is worthy of its location. It consists of an admirable tower and slender spire, nave, embattled south aisle, chancel and north and south porches. A notable elegance characterises the building. The top of the tower is rather more intricately embellished than is usual, with battlements and fancy pinnacles which have gargoyles at their bases and a ring of human heads where the crocketted upper sections meet the panelled lower sections. The octagonal spire is recessed and quite short, and approaches a needle form, with crocketts running up the angles. Nothing diagnostic in the present fabric appears to be pre-14th century, but much of the lower stonework is cobblestone which may point to an older foundation. A change in fabric can be seen at several points, especially in the south aisle, which was raised in height at some stage to accommodate a clerestory, and is crowned with battlements. The interior is most interesting and contains several fine items. In the chancel are several memorials and two recesses, one containing the effigy of a knight in impressive military costume with a lady by his side but outside the recess; a date of 14th century is ascribed. The other contains a very worn praying man. On the north wall of the chancel is a 16th century incised tomb chest lid showing an armoured knight with two ladies by his side. A wall tablet of 1831 includes a stylish representation of a graveyard. The font is a very old piece, the ornament of concentric lozenges suggests a 12th century date. A piscina of the 13th century with dog-tooth ornament can be found in the chancel; another is in the aisle. The medieval parish chest is located by the aisle west wall. Certain windows contain medieval glass fragments. There is much more in this fine church.

St Mary from the south east　　　**Tower and porch**　　　**Tower arch corbel heads**

Looking east and west along the church

Recess and effigies　　　**The font**　　　**One side of a medieval chest tomb**

Chancel piscina, sedilia, mural tablet　　　**Incised slab**　　　**Medieval stained glass**

The pleasing southern frontage of All Saints

Pickwell is only a small place located to the south of Melton Mowbray, and has a timeless feel and peaceful atmosphere. No main roads pass through it; it must be a nice place to live if you can manage without most facilities. All Saints stands four square in the middle and occupies pride of place, and is a building of some presence, having a 'full set' of tower, aisled nave with a rare Decorated clerestory, chancel and south porch. An added touch of style is provided by the fine Perpendicular limestone tower with its imposing bell openings in the top stage, which contrasts nicely with the ironstone fabric of most of the remainder of the church. A varied range of windows contributes more individuality. The chancel south wall has one unusually tall transomed window and a similar blocked one beside it with a memorial tablet in the filling, also a deeply moulded doorway. The south aisle has feature buttresses with empty niches and just a single window in its south wall. Nothing on the exterior seems older than 14th century but inside there is evidence of an earlier 13th century foundation in the north aisle arcade and the tower arch. The arcade has rounded arches, which are thought to be a late example of this style. One of the piers has stiff leaf carving on the capital. The south aisle arcade has pointed arches, the aisle itself was rebuilt during a restoration by R. W. Johnson in 1860. The south porch probably originated in the 14th century and has stone benches, it was also rebuilt in 1860. The south doorway may also be an early feature, but there is a venerable font with typical Norman arcading which may be the oldest thing in the church. Both north and south walls contain more recesses than is normally seen in a village church, but all are of simple design and empty. Near to the two recesses in the south wall is an ancient piscina, pointing to the probablity of a chapel being originally sited in the south aisle. Another piscina of simple outline is seen in the chancel south wall, with three equally plain sedilia, these may be 14th century. Much of the rest of the fittings and furniture date from the 1860 restoration, including the pulpit, seating and brass lectern. There are some good mural tablets, several of which are from the 18th century.

Tower and porch

Looking along the nave to the chancel

The nave looking west

The north arcade and stiff leaf carving on a pier capital

Piscina and sedilia in the chancel

Recesses, south aisle

Old parish chest

C18th mural tablet

Resited mural tablet

South arcade head

The font

115

St Helen sits prettily on a little rise

In the far north of Leicestershire a line of villages comprising Harby, Plungar and Barkestone-le-Vale man the frontier with Nottinghamshire like a row of border forts, but in truth these settlements are of a piece with their neighbours on the other side like Granby, Barnstone and Langar, as part of the distinctive geographical area known as the Vale of Belvoir. Plungar is small and compact and its church sits to the north east of the village in an attractive churchyard in a pretty setting. It will never win any historical church of the year contests, for it was heavily restored in the 1840's and 1850's and little that was medieval was left. But it has retained a tranquil ambience, with a restful and calm interior. It consists of battlemented tower, nave with south aisle, chancel, south porch and 19th century vestry, all completed in ironstone with patches of limestone repairs and dressings. Oddly, the 14th century tower is unbuttressed, while the 15th century aisle (rebuilt in 1855-6) and chancel sport quite substantial examples of the angle variety. The south aisle was enlarged to house a chapel as part of the main Victorian restoration. Built into the tower are three very worn carved stones which tell part of the old traditional story of Reynard the Fox, these are thought be 15th century in date, possibly finding their way here from Croxton Abbey. First impressions on entering St Helen are that the interior is very plain and very Victorian, but some of the details are pleasing, such as the fleurons and odd creatures around the inner chamfer of the tower arch. There is also a splendid, ornately carved wooden reredos in the south aisle chapel, a beefy pulpit of Caen stone and angels on the roof wall posts. There are few pre-19th century fittings but pride of place goes to some medieval bench ends which originated from Croxton Abbey, complete with lively and skilfully carved mythical beasts; these are on the right hand side of the chancel (looking east). On the other side are a complimentary set of very competent Victorian stalls with carvings on the arm rests, made to match. The 3-bay arcade is restored but basically original and the font probably 15th century. The latter is rather well done, with quatrefoils and battlements on the bowl and arcading on the stem.

116

The main approach **St Helen from the south** **Looking out from the porch**

From the west looking east to the chancel **Chancel arch and nave** **Tower arch**

Victorian (L) and medieval (C) arm rest carvings and medieval bench end (R)

C18th or C19th chair **Superbly carved reredos (temporarily detached)** **C15th font**

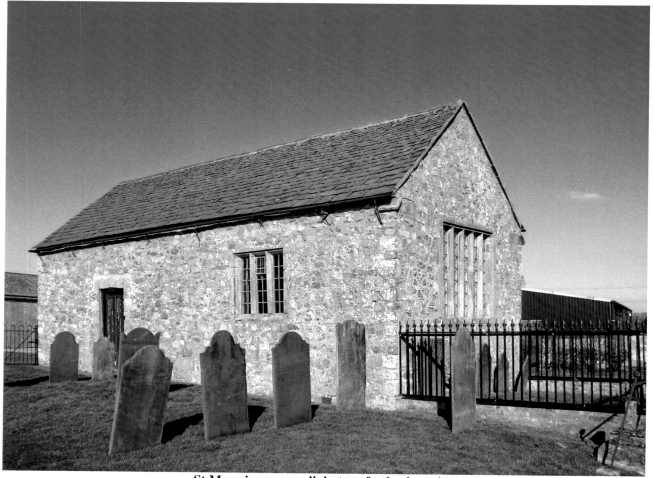

St Mary is very small, but perfectly charming

Potters Marston is not even a hamlet, just a cluster of buildings around Potters Marston Hall and farm, some of which have been expanded and converted for business use. St Mary is part of this complex and is the smallest church in Leicestershire to offer regular, if rather infrequent, services. A larger village once existed, traces of which have been located nearby, and as suggested by the name, there was a local pottery industry which flourished in the Middle Ages. Potters Marston lies to the south west of Leicester, and the nearest places of any size are Croft and Stoney Stanton. The M69 motorway runs nearby so despite the pleasant countryside setting, there is a constant drone of traffic noise which disrupts the rural idyll somewhat. There isn't much to St Mary, it is a single cell building of rather indeterminate age containing nave and chancel/sanctuary, but it dates from at least the 16th century. It resembles a barn rather than a church but is nevertheless a charming building, and clearly cherished by its congregation. It is built of random igneous blocks with sandstone window frames and dressings, and was restored twice in the 20th century, in 1908 and 1930. Clues to its age come from the kingpost roof, which is 16th century, and the mullioned windows have a Tudor look to them, despite the fact that their frames are plain squares. The heavy lintel above the south door could be old too. None of the interior furniture and fittings is older than 19th century, and many items are from the 1900's. Probably the oldest features other than the roof and three 18th century mural tablets for members of the Boothby family are the lectern, desk and chair set, and the altar rail. The pulpit is of indeterminate age, and was restored in 1950. A single Victorian pew has been retained at the west end, but seating these days is provided by modern chairs. There are just four windows, only one of which is on the south side, but despite that the interior is bright and airy. The pleasing modern font may be a war memorial, as it has the dates 1918 and 1945 carved on it together with the initials J. S. There is a small churchyard bounded by railings, within which is another railed and walled section in front of the east window for Boothby graves.

Views from the south and west

Interior views looking east and west

The east window　　　　　　　　**Detail of the C16th kingpost roof**

The modest pulpit　　**For Dorothy (d. 1712) and William Boothby (d. 1724)**　　**The modern font**

PRESTWOLD ST ANDREW

South frontage from the park

St Andrew is a classic example of an estate church, tied to the 'big house' (Prestwold Hall), just an easy walk away. The church enjoys a lovely setting at the edge of a copse of mature trees. There are very few dwellings nearby, but the villages of Hoton and Burton on the Wolds are only a short distance away. The interesting thing about St Andrew is that it wasn't built as a hall church, it's foundation comfortably predates the creation of the estate and it began life serving the medieval village of Prestwold. That unfortunate settlement was swept away to create the estate probably sometime after 1500 and the first hall was built a little later. It was further embellished and modernised in the early 1800's. The story of the incumbents of the Hall, first Skipworths, ardent Royalists in the Civil War, then Packes, equally committed Commonwealth supporters who acquired the estate after Cromwell's triumph, makes for fascinating reading, but must be pursued by the keen reader elsewhere. Once the Hall was built and the villagers removed, the church's affairs were run from the Hall, although estate workers and others from the area would have been permitted to use it. The building consists of a late 14th century tower with battlements, frieze and stubs of now removed pinnacles, nave of 1890, chancel of probably 13th century origin, organ chamber of 1890 and a kitchen and services extension north of the chancel. Entry is via a west door in the tower, above which is a Perpendicular style window. The chancel south wall fabric is interesting, very mixed and quite crudely fashioned. The walls contain all three major rock types, igneous from Charnwood, sedimentary Jurassic limestones and metamorphosed quartzite cobbles, in fact any suitable stone to hand seems to have been used. All that seems to indicate an early building date of probably 13th century for the chancel. The nave replaced an earlier one of 1743. Inside, the nave is spacious and attractively furnished, but all attention is soon directed to the chancel, which is full of memorials, mostly for members of the Packe family, some very large and ostentatious. It is a veritable treasure house, almost on a par with Bottesford, although several of the monuments are more recent.

St Andrew from the north east   **The tower through the trees**   **Top stage of the tower**

Looking east and west along the church

Tomb of Richard and Isabel Nele, late C15th   **Tomb of two mysterious ladies, c. 1520**

Sir William and Jane Skipwith (1631), Christopher Packe (1682), Frances Andrew (1800), Hussey Packe (1912)

QUENIBOROUGH ST MARY

St Mary has one of the finest spires in the county

Queniborough St Mary is a church that is full of interest, both externally and internally. The renowned pale limestone recessed spire is nothing less than a work of art, reaching almost 50m into the heavens and slender as a needle, but the rest of the building has scarcely less interest. Predominantly 14th century, St Mary's origins go back much further. There isn't much of it, but the evidence for that is secure, and it is found in the chancel and north east corner of the nave. The best of the evidence is the very narrow round headed window in the chancel, which broadens dramatically inside into a wide splay. This is probably Norman in age, but, equally, such windows can also be found in Saxon churches, and the monolithic arch externally which is carved from a single block might support the earlier assignment. Nearby in the base of the nave wall at its north east junction with the chancel there is a length of quoining which has the look of Saxon long and short work, although it is perhaps not totally typical of that style. Whatever the true origins of this part of the building, the general aspect of the stonework and its very mixed and roughly coursed nature point to an early date. Inside there is lots to seek out, although it has to be said that first impressions on entering the nave are of slight disappointment after the splendid exterior. The chancel has more atmosphere. It is the details that hold all the interest rather than the appearance of the whole. Firstly there is a fine 15th century (restored) screen, now seeing service as the east wall of a western room/vestry. The chancel arch holds two treasures, one is small and easily missed and is a short length of Norman ornament set into the south pier; the other is more prominent and is a rare carved wall tablet of Elizabethan age (1586) set into the northern pier. This is really quite lovely. In the chancel is an unusual memorial brass of 1633 mounted on the south wall with an imaginative design, although it is rather difficult to see due to the brass's reflective surface. High up in the nave north wall is the opening to the former rood loft. The east window contains an excellent example of modern stained glass, by Christopher Whall. And don't leave without looking at the bosses on the medieval nave roof, these are highly individual and vivacious.

Views along the nave from west and through the chancel arch

C15ᵗʰ screen   **Norman window, chancel**   **East window**

Margaret Bury brass   **Pulpit and rood opening**   **Norman fragment**   **Stone tablet of 1586**

A selection of imaginative(!) bosses in the nave roof

QUORN ST BARTHOLOMEW

St Bartholomew from the north west

Quorn St Bartholomew is Grade 1 listed and of very ancient foundation. However, the Mountsorrel granite building was so thoroughly overhauled in the 19th and 20th centuries, especially internally, that evidence is hard to find of those distant origins. It is externally that the evidence must be sought. That is in the form of two doorways on the south side, one, the main south doorway, is a fairly flamboyant Norman structure, complete with zig-zag in the arch and spiral ornament on the jambs. The other doorway is a narrow priest's entrance into the chancel, and while it is much less grand than the main doorway, it has a nice round Norman arch. Although not as old as the doorways, the chancel, nave, south aisle and porch are all of late 12th to early 13th century age. The porch possesses an upper room and fine vaulted roof. Other major elements of the church are a tower of 14th century date, a north aisle chiefly of 1842 though it was expanded from a much earlier one, an organ chamber of 1894, and a late 20th century complex which is wrapped around the west end of the north aisle and the tower. All that development has resulted in a sprawling ground plan of little aesthetic merit, although facilities for the church-goers of Quorn are now amongst the best in the county. The greatest treasure of the interior is the south aisle, for many centuries, and still today, known as the Farnham Chapel. It is one of a tiny number of chapels within parish churches that have remained in private hands, and it is still kept locked and separate from the rest of the church. It is also beautifully laid out and maintained, and is full of memorials and monuments to members of the Farnham dynasty, in a wonderful state of preservation. Though it is unfortunate in some ways that the chapel is usually inaccessible to the public, there can be no doubt that this isolation had led to the treasures remaining in excellent condition. Amongst the most eye-catching are a super table tomb of 1587 complete with very fine effigies on top, four 16th century incised slabs in grand condition, a typically Elizabethan mural tablet of 1574 and many other impressive memorials from later years. Elsewhere in the church there are several mural tablets in the chancel, none particularly good, a font with a medieval stem and base, and an old parish chest. Almost everything else is 19th century or later.

The C14th tower

The church from the south east

South doorway and roof

Looking east along the nave

The font

Three views of the Farnham Chapel

Sanctuary and reredos

'Courage'

Through the chancel screen to the nave

RAGDALE ALL SAINTS

All Saints setting is pure picture postcard

All Saints is one of the most charming of Leicestershire's rural churches, set in a lovely position in a tiny village in pretty, rolling countryside. Add to those attributes the mellow ironstone fabric that glows in sunshine and a cosy rustic atmosphere, and you have one very attractive church. It is quaintly small and consists of tower, nave, chancel, a south aisle and south porch. A most appealing approach path winds up to the churchyard gate from the Six Hills Road that runs through the village. The church is undoubtedly very old, because the south aisle contains an Early English lancet window in its west wall, and that would indicate that the nave is even older. The base of the tower is 14th century but the rather curious brick-built top stage with its low angle pyramid roof was added in the 18th century. The battlemented chancel also dates from that century, and what's more, a stone on the gable tells you the precise date – 1787. The porch also bears battlements and probably is contemporary with the chancel. There is a clerestory, of the usual Perpendicular date. The interior is small and homely, but there are several interesting features and fittings. The age-worn arcade is very low and the capitals of the piers are only 1.5 metres or so from ground level. One of the pier capitals, also that of the eastern respond, have heads and crocket-like carvings. The big, square font on its four odd legs is another item that the years have taken a toll of, and there is nothing diagnostic to indicate a precise age, but it appears no younger than 1300 or so. It sits on an improvised base of incised slabs, cut and fitted together to form a circle. The slabs themselves may be very old. Also very old, but difficult to date, is a fragment of a tomb chest lid or similar that resides in the vestry beneath the tower. On it there is a figure who is holding what appears to be a bishop's crozier. Some would assign a Saxon date to this stone. Accompanying the stone are two mutilated stone heads, also clearly old. The tower screen is curious, with panelled dado surmounted by unusual tracery which seems to depict two hearts. The tower itself, as built, impinges into the nave. The stained glass in an aisle window is only 19th century, but contains interesting heraldic motifs of the Shirley family.

Tower and clerestory

Looking east along the nave

Nave and tower arch

Chancel/sanctuary

Shirley arms in an aisle window

Saxon or Norman fragment

Carved pier capital

The font

East window stained glass

The pulpit

Old woodwork - faces carved on a settle and a poppyhead

Mutilated head

127

RATBY ST PHILIP AND ST JAMES

Beautifully positioned, St Philip and St James on its low hill

St Philip and St James is a fine, big church in a very spacious and attractive churchyard, the monolith-like tower can be seen for miles around. The church consists of tower, nave with south aisle, chancel, north porch and vestry. There is no clerestory. The south doorway is especially attractive, and has a string of fleurons running around an arch chamfer. The basal two thirds of the tower are mid-late 13th century, but the clear change in building stone and style signals that the battlemented top third is later, probably 14th century. The tower arch internally is relatively simple and unsophisticated and is Early English; it is offset to the south when viewed from the east as a result of later re-siting of the north nave wall. The five-bay south arcade with its round piers and capitals is also Early English. Only one pier has carving, and, oddly, that stops part way around the capital. A suggestion that the mason's work was interrupted by the Black Death in the late 1340's cannot now be proved of course. One of Ratby's highlights is the window tracery. The main chancel east window is a bold Decorated tour-de-force (though very much restored in 1881 and again after storm damage, in 1981), and the east window of the aisle (also restored), known as the Butterfly Window, is also very fine. Set into its glass are a few precious medieval fragments, some of these can also be found in one of the nave north windows. There are few memorials left in the church, but there is one very impressive alabaster monument of 1620 set against the chancel north wall, known as a sideboard tomb. This is for Sir Henry Sacheverall and he lies on top of the tomb chest in effigy, wearing typical clothes of the period. Beside him beneath a floor slab sleeps his son, who died young. Above the tomb is a rare 18th century plasterwork design depicting cherubs and flowers, it isn't known if this has any connection with the family. Set into the chancel south wall are a set of three sedilia and a piscina with cusped arches, these are 14th century. The 14th century font has not been treated kindly by the passing years, but its unusual design of crocketed ogee arches is still very pleasing to the eye. It is thought that it came to the church from Groby Hall around 1500.

St Philip and St James from the south

South doorway

Deep in thought!

Looking east along the nave

Looking from the chancel to the nave

Piscina and sedilia

Sacheverall tomb

C14th font

The Butterfly Window

Medieval glass

Arcade details

C19th pulpit

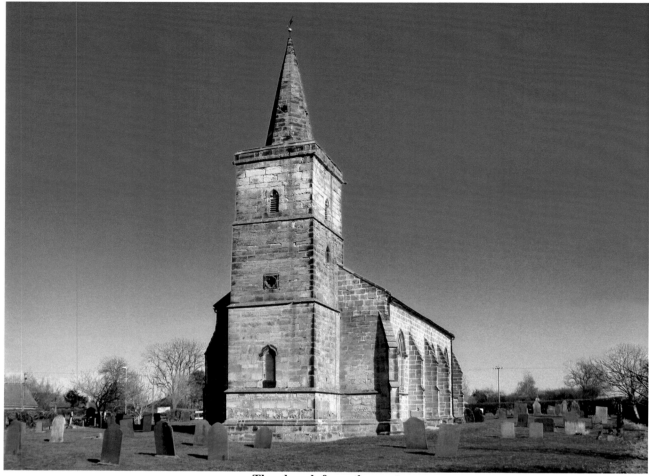

The church from the west

All Saints is a church that casts a spell over its visitors, not because of architectural merit or fine fittings, but for the sheer feel of the place. It is thought that the building was constructed in more or less one campaign in the 14th century, certainly there is an internal consistency in the style of the doorways and windows. The ancient atmosphere may be due to the fact that no overly robust changes have been inflicted on All Saints over the centuries, and it still feels distinctly medieval. The church of those times was fully fitted and colourful inside, but today the interior is sparse and the décor insipid, yet strangely that doesn't rob All Saints of its atmosphere. It sits beyond the edge of the present village, to the south in this case, and first thoughts are that the village has migrated north over the centuries. However, study of maps and aerial photos reveals the very close proximity of a moated site, with fishponds also nearby, so it may be that the church was once linked with a manor house or hall, and may even have been built primarily for the landed family that occupied it. The main patrons of the church were the De Culeys, and their arms can be seen on two stones with ogee decoration set into chancel buttresses. Ogee arches feature prominently at points all around the building. The plan of All Saints, which is constructed of sandstone ashlar, is simple - west tower with short, recessed spire, nave and chancel. There are no porches or clerestory, and no 19th century add-ons like vestrys or organ chambers. Buttresses running all the way around the church lend a distinctive appearance, and the window tracery is good. One window in particular stands out, and that is the second one from the west in the nave south wall. This bears imaginative tracery and may have been specially put in to light a chapel that once occupied the area of the nave beyond; a piscina can still be seen there. There are not many important features inside, but the set of 14th century sedilia in the chancel are very nice and several chancel windows contain collages of medieval glass, some with recognisable figures including an owl, a lion and a crucifixion scene. The font is plain but old. There is a recently uncovered text and a little painting on the south wall, and a George IV arms.

All Saints from the south west

Stone with Culey arms

Unusual tracery

Looking east

The fine sedilia

Piscina in nave

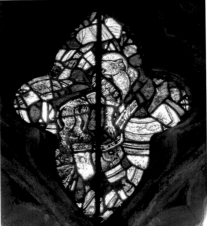

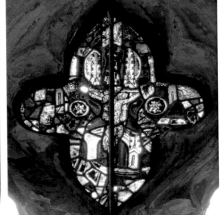

Medieval glass fragments collected together in chancel windows

Bell of 1778

Recently uncovered wall text

The font

Arms of George IV

The sun shines on St Botolph

There are only four churches dedicated to St Botolph in Leicestershire. Botolph was a 7th century abbot who founded an abbey somewhere in East Anglia, and became the patron saint of travellers. Beyond that, little is known about him, but clearly the number of churches dedicated to him (around 70) and the fact that Boston (Botwulf's town) in Lincolnshire was named after him, point to him being of some importance to the medieval mind. Ratcliffe's St Botolph has a plan of tower with slender recessed spire, nave, chancel and south porch. The undoubted highlight is the splendid octagonal needle spire of limestone, with crockets running up the angles. The building stone is mostly random or roughly coursed Mountsorrel Granite with limestone or sandstone facings and frames. The tower plinth is of sandstone. Until the late 18th century St Botolph had a north aisle. No trace of that can be seen externally, but inside the full arcade of four bays is preserved, each blocked arch except one containing a window. These are intersecting and Y-shaped and may well follow the pattern of the original aisle windows, or perhaps they could even be the reset originals with renewed tracery. The interior is long and narrow; the wide, high chancel arch is almost the width of the church, giving the impression of one continuous space. Immediately to the left on entering the south door is a bold and bulbous font, probably 13th century. It has four knobs that have been attacked and damaged at some stage. Inside the font is a rare survival, a plain but handsome pewter baptismal bowl which is certainly old, although difficult to date. Nearby is the parish chest, incised with the name of a churchwarden and dated 1721 but possibly a little older. Also at the west end of the nave are the workings of an old tower clock. The chancel is attractive and has several interesting features. Firstly there is a recess, quite plain with simple arch, containing the worn effigy of a priest, thought to date from around 1300. On the opposite wall are three fine sedilia and a piscina, clearly restored. The central south window contains several quarries of medieval glass of the rare grisaille type with simple but attractive designs of leaves, acorns, etc. There are also some coloured panes.

St Botolph from the south

Spire above the trees

Details of the top of the tower

Chancel and sanctuary

Nave and chancel arch

Blocked north arcade

Piscina and sedilia

Old parish chest

The font

Pewter baptismal bowl

Grisaille and other coloured medieval glass

Recess with effigy of a priest

The effigy

Enigmatic date set into the nave wall

RAVENSTONE ST MICHAEL AND ALL ANGELS B3, SK 402 139

St Michael's from the north east

The largely 14th century St Michael hides its attractions behind a screen of trees and it is hard to get a glimpse of the complete building. However, there is no denying that on a sunny day this arboreal setting is most beguiling. Not quite so on a rainy day! Ravenstone lies in the lee of the industrial and urban sprawl of Coalville, but is far enough away to feel detached and rural, though it too has its share of industrial development and tedious modern housing. As is so often the case, the best part of the village is around the church, and there are other historical buildings nearby like the Ravenstone Hospital Almshouses and Ravenstone Hall. This whole area, which is in the north of the village, is a Conservation Area. When the screen of trees is penetrated, one can soon appreciate a fine building constructed of a pleasantly hued pale sandstone ashlar thought to have been quarried nearby, consisting of a low tower with bulky broach spire, nave, south aisle, long chancel and south porch. There is a 15th century clerestory. The tower has a niche in its west face containing a modern statue of the winged St Michael, wearing armour. The spire has rather unusual quatrefoil-shaped lunettes. On the north side of the nave is a blocked doorway with slightly pointed arch and cushion capitals. There are no great treasures within, but the largely 19th century interior is pleasant enough and there are some items of interest to seek out. Near the main south entrance in the nave south wall is a rather worn head of St John the Baptist and also in the same area is the square font with its chamfered corners and solid base. The latter is difficult to date but may be contemporary with an original 13th century church which is hinted at by the apparent antiquity of some areas of stonework. The four-bay arcade is 14th century with unusual detail around the junction of the arches and capitals. The wrought iron altar rails are 18th century, and the wood panelling at various points around the church may be contemporary or somewhat earlier. There is an old three-lock parish chest, but most other fittings are 19th century, including the alabaster reredos with its figures of the Four Evangelists, the lectern and the stained glass.

134

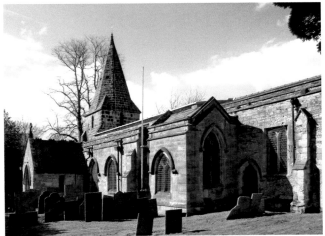

South side with its short aisle

The tower peeps out above its screen of trees

The churchyard in winter

War memorial and tower

Tower from the north west

St Michael in his niche

East end

Blocked north doorway

Lych gate

Looking east along the nave

Gravestone of 1746

135

Rearsby's white limestone tower catches the sunlight

St Michael has a lovely situation at the end of a quiet lane that leads up from Rearsby's well-known medieval packhorse bridge, and in many ways is an attractive church, but the eccentric and inconsistent choice of building stone for its fabric by its various builders and architects makes for an odd-looking exterior, particularly the north side. The tower looks grand in cream limestone ashlar but the adjacent nave and aisles are clad in red Charnwood granite, which was applied during a 19th century restoration. The chancel escaped that treatment, but is made of yet another type of material, a mixture of ironstone and sandstone rubble. The north aisle after recent work looks odder still, with granite east and west walls but with a light stone used for the north wall. Another building recently added at the west end of this aisle is also of light stone, but nearby a further building is constructed of a dark ashlar sandstone. And there's a wooden shed to the north of the tower! Of course, in a couple of centuries all this will have weathered in and will be admired for its individuality. With the cladding obscuring the original building stone of the nave, it is hard to gauge what is the oldest part of the building, but the chancel, though now with replacement Perpendicular windows, is of rough rubblestone laid in a style which looks early, suggesting 13th century. The tower with its battlements and corner pinnacles is Perpendicular. The south porch is Victorian and sports pretty ornamentation in the form of shafts with fancy capitals, foliage around the arch, a head at the apex and foliage-backed crosses either side. Inside is a nice 13th century piscina and sedilia set in the chancel, and an equally old piscina in the south aisle with cusped arch, which no doubt indicates the former presence of a chapel. The 13th century sub-square font on its far more recent columned base has seen some rough treatment over the years but is a highly individual design with clustered pillars at the corners and foliate carvings. There are a few quarries of old glass and a ?Jacobean chest. Of the more recent fittings the 19th century screen with stepped stone base, openwork top and integrated ornate pulpit is excellent, as is the noble war memorial.

Views from the north east and south west

From the west

Looking east along the nave

The south arcade

The font

?C17th chest

The pulpit

Five panes of old glass

Dignified war memorial

Chancel piscina

REDMILE ST PETER

St Peter from the south east and south

Redmile is one of the Vale of Belvoir villages, situated up in the north east of Leicestershire, and like almost every other church in that area, it is largely built of ironstone, but with significant use of limestone in the spire and tower. The prominent tower battlements, corner pinnacles, corbel table, gargoyles and broad diagonal buttresses are all of limestone. St Peter, which consists of tower with crocketed spire, nave, south aisle, chancel, south porch and 19th century vestry running north off the chancel, is almost entirely of the 14th century with some 15th century rebuilding, the earliest parts date from around 1300. The church occupies a prime position on Main Street in Redmile, opposite the village pub, demonstrating a very old association of key establishments. It also enjoys close ties with the local Church of England school, and is often visited by the children and included in their projects. Despite the overall attractiveness of the building externally it has to be said that except for some cheery gargoyles on the tower nothing really distinctive catches the eye, and it is probably inside that the most interest can be found. It is fashionable these days for churches to remove their old and uncomfortable pews, but Redmile did this before most others, and chairs were first provided in the late 19th century. They lend quite a rustic atmosphere to the interior and the stripped walls add to the basic feel. The four-bay arcade is old, of the late 13th or early 14th century, and has two octagonal and one round pier. Some authorities ascribe a Norman age to the round pier but it seems more likely to be Early English. The north wall of the nave, oddly, has no windows, so it is as well that there is a clerestory above. The 15th century font is a pretty piece, with quatrefoils and panel ornament on both bowl and stem; the base seems later. There are some nice, long medieval benches at various points, and they have retained their poppyheads, some with vine trails and grapes. Built into the sill of a window near the balustraded openwork pulpit is a grave slab, certainly very old and thought to be Saxon, with interlace ornament. The nave roof demands attention with its tie beams and braces, and is 15th century. The old 14th century tower arch is tall and narrow.

The tower from the west

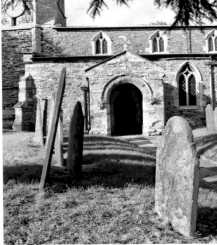

Looking towards the porch

The south doorway

Looking east and west along the church

The aisle

The arcade

The tower arch

Mural tablets

The font

Nave roof

Medieval poppyheads

ROLLESTON ST JOHN THE BAPTIST

St John's shady north side

If any church in Leicestershire demonstrates the ancient association of squirearchy and church, then St John does. Even today, there is a distinct feeling that one might be hauled up for poaching when one enters the grounds of Rolleston Hall to view it. The tiny village's use of the church in the past may have been more permissive than a right, although these days life is rather different. There's not much to St Peter, an old 13th century tower, with a nave and chancel in one rebuilt in the middle of the 18th century. A very shallow porch constructed in either the 18th or 19th century sits between buttresses and protects the disused south doorway. Everything has seen phases of restoration, and the main periods were circa 1740 when the top of the tower was remodelled, battlements added (also to nave/chancel) and the rest restored. The benches inside probably date from this time. There was another round of restorations in 1899 and more in 1962. The chancel and nave windows must date from the earlier of these two dates. Throughout, the original crudely constructed Early English round tower arch has survived, though with some remedial work clearly necessary at times. The next oldest thing, apart from areas of the fabric, is probably the hexagonal font, which coyly discloses no clues to its age by being totally plain, but which dates from at least pre-1400. The simple piscina in the chancel is of the same general age, but everything else except the 18th century stalls seems 19th century. Of the later features, the east window stained glass depicting saints is rather good and was donated in remembrance of one of Queen Victoria's ladies-of-the-bedchamber by her children in 1902. Three godchildren of that august monarch were present when the window was dedicated, as we are helpfully informed by commemorative brass plaques. Another plaque remembers the 1899 restoration inaugurated by Victor Albert 3rd Baron Churchill in memory of his father. The only other stained glass is in the small two-light tower west window, and shows Saint George and an angel effected in a quasi Pre-Raphaelite style. There is very little by way of a churchyard, but in the small area dedicated to graves is a cross with ancient head on a more recent shaft.

Tower and doorways

Ancient tower arch

The east end of St John

The font

Piscina in chancel

East window

Memorial brasses

ROTHERBY ALL SAINTS

All Saints is neat and picturesque

Rotherby is a small linear village set on a minor road that runs parallel to the main A607 road in the Wreake valley. The village has thus far avoided the 'commuterisation' that has spread up the Wreake valley from Leicester as far as Rearsby and therefore has retained a peaceful atmosphere. That sense of calm extends to the parish church of All Saints, which is a pretty building of limestone with minor ironstone, the latter most obvious in the tower. That is fairly unusual for these parts where it is more often the case that ironstone dominates in the main fabric, with limestone playing only a subsidiary part. The plan is fairly standard but there are a few oddities, the main one being that due to space restrictions to the west, the tower, added in the late 14th or early 15th century, was built within the western bay of the south aisle, its walls being visible internally. Thus it could be described as a south west tower, with the south aisle now being very short. The 13th century nave, which gives indication of an earlier foundation by the presence of a blocked Norman window high in its west wall, is rather high for its length. This is due to excessive heightening to accommodate a clerestory. An interesting melange of stone types and building phases is recorded in All Saints north wall, including a blocked square-headed doorway. Most 19th century vestrys/organ chambers are small affairs, but Rotherby's is quite large, and runs off the north wall of the chancel. The 19th century south porch is a charming, mostly wooden structure, founded on low walls. The interior was given a vigorous reworking and refitting by the Victorians and lacks impact, but there are interesting and occasionally unusual features to be seen. The chancel was decorated with a set of panels of saints, shields, etc, painted by a zealous rector in 1911-12, these are not great works of art but have a certain character. Medieval piscinas survive in the chancel and the south aisle, the latter has dogtooth and may be 13th century. A few rare old wooden humanesque corbels are dotted about in the nave walls. There are some good 18th and 19th century memorial tablets in the tower and on nave walls. The George IV arms on the north nave wall is much deteriorated.

All Saints seen from the south east and south

Nave north wall and vestry   **View from the gate**   **Looking down the nave**

Blocked Norman window   **Sanctuary details**   **Painting by the Rev. Beresford**

Seaman mural tablet   **Chancel piscina**   **Wooden homunculus**   **C19th pulpit**

ROTHLEY ST MARY AND ST JOHN

St Mary and St John from the south east

St Mary and St John is large and well-appointed, reflecting the fact that Rothley is both prosperous and a desirable place to live. There is much of interest to discover and that interest begins in the churchyard even before the church is entered. Here is a very fine Saxon cross shaft, which unfortunately lost its head in the mists of time. It is fairly well worn but the vigour of the carvings, which cover every face, is still apparent. Also in the attractive churchyard is a well-known gravestone that depicts a lively Last Judgement, beautifuly carved. The plan of the largely 13th – 15th century church is the 'full set' of grand tower, aisled and clerestoried nave, and chancel. The base of the tower may be Norman. Added in 1877 were a north porch and a vestry/organ chamber in an extension to the north aisle. The chancel was rebuilt in the 19th century. Many buttresses stand sentinel on the walls, those of the tower change in design at almost every stage. The west face of the tower boasts a splendid doorway with tracery in the spandrels. Tough, hard-wearing Mountsorrel Granite was chosen as the main building material, hardly surprising given that the quarries are barely two miles away. Limestone dressings were used from sources near (Ketton) and far (Corsham, Box). Like all churches constructed of Charnwood stone, weathering has had little outward effect on the fabric and thus the church presents a stern, unyielding face to the world despite its architectural merits. The interior offers several delights, not least of which are the numerous excellent monuments and memorials, many to members of the Babbington and McCauley families, including two fine chest tombs and an incised chest tomb lid. There are also lovely mural tablets, which span the years from the 16th century onwards, many of high interest and quality workmanship. The font is a Norman beauty, featuring an ornament of concentric lozenges. The screen has a fine 15th century dado, but the other parts incorporate later elements. Some of the 19th century glass is of good quality, and a few medieval fragments survive in the south aisle east window. This summary only scratches the surface, do go and see this fine church for yourself.

Tower and north porch

The Saxon cross

The Last Judgement (in the churchyard)

Looking east along the nave

Partly C15th screen

Norman font

Incised tomb lid and chest tombs, the last incorporated into a war memorial

C16th and C17th mural tablets

Medieval stained glass

SADDINGTON ST HELEN

St Helen's shady north side

The village of Saddington occupies a favoured situation in a fine hilly area of south Leicestershire. Nearby is pretty Gumley and other charming spots. The church of St Helen usually gets a tepid or even critical assessment from church experts, and this is down to the restoration by F. Peck in 1872-3, who according to his own words appeared to have little liking for the church and gave it a rather slapdash and uninspiring restoration. That is the received wisdom, but this seems unfair because St Helen is actually an attractive building in a pleasing blend of ironstone and limestone. The alternation of these materials in bands up the tower is especially pleasing and Peck's Decorated-style reticulated windows lend a nice unity to the exterior. The plan is standard, consisting of tower, aisled and clerestoried nave, chancel and north porch. The oldest parts are 13th century with 14th century additions, so Saddington originates from the classic time for Leicestershire church building. Subsequently, much was changed, renewed or removed, and after Peck's work, only a handful of medieval features remained. The top stage of the tower is 15th century and a date of 1707 on the battlements indicates a later phase of rebuilding. Externally, the best features are the excellent Early English north doorway and the similarly shaped, roughly contemporary west doorway of the tower. The patchy fabric of the chancel is interesting, and shows both original 13th or 14th century coursing and a lot of later rebuilding or refacing. Inside it must be admitted that the comprehensive 19th century restoration left little of interest and imposed a sterile feel, but some things escaped banishment or destruction. The 12-sided font on its unusual chamfered base is quite plain but could just possibly be the original from the 13th century church, and a lovely 14th century piscina can be found in the chancel. The south arcade is 13th century, and a very worn incised slab of 1628 is set into the chancel floor. Of the later fittings, there is a Hanoverian royal arms, an enigmatic wooden plaque bearing the date 1727 and churchwardens initials, an old chest and some variable wall tablets. Peck installed stone angels as corbels in his chancel and I think they are rather splendid.

Distinctive tower

Rebuilding date on the tower

North doorway

Two views of the main body of the church

Angel pillar corbel

Two mural tablets

1628 incised slab

12-sided font

Piscina in chancel

Wooden plaque

Hanoverian royal arms

147

SALTBY ST PETER

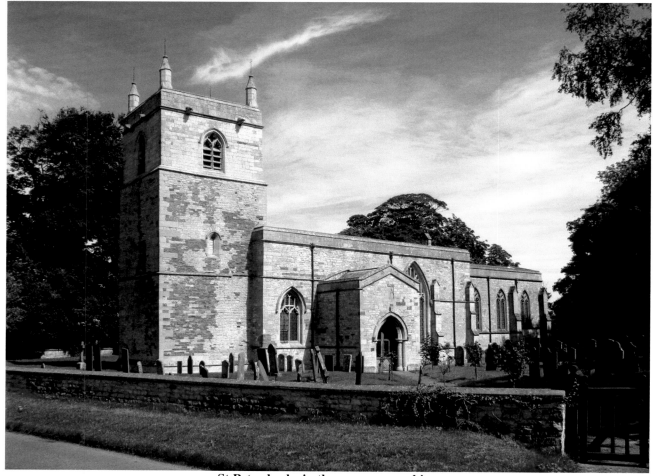

St Peter basks in the summer sunshine

In the far north east of Leicestershire the pale Jurassic Lincolnshire Limestone appears for the first time and the countryside immediately looks and feels different. In truth, the scenery has much more affinity with that around Grantham, nearby in Lincolnshire. Saltby lies on a high plateau of this excellent building stone and many of the local buildings are made of it, including the church of St Peter. Some ironstone is incorporated into the walls but overall this is a limestone church and never looks better than when bathed in sunshine. Its appeal is enhanced by its isolated situation in the angle of crossroads above the village to the north. Because it stands alone, it looks bigger than it is, in fact there are no aisles and St Peter is a simple tower, nave, chancel and south porch building. The latter makes an excellent beginning to an exploration of the church as it has a pretty outer doorway with shafted responds, whose capitals have interesting carvings of stylised faces, crosses and other motifs too eroded to identify. The inner doorway to the church proper is also worth a look as it is another 14th century construction. The porch was modified and its roofline altered in the 19th century and the chancel was rebuilt at the same time, but the tower is largely original 13th century work and the nave was built not much later in the early 14th century. The interior is light and airy due to the large nave windows, especially the southern one nearest the chancel arch which was probably made extra large to light the now vanished rood. The tower arch to the nave is unexpectedly flamboyant in the context of the restrained architecture of the rest and has Early English responds with two orders of shafts and typical 13th century capitals. Above the arch is a doorway which perhaps opened onto a gallery, now removed. The chancel arch is Perpendicular. The large font is likely to be the original one, but like all unornamented fonts, putting an actual date to it is difficult. Up in the nave roof are a delightful array of medieval stone heads, animated and full of life. Most of the rest is 19th century, oddly there are very few wall tablets. The Victorian stone pulpit and low screen came from a church in Essex in the 1930's. In the chancel the 19th century piscina and sedilia are beautifully done.

Views from the north east and east

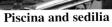

Views along the church from west and east   **Piscina and sedilia**

The altar   **Tower arch respond**   **Nave west wall**

Substantial font   **Four of the cheery nave corbels**

149

All Saints on a fine winter's day

Sapcote has fallen prey to the inexorable demand for commuter housing from nearby big towns, but little of that is sensed around All Saints, which is situated right on the southern fringes of the village away from the worst of the new housing. Nearby are the beautifully preserved Sapcote Almshouses. Across from the church is All Saints primary school, whose 150 pupils keep the neighbourhood from being too quiet. What immediately strikes the onlooker about All Saints is the dramatic effect of the tall, narrow tower and spire combination, which overshadows all else. The rest of the church consists of clerestoried nave, chancel, north aisle, north porch and Victorian vestry/organ chamber in the customary position running north off the chancel. Nothing undoubtedly pre-1300 survives from earlier buildings but it seems clear that the nave at least was constructed in Decorated times, and later in the 14th century the south wall was moved inwards and a new south doorway added. A north aisle was built in the mid-14th century to house a chantry chapel for the dynastic Bassett family, a college of chantry priests was inaugurated at the same time. A squint with quatrefoil opening from the north aisle to the chancel and a piscina in the aisle must also date from this time. The splendid tower and recessed spire were built in the 15th century. Nothing significant survives in the church from the period 1500-1800, but the 1800's saw much restoration and remodelling. A west gallery was erected probably early in the century, and then as was usually the case, was taken down in Victorian times (probably 1886). There were two major phases of restoration, the first in 1843 when the chancel was rebuilt and probably much general upgrading took place. Then in 1880 the nave and aisle were reroofed, followed in 1886 by a wide-ranging refit when most of the windows received new tracery, the chancel was refitted and much else removed or replaced. After all that few medieval fittings remained. Even the uniquely styled and richly carved Norman font was outed in 1794 and had a hard life outdoors until a glorious reinstatement in 1842. There are some good wall tablets from both the 18th and 19th centuries.

All Saints from the south east

Sunshine and shadow

The lych gate

Looking east and west along the church

The squint

Piscina and aumbry

Mural tablet

The font

The sanctuary

St Peter from the north

Saxelbye seems to have settled these days into having an 'e' on the end of its name, but has had spells in the past of doing without it. It is a tiny village, just a hamlet really, around 2 kilometres as the crow flies west of Melton Mowbray. Nearby is a railway test track from Nottingham to Melton. It has, according to one source, just 27 inhabitants. St Peter is not a large church but Saxelbye is lucky to have such a building to serve its few residents. It is beautifully set off the narrow Church Lane, yet due to abundant tree growth and a restricted churchyard in certain directions, is one of those churches that is difficult to photograph as a whole. The outline and construction are very familiar for east Leicestershire with a plan of lovely ironstone tower with battlements, quatrefoil frieze and gargoyles at the corners, recessed crocketted limestone spire, nave with south aisle, chancel and south porch. The body of the church is of ironstone, beautifully sculpted by the centuries. There is undoubted early 13th century work in the four-bay arcade, some of whose pier capitals have leaf carving while another has nailhead. The nave north wall is of around 1300 and has some interesting features such as what looks like an original Y-traceried window and a low, narrow, blocked doorway with incongruously large arch and imposts. The chancel may well also be originally 13th century, but was restored during the inevitable 19th century restoration in 1856-7. The tower and spire are 14th or 15th century Perpendicular, as is the clerestory and south aisle windows. The south porch is probably medieval, but was also restored in the mid-19th century. It has two slit windows with a holy water stoup below the eastern one. The south doorway has a late Perpendicular rectangular arch. The probably 15th century font is a very unusual piece, with quatrefoils around the bowl and battlements, on a fluted stem. The pulpit is another of the highlights of the interior, and is either 15th or early 16th century in date, with fancy tracery in the heads of the panels. One source at least suggests that it was made up from panels of a dismantled 15th century screen during the 1856 restoration. Several excellent memorials include an incised slab (1531) and part of a brass (1523).

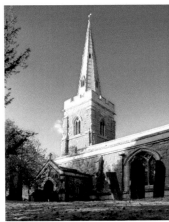

From the south east   **Top of tower and spire**   **The porch**

North wall of the nave   **Blocked north door**   **Nave north window**

The two slit windows in the porch

South doorway   **Belvoir angel gravestones**   **Church Lane**

153

St Egelwin is another fine, big ironstone church

Now here's something unique not only for Leicestershire, but also the country, a church dedicated to St Egelwin. St Egelwin was a Saxon martyr of the 7th century, brother of a king of the west Saxons, but that's about all that can be discovered. How a church in the deep Leicestershire countryside acquired this dedication is a mystery, but at least one source suggests that St Egelwin is buried in the churchyard. That presupposes that a very early Saxon church or other religious establishment stood here. Today's church has no Saxon fabric from that period, but, interestingly, there is a carved Saxon stone in the church set into a wall near the pulpit. St Egelwin is a large church, consisting of a classic East Leicestershire ironstone tower (rebuilt 1639) with limestone buttresses, battlemented parapet with pinnacles, gargoyles and a frieze, aisled nave, chancel, organ chamber and a super medieval south porch. Lincolnshire Limestone battlements bristle on the nave and south aisle. The earliest fabric is the early 13th century arcades which have some stiff leaf ornament in the capitals. The chancel arch also has stiff leaf carving interspersed with quaint heads in its capitals. The south aisle is from later in the 13th century. The porch is one of Leicestershire's best, probably 14th century, embellished with big niches above the fine doorway and more niches in the buttresses. It was originally two-storey, with an upper parvise. The chancel was rebuilt in 1845 (date above east window) and major restoration took place in 1858 when many of the windows were replaced and the interior was thoroughly refitted.   Despite this aggressive makeover, several excellent features survived. There are two 14th century tomb recesses in the north aisle with ballflower ornament, a rood loft entrance with steps, some good brasses from 1520, 1624 and 1651, early piscinas in both aisles and a clock mechanism of 1750 in the south aisle. Of the Victorian fittings, the marble font with its inlaid terracotta panels is superb, and the pulpit is nicely done. A simple tablet in the chancel south wall records the death at the age of 19 of Basil Mogridge in 1915, killed in France, one of thousands of such touching memorials to be found in churches throughout the land. A major internal reordering is currently in the pipeline.

Southern approach   **The grand porch**   **Tower, rebuilt 1639**

Views west from the chancel and east from the nave   **Pulpit and chancel pier**

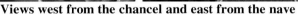

The Saxon stone   **Victorian font**   **Tomb recess**

The sanctuary and altar   **Rood opening**   **Mogridge tablet**   **Reredos detail**

Chancel arch capitals   **Brass of 1624**   **Churchyard cross**

All Saints looking lovely on its hill

All Saints is a rustic, largely ironstone church mainly of the classic 13th-14th century period. Usually such buildings are found in the picturesque villages of east Leicestershire, and indeed for most of its existence Scraptoft was exactly that, but it had the misfortune to be close to Leicester, and that has been its undoing. The city has crept nearer and nearer in the 20th and 21st centuries and to the immediate west of Scraptoft is a mass of dormitory housing. But the old village still retains some separation and sense of identity despite suffering development to the north east of the old centre. The grade 1 listed All Saints has also been lucky so far and has not been encroached upon, and it has the advantage of being alone on a high point, aloof from the rat race taking place beneath it. It really is a very pretty, well-balanced edifice, consisting of low west tower, 'Perpendicularised' in the top stage, aisled nave, chancel and south porch. Interesting blocked windows, doorways and bits of windows occur around the building. Despite having a rather quaint porch to the south, these days the north door is the main entrance. All or nearly all of the windows are replacements, but they have authentic Gothic stylings. Inside, the church saw extensive refitting and redecoration in 1991 when all the pews were removed and modern furnishings and amenities were installed. All of that was very well done and the church radiates a comfortable, welcoming atmosphere, while still retaining the best of the old features and fittings. Amongst those features are a suite of very fine wall memorials, many to members of the Wigley family. The oldest is a handsome tablet to Sir Edward Wigley and his wife from the early 18th century, featuring the two as busts. Also very attractive are two from the middle of the 18th century, one to Andrew Noel which has an angel leaning on an urn, and another to James Wigley which shows Britannia reclining on a sarcophagus carved with a scene of James supervising tree planting. The 13th century plain font, like many others, spent time in exile in the churchyard. The effigy of a 13th century priest is set into the south chancel wall. There is some good stained glass, including some typical 20th century examples in the south aisle.

All Saints from the north east

Tower doorway and reset window

Font, nave and chancel

Looking west from the chancel

Effigy of priest, C13th

A gallery of mural tablets in the chancel

Roof boss

Examples of the stained glass

157

 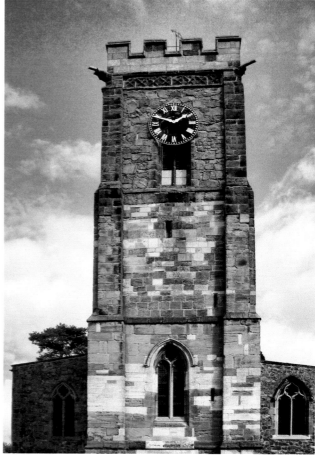

All Saints and its multihued tower

Seagrave is a prettily set village tucked into a valley on the gentle slopes that climb eastwards out of the Soar valley, and has the feel of remoteness despite proximity to densely populated areas such as Loughborough and the many villages of the Soar valley itself. The village name derives from the medieval Segrave family who ruled the roost in these parts from the 12th to the 14th centuries. The church of All Saints is just what you'd expect of such a village, honorably abraded by the centuries, but full of the character as a result. One only has to look at the tower, with its freize, battlements and remains of gargoyles, to see a pocket history of the changes that time has wrought. The west face is a patchwork of different types of stone. Once maybe the whole tower was of ironstone, but necessary repairs have been effected in limestone and then, possibly during the de rigueur Victorian restoration of 1890-1 the top stage was clad in local granite, whilst the three other sides received a complete refacing in that material. The rest of the church, which consists of aisled nave, chancel (rebuilt 1890-1) and north and south porches, is finished in mostly granite rubblestone, but many other types of cobbles can be seen in the fabric. One of the highlights of the interior is the splendid tower arch, tall and narrow. The arcades have no great merit, but are old, the northern one with its circular piers and capitals is 13th century while the southern one has octagonal piers and capitals and is early 14th century. Older still than the arcades, and everything else as well, is the rugged and crude font bowl with its pattern of arcades. Hard to date, but certainly no younger than Norman. The stem and base are more recent. The ancient doorways are seemingly original 13th (north) and 14th (south) century work. Overall, the interior is rather dull, but there are other good things to be discovered, one of the most interesting being the stone altar slab, almost certainly an original mensa from the mists of time. Two consecration crosses can still be seen. The venerable and capacious parish chest has the customary three locks. Once upon a time the sound of a church band would have been heard inside these walls, as in most churches, but very rarely do its authentic instruments survive. Here, however, displayed in a case, are a serpent and an ophicleide (a curious sort of brass bassoon).

Tower and south porch

The altar with mensa

An agnus dei in stained glass

Looking east and west along the body of the church

The parish chest

Serpent and ophicleide

Decalogue and Creed boards

The Norman font

Outstanding Victorian woodcraft

SEWSTERN HOLY TRINITY

Holy Trinity has a modest, but nicely realised design

Sewstern has the distinction of being the most easterly village and parish church in Leicestershire, with Lincolnshire but a few hundred metres away. The area around already has the unmistakeable but indefinable air about it of England's fourth biggest county. Yet for all its small size, Sewstern has a little fame due to giving its name to a well-defined prehistoric trackway, Sewstern Lane or Drift, which passes nearby and forms the boundary between Leicestershire and Lincolnshire for much of its length. It may be an old drove road for bringing animals from the north to markets in the south of England, although some sources call it a salt road; probably it served as both. The church is also a rare beast for Leicestershire, in that Holy Trinity was built by Salvin in 1842 to a Romanesque (Norman) design. It replaced an earlier chapel demolished many years before. The architect's plan was not ambitious as befitted a commission for a chapel at ease (to Buckminster), but it is effective and pleasing. The exterior especially has a satisfying unity of design, and the interior an intimate atmosphere, although the benches don't look especially comfortable! The ironstone-built nave and chancel are under one roof and at the west end is a projecting bellcote in contrasting limestone. It contains only one bell but the line of the bellcote is continued downwards through a middle section with narrow round-arched window and two jolly heads at the ends of a string course to embrace the doorway, the latter being a typical Romanesque round-headed design with several orders in the arch, but no ornament. The shafts have scalloped capitals. Along the nave/chancel are rows of four identical round-arched windows, with shafts and scalloped capitals, like the west doorway. At the east end are two long, round-headed windows above which is a small, circular window. Clasping buttresses stand at the four corners of the building. The interior is small, but despite that, there are some nice things here. Firstly, on entering through the west door, one almost bumps into the font, plain but nicely integrated into the overall Romanesque design with its pier and capital type stem and bowl, with scallops. The pulpit is even better, a lovely, ornate, classically Victorian Gothic design in pale limestone and marble with graceful arches and ammonitico rosso shafts.

Holy Trinity from the south

Two lively creatures

Views along the church, looking east and west

The tiny chancel and altar

The beautiful pulpit

1914-19 War memorial and scroll

The font

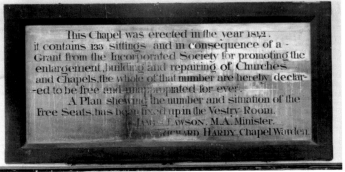

Plaque from the time of the building of the church

C17th chair

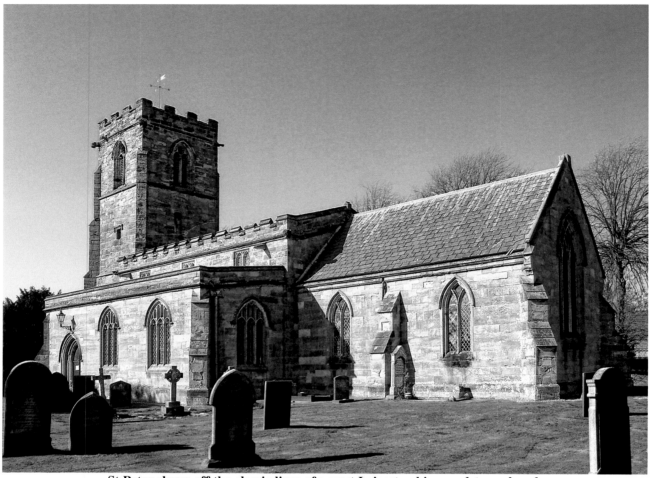

St Peter shows off the classic lines of a west Leicestershire sandstone church

Shackerstone over in the west of Leicestershire is a very small village of only 200 souls or so, but has every reason to feel proud of itself. In 2004 its church of St Peter, the treasure of the village and sited in pride of place in the centre near the pub, was in a state of delapidation and it seemed that it would no longer be given insurance. Closure and possible demolition loomed, but the villagers were having none of it and a group of five trustees was set up to mastermind the raising of the large sums needed to restore St Peter. They were gloriously vindicated when at least £105,000 was raised, and since then great things have been done to this church and it once again is a fit and proper place for worship, and the jewel of the village. As always, more needs to be done, especially to the sandstone fabric, but with that sort of determination, who's to say it won't be achieved? So successful was the village that the project was nominated for an English Heritage award in 2011. St Peter is not an important or especially interesting church architecturally or historically, except to the inhabitants, and conforms to a familiar Leicestershire pattern of surviving medieval tower, attached to which is a heavily restored or rebuilt church body of aisled nave and chancel. However, aesthetically, it is a fine building. The tower is probably late 14th or early 15th century and has standard details, including battlements. The rest was completely overhauled under the direction of Earl Howe of nearby Gopsall Hall in 1845, and it is difficult to establish where rebuilding stopped and restoration began, but it is clear that almost everything was renewed. The great thing was that St Peter has retained nearly all of the fittings installed at that time, so presents a complete scheme of early Victorian furnishing, including a full set of box pews, openwork reading desk, pulpit, west gallery and chancel furniture. It is interesting that even as late as 1845, in the deep countryside, old ideas persisted and it was deemed appropriate to install box pews and a gallery. Thankfully for us they are still in place for us to admire. A notable survivor from the medieval church is the excellent Perpendicular font with its fine carvings.

St Peter from the north east and south east

Looking from nave to chancel and vice-versa

The west gallery

The wonderful set of doored pews and furnishings of 1845

The font

Parish chest

Arms of Howe

SHANGTON ST NICHOLAS

Where sheep may safely graze, St Nicholas in Spring

Churches in east Leicestershire frequently have splendid positions, but St Nicholas is up there with the best, nestled into the side of the hill that ascends to the small settlement of Shangton, deep in the Leicestershire countryside. The views from the high, east-west running Mere Road to the south (gaps in the hedge permitting!) are terrific, as are those from the approach road from the south as it descends to the valley of the tiny stream that runs in front of St Nicholas. It is another church that seems to have fallen out with its village and it sits quite aloof some distance to the south of the main cluster of houses, with only the impressive Shangton Manor for company. However, the field to the south and the immediate surroundings are full of humps and hollows, and it is tempting to surmise that the old village lay all around St Nicholas. The mostly ironstone building consists of nave with two-bell bellcote, chancel, south porch and vestry/organ chamber. At first sight the church appears very ancient and untouched by the hand of the restorer, but in fact St Nicholas has seen many changes over the centuries from at least 13th century beginnings, not least a series of 19th century rebuildings, refittings and restorations. New nave furnishings, floor and door were installed by Henry Goddard in 1845-6, the chancel was restored in 1851, the east wall of the chancel was rebuilt in 1863 and a vestry/organ chamber added on the north side in 1874. Apart from the fabric itself, traces of older medieval work are confined to little touches here and there, like the ballflower on the inside arch of the east window and another south east window, and two lengths of quatrefoil frieze commandeered for use as reredos for the altar. The font has a fairly primitive design, being a deep tub which sits directly on the base with no stem; it could date from anytime from the 13th century onwards. There is only one important memorial, a handsome, large wall memorial in the chancel commissioned by Matthew Saunders for his wife Margaret in 1612, with typical strapwork, squared columns, lots of curly ornament, finials and the dedication in a central tablet. The grave slabs of both Matthew and Margaret are set into the floor immediately west of the altar. There are two other slabs in that area, an older one partly concealed beneath the altar and carpeting, and one of 1757 to the Rev'd Walter Allicock. Another grave slab lies near the font, to Joseph Chambers (died 1726). Despite the Victorian interior, St Nicholas has retained an engaging, antique atmosphere.

St Nicholas from the south

South doorway

Lizard headstop

Views along the church looking east and west

The sanctuary and altar

Arch to organ chamber

Saunders memorial (1612)

Fonts large and small

The east window

The pulpit

St Helen as seen from Leicester Road

Sharnford is a very handy and pleasant place to live if you commute to Hinckley or use the A5, and these facts have not been ignored by the developers, and the village has grown to a population of around 1000 these days. The eastern part of the village is the oldest and naturally that's where its oldest and most important building is situated, close to the village's boundary. St Helen has pride of place next to the main thoroughfare, the B4114 Leicester Road, and makes a pretty picture in its arboreal churchyard. It is not a particularly distinctive building and was thoroughly 'worked over' during Victorian restorations to the point where only the tower has retained substantial medieval elements. That is of mainly 15th century origin, although perhaps it has even older foundations. The battlements are Victorian additions. The rest of the church is simple in plan, with a nave, chancel, south porch with stone seats and 19th century vestry. On the south side central buttress is a scratch dial. The 19th century fenestration is a mixture of Decorated (see the main east window) and Perpendicular stylings. The main Victorian restoration took place in 1866 under the direction of W. Smith. The chancel prior to 1984 was a construction of 1846, but in February 1984 disaster struck when a fire more or less destroyed everything in the chancel, which required a new roof and complete internal refitting. But the village rallied round, the money was raised and a gleaming new chancel was opened in 1985. The interior fittings are all Victorian, although base elements of the building like the chancel arch are original medieval work. There is little to arrest the attention inside, but St Helen is obviously well cared for. The most interesting feature is the set of Victorian doored pews with stylish hinges and carved doors, which probably date from Smith's restoration. The octagonal font is quite plain except for a text around the bowl. There are a few mural tablets in the chancel, but none are exceptional, probably the best is a marble and slate piece of 1839. Two slate commandment boards which used to be in the nave are now mounted on the east wall either side of the altar. The churchyard is one of St Helen's best aspects and is particularly attractive in Spring.

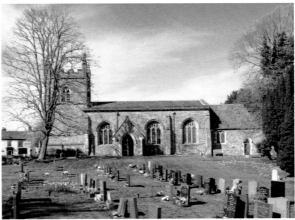

From the west

From the south

Porch and tower

Looking east and west along the church

The pulpit

The sanctuary

Doored pews

The eagle keeps watch

The font

Wall tablets

SHAWELL ALL SAINTS

C5, SP 541 797

All Saints from the north west

Oddly, we have two consecutive entries here where the architect of Victorian restorations was William Beaumont Smith, and indeed, he restored All Saints at the same time (1865-6) he was masterminding St Helen at Sharnford, around 10 miles away. A glance at the map reveals that the two villages lie close to the major A5 road and it is easy to imagine Smith mounting his horse or taking the stage coach to journey to and from his two commissions. There's nothing to say he was working on both simultaneously, but with such easy communication between the two, who knows? Be that as it may, All Saints has a standard layout and is rather similar to St Helen, but as well as the usual west tower, nave, chancel, south porch and north vestry, it has a north aisle. But, like St Helen, Smith was quite ruthless with the old church, leaving in this case only the medieval tower, and completely rebuilding the rest. He chose a mostly Decorated template, but the north aisle is simpler in conception and tends to an Early English style, and the tower west window is Perpendicular. The tower is very similar to Sharnford's and also would appear to be mainly Perpendicular with older roots. It is built of grey sandstone and it seems a little perverse that for the church body Smith chose pinkish intrusive igneous rock blocks, but he knew well that such a stone would last for ever. He used pale grey limestone for contrast in the window frames, doorways and dressings. Inside, if the visitor has already seen Leire St Peter, the appearance will seem familiar. Smith was very fond of polychrome stonework and he used it here, as he did at Leire in 1867-8. He also chose similar building materials. Another characteristic of Smith's is a certain Victorian stiffness and formality, and the interior has both of these faults. It is also quite gloomy due to copious stained glass and lack of clerestory, but there are some diverting features and fittings to be discovered, including quality Victorian stone carving and woodwork, and a marble and mosaic reredos. The font is of drum type. The wall memorials are notable, with some 18th century examples which derive from the earlier church. Near the church are the earthworks of a 12th century motte and bailey castle.

From the south west and north

Tower and north aisle   **Details of the south side**

Earthworks of the nearby motte and bailey castle

SHEARSBY ST MARY MAGDALEN

C4, SP 623 910

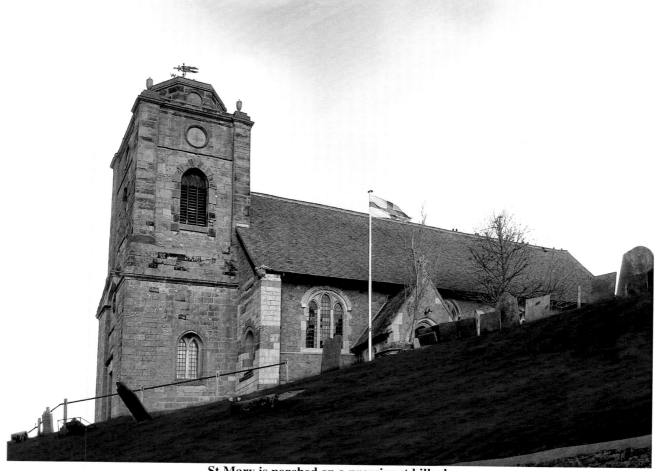

St Mary is perched on a prominent hillock

St Mary is an unusual church, not like any other in Leicestershire. It is almost a complete rebuilding of a medieval original, but small areas of medieval fabric and some artifacts survive. The building promises much when seen from the steep approach path, for the unique tower of 1789 is a detailed Classical design, and hopes rise that things will be similar inside. However, that thought is quickly dashed when the undistinguished, insipid Victorian interior is seen. So it is probably best to concentrate on that fascinating tower. Many complex architectural terms could be expended on the design, but basically the highlight is the west front which features a first stage with pediment under which is a quatrefoil opening which sits above a typical Georgian doorway with voussoirs and keystone. There is an inscribed tablet above the doorway referring to the rebuilding. The second and third stages have more characteristic Classical details, which include fine bell openings. Then things get a little strange, because the last unit of the tower is a stumpy octagon which almost looks like the beginnings of a spire that was never finished. The Classical west frontage is completed by large, empty niches in the nave west wall which seem to cry out for Grecian statues to be inserted. The rest of the church is mostly Victorian and consists of nave and chancel under one roof, and porch with sharply angled roof. The windows are Early English inspired, the east one a group of three lancets. The nave/chancel walls are faced with granite, but the east wall is original rubblestone and the tower is sandstone. At the external corners of the nave/chancel are lively gargoyles, possibly griffins. Much of the 19th century restoration and rebuilding was done under the direction of Ordish in 1880. Almost all the interior fittings are 19th century, but for some reason an unpleasant looking medieval figure remains from the earlier church and now resides in the north wall of the chancel. The piscina and sedilia were also retained, and the chancel screen is 15th century. The font is a worthy piece, with bulbous bowl, carvings of four angels and ropework around the lip. Behind it on the west wall is mounted a large, rather battered gravestone.

Three views of St Mary from the west, north west and south

From the north

Seen from the south over Shearsby's rooftops

Super 'Hammer Horror' gargoyle

Early English inspired

Classical niche

Scenes from the churchyard

All Saints as seen from the approach path

All Saints serves the villages of Sheepy Magna and the much smaller but almost contiguous Sheepy Parva and lies very close to the Warwickshire border, about 2 km north of Atherstone. It is by no means a glamorous or architecturally interesting church, a rebuilding in 1788-9 left untouched only the medieval tower and the fabric of the chancel, while the body of the church was reconstructed in a very uninspired style. Yet interestingly, despite the date of 1788, there are no obvious Classical details, the form is purely Gothic, although it may be that Victorian alterations eradicated an earlier layout. The plan is 15th century west tower, nave with north aisle, chancel, northern vestry and north porch. The aisle and porch date from 1859 during a makeover by Robert Jennings, when the nave windows were replaced by others in a Decorated style. The tower west face shows distinct traces of a large arched opening, which would have had doors and formed the main entrance to the church before the 1788 rebuilding. Today the upper part contains a Perpendicular style window; beneath it are twin lancet windows and at ground level is an obviously resited recess containing a worn effigy. Nearby is a resited stone grave slab with Maltese Cross engraving which appears to be 13th or, more likely, 14th century in date. Unless the lights are switched on, the interior is a very gloomy space, due to the lack of clerestory and widespread use of stained glass in the windows. Yet, paradoxically, it is the stained glass that is the highlight of the building. Three of the greatest late Victorian talents in the field were involved in its provision for four windows in the south wall. Two were designed by Edward Burne-Jones (1833-98) and manufactured by the William Morris (1834-96) Studio in 1879, while the two more westerly ones were designed and executed by Charles Kempe (1837-1907) in 1897. All are gems and redolent of the essence of Victoriana, with deep glowing colours, sharp detail, and sensitive and evocative portraiture. Of the other fittings, there's a nice spread of wall tablets, mostly in the chancel, many commemorating members of the Fell family, and a decent font which may be 15th century. A wide-ranging refitting of the interior is planned to start soon.

The tower from the south **Recess and effigy in tower west wall** **Medieval grave slab**

Views along the nave looking east and west

The font **Parish chest (4 locks!)** **Ornate Edwardian, and Fell family tablets**

Snapshots of the marvellous stained glass

St John from the north east

Dedications to St John the Evangelist, as opposed to St John the Baptist, are not common. Only two others can be found in Leicestershire, at Hinckley and Donisthorpe. St John Shenton was constructed in 1860-1 on the site of a modest medieval forerunner. Stone from the earlier building was used for the inside walls. The plan is fairly unusual in that there are two transepts running off the nave, the rest of the church is standard in conception and was completed in a classic Victorian Gothic style, loosely Decorated, which is continued inside in a largely original furnishing plan. Amongst the fittings is a very fine stone pulpit, and reredos with texts of the Lord's Prayer, Creed and Decalogue. The church has a very long association with the inhabitants of nearby Shenton Hall, and St John's is a grander church than might be expected for such a small hamlet solely thanks to the sponsorship of the Wollastons in the 'big house'. St John was designed by the Rev'd H. J. Wollaston and largely paid for by himself and other members of the family, the architect was W. H. Knight of Cheltenham. The Hall itself was built by William Wollaston in 1629. The Wollaston family retained a fine memorial from the old church and installed it in the present one. It is one of the highlights of the interior and is for William Wollaston and his wife Ann (who unfortunately died the year the Hall was built) from around 1666. The large, flowing memorial features the two as busts, beneath a broken pediment with garlands. Also of good quality, but simpler, is a white marble scroll-type tablet of 1871 with Royal Navy emblems for the much decorated Sir Alexander Dundas Young Arbuthnot, who died at Shenton Hall and whose daughter married a Wollaston. In a connection with the previous entry for Sheepy, that daughter's memorial, plus other Wollaston memorials, can be found in Sheepy All Saints. Another connection is the presence of excellent stained glass by Kempe in both buildings. Here at Shenton the theme is St Michael and the Archangels and the 1918 window is a memorial to Frederick Wollaston. In the north transept are 16th century wall brasses and there are texts around the chancel arch and a north transept window.

From the east

From the south

Tower and porch

Looking west and east along the nave

Chancel arch with text

The sanctuary

The pulpit

The font

Wollaston memorial

Arbuthnot tablet

Fine Victorian stained glass

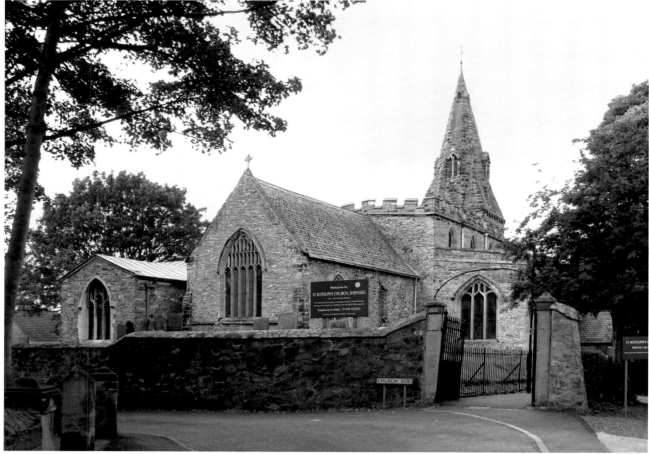

St Botolph seen from Church Side

St Botolph is a fine old church, still in the centre of things in Shepshed, as it has been for a very long time. It is sited on the highest and most dominant point in the oldest part of the village, and there's little reason to think that a church hasn't been here since Saxon times, especially as the dedication is to a Saxon saint, although no trace of that early building remains. There is nothing indisputably Norman either, but the rugged tower and very early broach spire were constructed as that period was passing into the Early English interval. The long chancel is also 13th century, as must be the core of the nave. The aisles are 14th century. There was further expansion as late as 1935, when a south transept and vestry were added to increase seating capacity when the old side galleries were taken down. The west gallery is still in place and accommodates the impressive organ. Changes in the 19th century imposed a Victorian look and feel to the interior, but that atmosphere was swept away by a comprehensive modernisation in 2008, which resulted in one of the most successful upgradings in the county and the comfortable, attractive space we see today. From the start the plan included the retention of the many medieval and later treasures, and the desire to make more of them, so a visit today is even more rewarding than prior to 2008. There are many fine things to admire; this is a super interior for the church explorer. Pride of place must go to the Phillipps memorials which adorn the chancel and other areas of the church. The family occupied nearby Garendon Hall and were a powerful and successful dynasty from the late 17th century until hard times led to the demolition of Garendon Hall in 1964. St Botolph's Phillipps memorials are from the period 1696-1830 and they are very grand pieces, in excellent condition. There is one old brass in the church, dated 1592 and commemmorating Thomas Duport, a patron of St Botolph. There are medieval benches with poppyheads and faces, an ancient font restored to the church in 1961, fine corbels including a rather rude one and a sheep's head ('Shepshed'), fragments of medieval glass, some good 20th century stained glass, an ornate Elizabethan pulpit, heads and 17th century churchwardens initials in the nave roof, bits of medieval tile, and much more. A fascinating church.

From the west

Spire through the rooflines

South transept foundation stone

Looking from the nave to the chancel, and vice-versa

Medieval stained glass

Snapshot of modern stained glass

Churchwarden's initials, heads and bosses on roof beams

The Duport brass

Phillipps memorials

Sheela-na-gig

Sheep's head

Bench end carving

C16th pulpit

Old font

St Botolph's Classical tower contrasts with the red brick of the nave

Sibson St Botolph, alphabetically, follows Shepshed St Botolph. There are only four St Botolphs in Leicestershire, so it is odd how these two fall together. But there the similarity ends, as they are completely dissimilar churches. Sibson is an unusual building, like sections of three separate churches bolted together. There is a very attractive Classical tower, built in 1726 when the medieval one fell down, bringing the nave with it. The tower was rebuilt smartly with sandstone ashlar blocks, and has several typically Classical details, like the west doorway, vases at the corners on top and three round windows or oculi, which are mirrored in the design of the later Georgian clock of 1789. The windows in the lowest stage are a curious classical version of Y-shaped Gothic. The nave is a quite different concept, built wider than the tower and the surviving 13th century chancel, and of brick. Perhaps the builders of 1726 wanted to maintain old traditions with a stone tower, but use the then fashionable (and cheaper) brick for the nave. The nave windows are all Decorated-style insertions of 1877, it is unknown what preceded them. The chancel was restored about 110 years ago, but retains interesting window tracery, apparently renewed but probably based on the originals. The main east window is most imposing and has intersecting tracery. The largely Victorian interior is light and airy due to the large windows and contains several items worth seeking out. Most of these are concentrated in the sanctuary. The oldest feature in the church is a reasonably well-preserved 13th century effigy which lies against the south wall; the figure, almost certainly a priest, holds a heart. Above his head is a canopy. Set into the floor is a fine one metre long brass of 1532, depicting John Moore. He holds two scrolls with texts which wind upwards to the figure of Christ in Majesty. Also in the sanctuary is an old chest, possibly 17th century. There is a piscina in the sanctuary and a three-seater sedilia which is original and in excellent condition, with piers at the divisions and hoodmoulds above the arches. There are few wall tablets, but one of them is a stylish late 18th century sarcophagus design in white marble on a black backplate, to Benjamin and Mary Grew. The font is Victorian and has a vintage bath chair for company.

The nave, chancel arch and roof

The chancel and screen

The sedilia

Pulpit and lectern

Grew wall memorial

John Moore brass

C13th priest effigy

Old chest

Font and wicker bath chair

Stained glass

The east window

Imposing from any angle, Sileby St Mary

Though these days referred to simply as St Mary, the full dedication of this impressive and dignified 13th to 15th century church is the Nativity of the Blessed Virgin Mary, a harkback to the days before the Reformation when Catholicism was the only religion in the country, and the Virgin Mary was a very important figure. Such a grand building speaks of rich patronage in its medieval days, and as well as the usual tower, nave with aisles and chancel, St Mary has two chancel chapels (the north one now adapted to take the organ) and a particularly imposing south porch. The latter is a rarity for Leicestershire in that it has an upper floor. The chapels were probably created by rich patrons as chantry chapels, where prayers were said every day for their souls. St Mary is a particularly harmonious and refined design, and highlights are the large (renewed) windows, which have a variety of imaginative, mostly Decorated, tracery. The use of stone is interesting, and both sandstone and granite are widely used. The two main areas of sandstone are the porch and west face of the tower, but possibly the whole of the church was once of this material and the granite was used for cladding or rebuilding later. The interior is excellent and a concentrated investigation is needed to appreciate everything. The nave roof is very fine, and now with recent cleaning, the details can be seen clearly; these include humorous corbels, on which perch a variety of figures holding shields, instruments, mitres, etc. The corbels are certainly medieval and maybe the figures too. Other ancient worn faces and beasts lurk in other corners of the building. The roof bosses have a variety of designs and are picked out in gold and other bold colours. The north arcade is 13th century and the south a little later, the former has dogtooth and nailhead in the arches and on the capitals (the north doorway also has dogtooth). The font is a crudely hewn, monolithic piece and is 13th century or earlier. A rood loft opening is still in place in the chancel. A medieval recess is partly hidden by the choir stalls, and there are a few decent wall tablets. Above the narrow door to the tower stair is a very odd corbel which looks like an extra from a sci-fi film! There's much more.

Looking from across Main Street

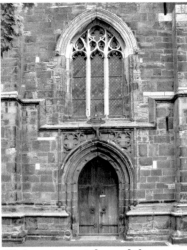

Elaborate west face of the tower

The north doorway

View along the nave to the chancel

The chancel with nave beyond

Nave roof

Jolly corbels and their 'minders'

Memorials of 1807 and 1856

The font

Hanoverian royal arms

An interesting corner

Rood opening

SIX HILLS MISSION, ST MARY

From the west

Six Hills is an interesting place despite the baleful presence of the race track known as the A46. There is no village, very few people actually live there, yet a study of the map reveals a fascinating nucleation of roads on the site. They come in from far and wide like the spokes of a wheel, but why? One theory is that the site has long been a place of meeting or celebration, possibly going back to pre-Roman times. But there never was a settlement as far as can be established. Thus it is a bit of a mystery why a church, or perhaps in St Mary's case, we should say chapel at ease, exists at all at Six Hills. Six Hills today is just a loose association of a large hotel on the A46, a small business park, a derelict farm and a petrol station that flickers in and out of business. Why build a church here in 1837? The answer is that in 1835, nearby Old Dalby church was rebuilt by the Rev'd George Sawyer, and as part of the evangelical fervour associated with that event the noble Reverend decided to establish and pay for a plant of the big church at Six Hills, a mission indeed. What perhaps is more remarkable than the initial building of the chapel is that it is still in business today, which is a tribute to the dedicated band of people who turn up from the surrounding area for the infrequent services. The building is unpretentious and small, constructed in red brick with sandstone capping on the buttresses and as dressing. To the west is a shallow vestibule projecting from the main building, which seems to have been designed to mimic the west face of a conventional tower, and continues upwards to a one-bell sandstone bellcote. Inside, St Mary is a preaching box, no frills. There is a nave and a small chancel with the altar protected by white wooden railings, all under one roof. The double-door main entrance opens into the vestibule from the west. The windows are modest lancets. The small churchyard is demarcated off at the front by an iron gate and railing fence set on a low wall, which could be original. All around the oasis of the chapel and churchyard, the environment is running wild or has been despoiled by industrial activity, but let's give three cheers for the continued existence of this brave outpost.

From the south west

Lancet window

Main west doorway

Iron fence and main approach

A glimpse inside

The bellcote

Back to nature on the north side

SKEFFINGTON ST THOMAS A BECKET

D3, SK 741 026

St Thomas from the south

St Thomas is another grand east Leicestershire ironstone church, but with a lot more limestone in the fabric than most. Despite a wholesale restoration and partial rebuilding of the 13th to 15th century building by W. Millican in 1860, a glowing patina of age seems to envelop the building. A plan of medieval west tower with regulation issue battlements and pinnacles, aisled nave, chancel and south porch is standard but there is one other element of the church that is a little unusual. That is the large 15th century chapel which runs off to the north of the chancel, the so-called Skeffington Chapel. These days it has been adapted as a vestry, but originally it was built maybe as a chantry chapel or more likely a repository for Skeffington family tombs and memorials. That dynastic family were all powerful in these parts, so powerful that the village was named after them. Those days are long gone but the memorials of several Skeffingtons remain, slowly mouldering and disintegrating. None of the memorials is especially good, but they are very much of their time and deserve better. The oldest is a very battered incised slab of 1543 set into the floor, for Thomas Skeffington, his wife and 13 children, but the carving is so worn that little can be made out. A couple of tombs, or their remnants, are set into recesses in the wall. The one for William Skeffington (d. 1571) is purely heraldic with shields and arms, unless a detached female figure to the right belongs with it. This is probably the best of the set. The other recess is occupied by detached figures from a much larger memorial which was dismantled at some time, this is for another Thomas Skeffington who died in 1600. The last memorial of note is a large showy wall memorial for John Skeffington (d. 1652) and his wife, with angels drawing curtains to reveal the eulogies on two tablets. The well fed angels look more like 17th century serving maids than celestial beings, but they add character. There are medieval corbels in the nave and excellent 14th century glass in the chapel, but more or less all the other fittings are Victorian, including good quality pulpit, font, fine east window by Wailes and pretty carved stone and marble reredos. Amongst the remaining medieval fabric is the chancel arch of around 1300.

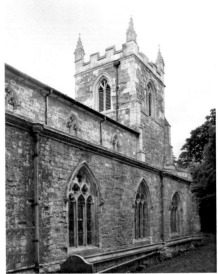

North aisle and tower

Renewed Perpendicular window

Victorian font

Pulpit, chancel and sanctuary

Looking west along the nave

South arcade

Two Skeffington memorials, John (left) and William (right)

Part of the reredos

Nave corbels

Medieval glass

SLAWSTON ALL SAINTS

From the south west

The description of churches tends to repeatedly lure the same adjectives from church lover's pens, and it is very easy to overuse certain words and phrases. However, that's the nature of the subject, similar buildings and settings are under discussion each time. Some of the commonest are 'pretty', 'picturesque', 'lovely', 'beautifully set', but sometimes there's no escape and a church simply begs to be described thus. Slawston is a case in point, it really is beautifully set and it IS pretty. Sited right on the edge of its highly desirable picture book village, the ironstone All Saints enjoys grand views to the nearby 131 metre high Slawston Hill, while the churchyard is peaceful and well-tended. An ideal place for contemplation. Externally it has all the requisites of the classic rural church painting, with well-proportioned tower and handsome broach spire, nave heightened with a clerestory, north aisle, chancel and south porch. The tower/spire probably date from the early to mid-1300's, as does the unusually early clerestory. The chancel was rebuilt in 1864. The porch and vestry were built new in 1864, the organ chamber in 1890. Internally All Saints is a disappointment, and it's the Victorians again who must be called to account. Spearheaded by local firm H. Goddard and Sons, the interior was stripped of almost all interest, most fittings replaced by bland 19th century substitutes. Only the plain medieval font survived. Of the 19th century fittings, only the pulpit has any character, but on the plus side the layout is ordered, uncluttered and well-balanced. There is some architectural interest, it seems that early in its history All Saints possessed two transepts. The eastern arch of the arcade is different from its companions, and corresponds to a similar blocked arch in the south wall, there seems no reason to doubt that these once opened into transepts. The north transept is now absorbed into the north aisle. There is no chancel arch, which may have been taken down at some stage. In its place is the end member of the chancel roof, extended upwards to a sturdy cross-beam, which provides support. Some old corbels can still be found in the north aisle, but two of the best heads can be found as headstops by the south doorway.

From the west and south

Faces from many centuries ago

Blocked north doorway

Clerestory and nave windows

The porch

Two glimpses of the interior

187

SMEETON WESTERBY CHRIST CHURCH

All Saints from the south

Smeeton Westerby Christ Church is a quintessential Victorian church, in much the same condition as when built in 1848-9. It is a summary in stone of Gothic Revival precepts (though modestly expressed here, perhaps due to financial constraints), designed by the deeply religious ecclesiologist and architect Henry Woodyer (1816-96), his only new church commission in Leicestershire (he did, however, extensively restore Sproxton St Bartholomew in 1882-3). Woodyer was a follower of the much better known architect A. W. N. Pugin and was a fascinating man; he has a recent biography to his name. Based in Guildford, he never advertised, and rarely ventured out of the south of the country, working mostly from personal commissions from friends or churchmen. Clearly some influencial figure brought him to Leicestershire for this work, or perhaps it was the first vicar of the new church, Richard Fawssett. Christ Church cannot be placed in the forefront of his achievements, but it is a harmonious building, with a few typically Woodyer touches, like the ornate font cover. The plan of the church is a wide nave with two aisles, chancel, south porch and vestry running north off the chancel. On the west nave roof is an octagonal bellcote with mini battlements and spire. The west wall of the nave features a large arch externally, beneath which is a window inserted into the filling of the void, with buttresses to either side. Such an arrangement suggests that a tower may once have been visualised, but no indication of that appears in Woodyer's original plan. The template for the design and its details is Decorated, and all the windows, arcades, etc are in that style. The font is an undoubted highlight and is an unusual design with two rows of arches, with shields and heraldry. The tall, wooden cover is very stylish, with two tiers of acutely angled Gothic arches with crocketts, pinnacles and small crosses. The attractive marble reredos is of cultured design and features five circles containing floral, quatrefoil and cross motifs. In fact, all the fittings are done in excellent taste, and the stained glass, which includes some by Kempe, is also good quality. However, with this glass and the lack of a clerestory, the interior is rather gloomy.

From the south west

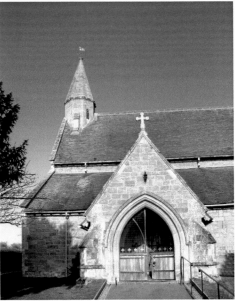

Porch and west end

Looking east along the nave

Sanctuary, east window

Altar and reredos

Ornate window and sedile

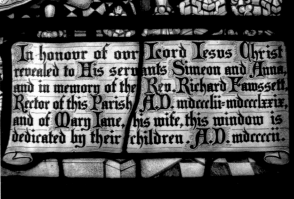

In honour of our Lord Iesus Christ
revealed to His servants Simeon and Anna,
and in memory of the Rev. Richard Fawssett,
Rector of this Parish A.D. mdcccliii-mdccclxxix,
and of Mary Lane, his wife, this window is
dedicated by their children. A.D. mdccccii.

Dedication in stained glass to the first rector

Stained glass snapshot

Organ details

The font and cover

Closer view of the font

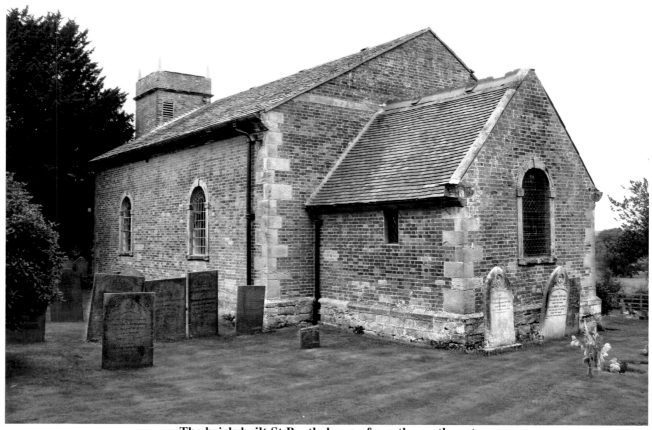

The brick-built St Bartholomew from the south east

St Bartholomew stands alone just off the B4116 to the north west of the main village of Snarestone, well away from most of the houses. It is a plain, unprepossessing, brick-built Georgian church, which some might think unattractive. But like all churches there are things of interest here, not least the building being very much of its time. It was built in 1752 and faithfully reflects the architectural style of the time i.e. classicism. The windows are all round arched with keystones and glass in small regular panes, a style reproduced in the arch of the wide double-door west doorway. Above this doorway is a commemorative date stone and another Georgian favourite, the oculus-type window. Around 1834 it was deemed necessary to increase capacity, and in order to do this the north wall was rebuilt further out. This was not an aisled extension, as there is no arcade and the nave roof forms a continuous covering. The windows match the earlier ones, but the frames are now in brick instead of the sandstone of the 1752 set. As a result of the extension the nave roof had to be reset to accommodate the widening and the thin, low tower is now offset to the south, off-centre of the nave. This tower has a gabled roof and simple, modest pinnacles. The rest of the building consists of nave and chancel only. It is unknown what sort of building preceded the present one, but some authorities claim that it was rebuilt while others imply that St Bartholomew was a new construction. The church registers go back to 1559, so at least it is known that there was an earlier church. It seems clear that if it was a rebuild, then it was almost complete, the only possible earlier fabric is the stone plinth that the brick building sits on. The interior is a simple space and it seems that no items were retained from any earlier church. The font is small and may be contemporary. Three 18th century mural tablets adorn the walls. The churchyard is of moderate size and there is an extension to the north. The villagers of Snarestone have worked hard to maintain the appeal of St Bartholomew with community events, and in 2001 new seating and carpets were installed. There are plans for the provision of kitchen and toilet facilities in the near future.

From the north

From the west

Details of the west end

Details of the tower

Original nave window

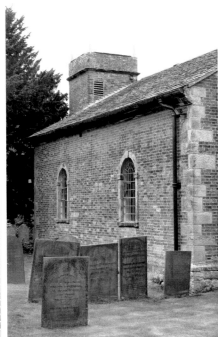

Nave and tower

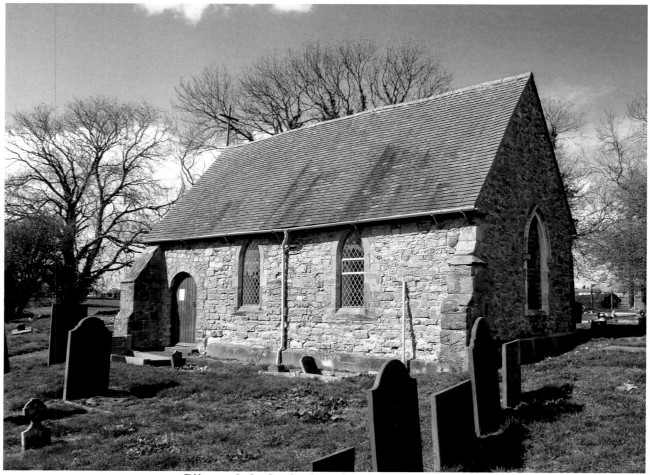

Bijou and absolutely charming, Snibston St Mary

Now here's a lovely little church in a rather unlikely place. The conurbation of Coalville is not renowned for its beauty, but here, barely two kilometres from the town centre is a distinctive ancient building in a sequestered spot. It is a very tiny church, one of the smallest in the country, just a single cell less than 10 metres long and six metres wide. It was not always so, old drawings indicate that a tower stood at the west end (its foundations were discovered in 1930) and there was a chancel. St Mary stands more or less alone, with just Grange Farm nearby, and is isolated from its village. Yet it is believed that one of the tracks or roads that runs nearby was previously a main artery between Leicester and Burton, and the undulations in neighbouring fields may be the traces of a long deserted village, so St Mary was not always so alone and tranquil as it is today. As recently as 2007 there was another church in Snibston, St James, bigger, more modern, far better situated and appointed than St Mary. Now that building is redundant and up for sale, a victim of falling numbers in the congregation and increasing costs. The pascal candle near the altar sits in a stand made from wood from the altar of St James. So St Mary sails on alone to grace another century, to go with the nine or more it has already seen. There is nothing in the present building to give an accurate date for its building but the late 12th or early 13th century would seem a good guess. The first recorded incumbent was in post in 1220. Everything except the fabric has been replaced and the windows today are simple Early English style lancets, most of the fittings are 19th century and it is very much a Victorian church inside. That does not detract from the calm, reflective atmosphere, in which the distant past feels very close. The only ancient item in the church is the font, and it may be as old as 13th century, but its overly pristine condition indicates that it has been recut. A band of intertwining foliage runs around the middle of the bowl, in which are hidden a small face and a snake. Two of the windows have rather undistinguished Victorian stained glass, including the east window. There is only one notable mural memorial, a touching tablet to a six year old girl who died in 1840.

St Mary from the south and north west

Looking along the church from the west, and east　　　**Altar and east window**

Wall tablet　　　**Sunlight and shadow**　　　**The altar cross**

The font　　　**Pascal candle**　　　**A simple but moving window display**

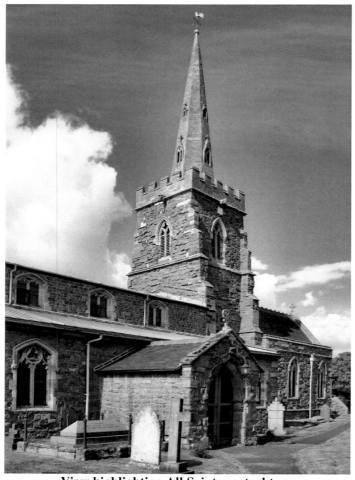

View highlighting All Saints central tower

The north aisle doorway of All Saints

Somerby is a picturesque village set amongst the hills of east Leicestershire and close to that area's scenic highpoint, Burrough Hill. Somerby's church is as appealing as its surroundings. Unusual too, as the church has a central tower with spire and a north transept, as well as the more customary aisled nave with clerestory, chancel and south porch. Local ironstone was used for the fabric and the familial relationship with other east Leicestershire churches is marked. Despite a general restoration in 1865-6 and rebuilding of the chancel in 1883 by local architect R. W. Johnson of Melton Mowbray, the church has retained its medieval appearance, and it is believed that a central tower has always been part of the design. That and the transept suggest a Norman forerunner, perhaps a southern transept also once existed to complete what would have been a classic Romanesque cruciform plan. However, the present transept was built in 1887 (as a vestry), so it remains supposition whether there was an earlier version. Little of the early church remains, maybe the round-arched doorway in the chancel north wall, but a lot of the present building was constructed in the 1300's or earlier. The south doorway is Early English, with dogtooth and fleurons in the arch and thin shafts, and the handsome north arcade is of similar age. This has piers with eight shafts and ornate capitals with luxuriant foliage which varies from pier to pier. Johnson (presumably) was responsible for the matching south aisle, which does a creditable job of complimenting the original north one. The delightful font, with its pointed arches, big leafy ornament and heads around the top, may be the same age as the other 13th century features. Inside the pointed arches are curved ones. There's a fine 13th century triple sedilia set in the chancel, with ogee heads. Set in the back wall of the middle seat are pieces from an early coffin lid including the top part with very damaged head, ornament and part of the peripheral inscription. A rood loft opening remains high up next to the chancel arch and there are corbel heads at the apices and in the springers of the nave arches. Of the Victorian fittings, the pulpit, and especially the marble reredos, are splendid pieces.

South doorway

Chancel doorway

Pretty stained glass

More fine Victorian glass

The nave looking east

Expressive corbel

Altar and tasteful reredos

North arcade capital

Triple sedilia

The font

SOUTH CROXTON ST JOHN THE BAPTIST

From the south east

South Croxton is not far from the north east edge of Leicester, but here is a different world, the world of east Leicestershire, a little visited area but one whose scenery will drive away 21st century stresses. The village is diminished by the usual recent infill housing, but it is tranquil, and one is tempted to linger, even more so with a fine church like St John to explore. It has an enviable position on the crest of a hill on the eastern edge of South Croxton. The building is archetypal east Leicestershire, built mainly of ironstone with limestone facings, buttresses, battlements and spire. The familiar plan is tower/short spire, nave with south aisle, chancel and south porch, nearly all 14th century. The round headed doorway in the chancel south wall is older and may have been retained from an earlier Norman configuration. Traces of an arch in the nave north west wall indicate that a north aisle was either built and later taken down, or never reached completion. At least one authority suggests that the two reticulated windows in the nave north wall were resited there from a demolished north aisle. The blocked west window of the south aisle has intersecting tracery with cusps. The chancel doorway and north nave doorway are also blocked. Near the aisle west window is an oddly sited gargoyle, much eroded. The tower was struck by lightning in 1936, necessitating repairs that took two years to complete. A memorial recording this event and the reopening can be found close to the south porch. The interior has an antique atmosphere due to there having been little pervasive restoration. The walls have been scraped but that only seems to reinforce the ancient feel. There are several treasures, and the first one greets the visitor immediately. That is a lovely but very crudely ornamented Norman tub font, with arches and a sinister head with long thin neck, very E.T! The pulpit is 18th century and quite plain, and the altar rails are at least the same age. The east window seemingly retains its original simple intersecting tracery and has two small roundels of medieval glass in its head. Up in the 15th century nave roof are wooden figures holding shields, possibly medieval. The piscina and aumbry in the chancel are either 13th or 14th century.

St John from the south west

North side of the nave

Looking west from the chancel and east from the nave

Nave architecture and furniture

Medieval roundel

The rugged cross

Figure in the nave roof

Two views of the font

Medieval piscina and aumbry

197

SOUTH KILWORTH ST NICHOLAS

A glimpse of St Nicholas through the wall of trees

A statue of St Nicholas survives on the tower

St Nicholas is nicely set in the bosom of the small village of South Kilworth and yet it is a shy church, hiding itself away behind a surrounding screen of trees. Even when near by in the village, it is difficult to see how to approach it. That's until the unobtrusive entrance is spotted on Walcote Road and even then you are not sure you are on the right path until the trees open out and you arrive at the porch. The next problem is how to photograph the whole building, or even a reasonable proportion of it, because the aforesaid trees block almost every vista. Yet this is a church that should be persevered with, it has a great deal of interest. Firstly, there is the plan, quite unusual as the 15th century tower with its handsome broach spire is positioned to the south west and has a south porch. This is the main entrance to the church, so the visitor must traverse the tower and enter the nave through a north tower arch. There is another eastern tower arch into the south aisle. All that adds an air of distinctiveness to the interior. Despite appearances which suggest that St Nicholas is an authentic medieval church, almost all of it was built new or rebuilt by G. F. Bodley, a doyen of church architects, in 1868-9. Apart from the tower/spire and north arcade, the only old fabric still apparent is in certain areas of the walls. Bodley was rightly praised for doing a sensitive job, a good example is the narrow north aisle which was made thus to compliment one of St Nicholas's best features, the round-arched Norman north arcade, which was retained from the old church. There are other ancient items that survived into the rebuilt church, including a large Norman font, probably recut, in the form of a Greek capital, with leaf ornament. Next oldest would be the two 13th century stone coffin lids which lean up against the west wall, one badly deteriorated but the other with foliate crosses. From around the same time is a poorly preserved side piece from another coffin, richly carved with a crucifixion scene in three panels, the central one showing a 'Lily crucifix'. Another panel with heraldic ornament is mounted alongside. These panels can be found in the south aisle, seeing service as a reredos. A worn effigy of a priest resides in a niche in the sanctuary.

Tower and south aisle

Views along the nave from the east, and west

The sanctuary

North arcade

Eastern tower arch

Eye-catching chancel roof

The organ

Section of C13th tomb, used as a reredos

The effigy in the sanctuary

C13th coffin lid

Norman capital font

St Batholomew seen from the north

The mostly 13th to 14th century St Bartholomew is one of Leicestershire's more isolated churches and stands in a scenic high position on the road to Saltby, with rolling views. The village is some way to the south. Why the church is so far from its village is an interesting question, but there used to be a 'big house' near the church in earlier times and perhaps its occupants dictated that the church should be near them, or possibly there was a settlement around the church, which has now disappeared. A quirk of the building is that its alignment is some way off the approved east-west axis, it sits more south west-north east. St Bartholomew has a special treasure in the churchyard, the only complete Anglo-Scandinavian cross in the county, which is situated near the porch. It wears its years heavily, and its condition wasn't helped by it being used as a footbridge for many years, but it is nevertheless a powerful statement, with the faint figure of a beast on the west face (plus another even fainter one higher up), and interlace work. The church, which consists of tower, nave, south aisle, chancel, organ chamber, vestry and south porch, was thoroughly restored and added to by H. Woodyer in 1882-3 at a time when much of the fabric was in decay, and a fine job he made of it. During that restoration the top of the tower, much of the south aisle and the south porch were rebuilt, plus much work inside. It may have been at that time that a length of Norman chevron work was inserted into the west wall of the aisle. Further evidence of an earlier Norman church is demonstrated by the recycled capitals with volute ornament in the chancel arch and the round-arched, deeply splayed tower lower stage slit windows. One of the highlights of the interior are the nave corbels, a cheery group drawn from reality and myth. They are usually all claimed to be medieval, but some look too pristine for that. In the aisle mounted on roof wall plates are wooden lozenges of green men and other enigmatic faces. An unusual naïve rustic memorial can be found in the wall near the pulpit, and there are two good benefaction boards. The busy font is said to be late 14th century, but has been recut, making it appear more recent.

View from the south east

Norse cross, porch and tower

The Norse cross

Fragment of chevron stonework

Views from the west and east ends of the church

Creatures real and creatures mythical, in stone and wood

The rustic wall memorial

Benefaction board of 1830/47

The font

From the south

St Mary is a small and unprepossessing building constructed in 1908-9, but its uninspiring exterior belies the welcoming and comfortable interior. There are no great treasures, in fact little to detain the casual visitor, but it is a church that makes you glad you called. There is an implied story associated with the origins of the church and that involves the time of its building. In the Edwardian age, the evangelical and religious revival of the 1840's onwards was fast petering out. Grand ecumenical schemes were finding it difficult to find sponsors or supporters, and money was tight. In the early years of the last century it was clear that Stanton needed a new church for its growing population, and hopes must have been high when the go-ahead was given for a moderately expansive church. Its plan included a south aisle and an ambitious west end, but the money must have failed and neither were ever realised. The brick filled arcade in the south wall bears mute testimony to that failure. The modest bellcote perched on the roof at the junction of the nave and chancel must have been a poor substitute for the tower or whatever was planned for the west end. But at least a church was built and has served Stanton well since then, and indeed recently an extension was added for lobby, kitchen and toilets at the west end, so everything comes to he who waits. The building material is durable igneous Charnwood stone, probably quarried from the local Bardon quarries, with red tile roofs and sandstone frames, facings and quoins. The division between nave and chancel is only hinted at outside but inside there is a big chancel arch which enlivens the interior and gives a touch of grandeur. The altar is made of stone blocks and the font is a very unassuming sandstone model without ornament. One modest touch of flamboyance is the organ and the piscina in the sanctuary is also quite smart, with its bowl on a column and a nice scalloped arch. A modern rood group sits on top of a thin rood beam set high up across the chancel arch. There was a forerunner to St Mary in Stanton, a chapel that was sited south of the village. The last mention of business there was in 1682 and since then it fell out of use and has now disappeared.

Views from the north west and east

St Mary from the south east

The blocked south arcade, external view

The blocked south arcade, internal view

Chancel arch and chancel

A corner of the sanctuary

The font

The sanctuary and altar

The organ

203

STAPLETON ST MARTIN

St Martin is tucked away in a pretty spot

Small, ancient churches have a charm all their own and St Martin falls into that category. It is a building of simple plan, just a tower with dainty spire, and nave and chancel under one roof. It is set just off the busy A447 in a small settlement in the south west of the county. The nearest large villages are Barwell and Earl Shilton, around two and a half kilometres away. Like most churches in that area, it is built of the local sandstone. Despite a scarcity of hard structural evidence, the church's origins are probably 13th century, judging by a blocked Y-traceried window in the south wall and a blocked lancet window on the north side. There is evidence of other structural alterations regarding windows and doors, with blocked examples of both around the building, for example the traces of a square framed window on the south side, the aperture now occupied by a much later Edwardian window. Also, to the north are vague traces of an old doorway with later window above it, its outline marked by a few surviving pieces of the frame. Inside a surprise awaits, for much of the interior retains fittings from the early years of the 19th century, when box pews and a west gallery were installed. The feel is very much of a chapel of that period, and the surprise is that these fittings weren't ripped out during the period of Victorian ecclesiological revisionism when such items were very much frowned upon. Nothing medieval remains except the tower arch, which is now the only doorway into the church. The restoration, when it came, was in 1904 and many features were replaced, including the windows, while the interior was left rather stark and functional. The spire was also rebuilt. The small plain font probably dates from that time, perhaps the decent pulpit too. The east window dates from 1936 and contains Stapleton's only stained glass, a solitary small roundel incorporating the IHS symbol. The organ looks Victorian or maybe dates from the restoration. It is only of moderate size yet in such a small interior it is a significant presence. The walls are largely bare, the only mural tablet of any note is a simple memorial to a soldier killed in the 1st World War. The churchyard is very pleasant, although the noise from the A447 detracts.

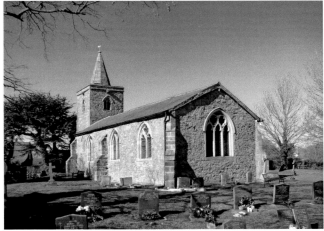

The view from the south west

Window detail on the south wall

Looking east from the tower doorway

West from the altar

Box pews and gallery

The east end

The organ

Organ detail

The pulpit

The font

IHS roundel

Mural tablet

STATHERN ST GUTHLAC

From the south east

Stathern is a moderately sized village on the edge of the Vale of Belvoir in north east Leicestershire, sited where the topography changes suddenly from the flatlands of the Vale to a steep escarpment with rolling hills beyond. The church is Leicestershire's third and (alphabetically) last St Guthlac. All are handsome churches, and this is one of the best. It has the full set of building elements – tower with limestone battlements and big pinnacles, aisled nave, chancel, north chancel chapel (now a vestry), north and south porches and a clerestory. All elements are constructed of the local ironstone, with limestone dressings and frames. The church has ancient roots in the early years of the 13th century and it is believed a predecessor stood on the same spot. Evidence for this comes in the form of a fragment of Saxon interlace built into the external wall at the north west angle of the north aisle. The aisles are 13th century and have deeply splayed west windows, but at the core of the church the nave is presumably older, the chancel too probably. The south doorway is arched but has prominent dogtooth ornament, suggesting it is 13th century like the aisles. The tower is from the late 13th or early 14th century, the clerestory and probably the porches some tens of years later. How much of the fabric of the building was restored or rebuilt by the Victorian restorer R. W. Johnson in 1867-8 is uncertain but his hand lies quite heavily on the interior, where most of the fittings and furniture were replaced. The north chapel, which saw service as the village school in the 19th century, has a blocked fireplace and the expected piscina, but there are also the remains of a piscina in the south aisle, thus a chapel was probably established there too. The chancel boasts the third piscina in St Guthlac. The tower arch is a powerful statement with heavy triple-chamfered arch on more gracile triple shafted responds. The arcades, though old, are unexceptional. Fittings of note include the Perpendicular octagonal font which has window-style tracery in its panels. A posse of glum corbels occupy the nave roof, although the pig is a cheery character. There are two good mural tablets, one in latin in the chancel from 1704, and another in black slate from 1839.

St Guthlac from the south

………. and the north

The south doorway

Views along the nave from west and east

Remains of rood opening

Sanctuary and altar

A selection of corbels

A collection of artifacts

Two mural tablets, 1704 and 1839

The font

C19th pulpit

St Peter from the south

Stockerston is a delightful little outpost very close to the Rutland border and the Eyebrook Reservoir, and its church is a fine example of a 'hall church', whose affinities and location lie closer to Stockerston Hall than its nominal village. These days those traditional ties have all but disappeared and St Peter spends most of its time in wistful slumber, disturbed only by its indigenous fauna and a service once a month. Yet this is a building that is most rewarding of a visit, with some features that are the best of their kind in the county, and many reminders of its more gracious past. The setting could hardly be better, a truly sequestered spot at the end of a quiet drive, and the church itself is equally attractive, finished as is invariably the case in east Leicestershire, in ironstone and limestone. It has a satisfying, symmetrical plan with tower, nave with short aisles/broad transepts and chancel. The oldest parts of the building are the 13th century arcades, but some of the piers sit on rubbly masonry bases which look like remnants of earlier walls, thus it seems very likely that an aisleless predecessor stood here at least in Norman times. Much of the church was refashioned in the 15th century by the incumbent of the Hall, including rebuilding the aisles, and most work on view today is in the Perpendicular style. Most windows have flattened 'Tudor' or square heads which date from later Perpendicular times. St Peter's chief treasures are its brasses and stained glass. There are two pairs of excellent brasses from the 15th century, one pair is John and Isabella de Boyville (he is headless), the other Henry and Anne Southill. These are mounted most unsatisfactorily on stark wooden boards near the south entrance. Nearby is an early stone coffin lid with cross motif, an old parish chest, plus seven medieval bench ends. The south aisle was originally a chantry chapel but has subsequently became a repository for the massive Walker family tomb and vault. Also in this aisle are the effigy of a cross-legged knight and various other gravestones and memorials. The stained glass is superb but is only a shadow of what it once was. The figuration that remains is far more complete than is usually seen, and includes a St Christopher, a crucifixion scene, a pontiff and local gentry. In the chancel is a very fine floor slab from 1633 and in the north aisle a battered effigy and equally distressed incised slab. There's much more to discover in this superb church.

The tower

Looking west from the sanctuary

Looking east along the nave

Examples of the exceptional medieval stained glass

Pew end

Southill brass

Effigy of a knight

Elizabeth Havers slab

Stair turret, rood remains

Rare pristine C18th gravestone

A C19th tradesman left his mark

Two shots from the south east and south

Stoke Golding St Margaret is one of Leicestershire's most celebrated churches, universally admired as an example of a largely Decorated church which retains significant elements of its early layout. The plan is west tower with spire, nave, south aisle incorporating an east chapel, and chancel. Although only a parish church, the building is ambitious and finely realised, clearly there was money available to fund a great and expansive redevelopment between about 1280 and 1350. During that period the church was transformed and the long, grand south aisle with its chapel and openwork parapet was built, matching the nave in size and giving rise to a 'twin nave' appearance. One of St Margaret's most spectacular features, the windows, were largely put in at the same time, and inside, the richly developed arcade also. The best of the windows adorn the south wall of the aisle, a quite lovely and varied series of six geometrical and cusped designs, bound together by the similar shape of their frames. The windows on the north side are later and are mostly more curvilinear in conception. Inside, the church has a distinctly unrestored and ancient feel, and many medieval features and fittings remain. St Margaret did not escape restoration entirely, the chancel was rebuilt in the 19th century, the seating in part is Victorian, as is the pulpit and chancel screen. The box pews are probably pre-Victorian. The nave and aisle roofs are late medieval and have rather enigmatic bosses. The highlight of a fascinating interior is the marvellous Decorated arcade of four bays, with arches of many orders and multiple shafted piers, with finely wrought capitals ornamented with foliage through which peer human heads. The richly carved font is from the later years of the 13th/14th century remodelling and has panels with tracery or standing figures. The south aisle chapel sanctuary has a nice double piscina with a triangular head and at first sight there is another further west along the same south wall, but it has no drain and is probably a niche. To the left of the aisle altar is an odd, but clearly old, short column resting on a corbel head whose affinities are uncertain. Nearby, next to a lancet which survives from the early 13th century church, is a large, bold monument standing by the wall which dates from 1690. Many other treasures await the visitor.

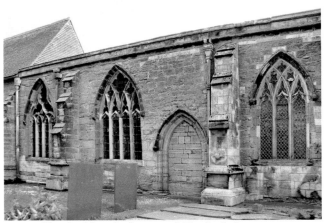

North side windows and blocked doorway

Looking east along the nave

The arcade

Arcade capitals

Roof bosses

A view across the nave

Recess in the south wall

Chapel piscina

The font

Enigmatic moulding

Fairbrace memorial (1690)

Commemorative tablet

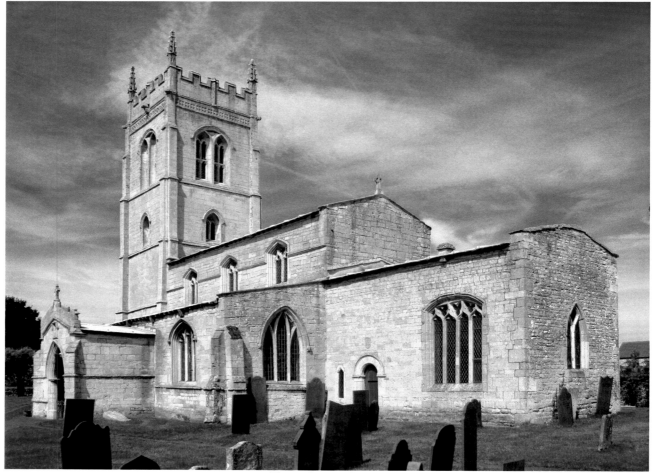

From the south east

There are only a small number of all-limestone churches in Leicestershire, but like St Peter, all benefit from the beautiful cream colouration of this stone, which takes on a glorious radiance when bathed in sunshine. The stone is Lincolnshire Limestone, which only crops out in a small area in the far east of Leicestershire, but is more widely exposed further east beyond the county boundary. It has many local names, several very famous as building stones, such as Clipsham, Ketton and Collyweston stone. St Peter is one of the finest churches made of this stone in the county, and also benefits from a picturesque setting in a pretty village with many limestone houses. The plan is nicely symmetrical, with two aisles of almost the same dimensions to go with the handsome Perpendicular tower, high clerestoried nave, chancel and south porch. The origins of St Peter are ancient, there is still a little Norman work to be seen, such as the reconstructed priest's door into the chancel and the fine font. Much work from the decades immediately following this period can be seen, such as the north arcade and some Y-shaped windows. The south arcade is a little later. The porch may be 14th century and is quite impressive, with a parapet on the gable and two buttresses either side of a good doorway, which has a small niche above it with square head and headstops. The tower is imposing and refined, with the de rigueur battlements, pinnacles and narrow quatrefoil frieze. The chancel has the look of antiquity about it, with rubbly fabric in the east wall and only three windows, a large Perpendicular one to the south, a small narrow 'low-side' window to the west of the chancel doorway and an unusually small, possibly original, early 14th century Y-traceried east window. Inside is bright and airy thanks to the clerestory and generous aisle windows. The excellent arcades set the tone for an interesting interior, where the highlights are the recut but still attractive font and the tall, stately tower arch. The north aisle has a mysterious configuration of an old roofline cutting into a blocked doorway in the stonework of its east wall, clearly there was once an extension to the east, probably a chapel. Three old benches survive in the nave, note also the genial corbel heads.

Views from the south and east

Looking from the chancel to the west end

Font and nave

Nave and south arcade

Nave and arcades

Font and tower arch

Mysteries of the north aisle

The font

Medieval bench arm rest carvings

Bearded twins

STONEY STANTON ST MICHAEL

Posed behind its boundary wall, Stoney Stanton St Michael

Some churches lurk inconspicuously amongst narrow streets or behind a screen of trees, but not St Michael, it shows off its bold southern frontage to the passing world with confidence, and a grand sight it is too. A tall tower and delicate spire help a lot, and these are supported by a fairly large church of two aisles, nave with high clerestory, chancel and north and south porches, all set in a generous churchyard. The village of Stoney Stanton, as befits its name, is situated in what might be called the southern Leicestershire stone belt, although this is not a stone that shows itself above ground very often, rather it a very hard magmatic rock which exists as masses below the surface, and has to be quarried. The largest of the present day quarries is at nearby Croft. Naturally St Michael is constructed of its local stone, with sandstone for the spire, facings, battlements, frames, etc. Like so many Leicestershire churches, St Michael was heavily remodelled in the 19th century, and almost nothing substantial of the pre-1840 church remains, except the tower and spire and the north arcade (all Perpendicular). The chancel, south aisle and clerestory date from 1842-3, the south aisle was extended to form an organ chamber in 1882 and the north aisle and vestry are from 1888. Above the vestry door is a remarkable primitive tympanum which has survived from at least Norman times. It depicts a strange battle between an assortment of weird creatures, presided over by a bishop with his crozier. Experts have offered many interpretations of a scene which includes a winged beast with two tails, a dragon (which is the object of the attack by the others), a lion and some sort of bird (?cock), but it is all very arcane. The interior is a good one but contains little of great historical significance, although the font and parish chest are medieval. Outside the east window is an easily missed memorial to a Rev'd John Bold who died in 1751. He, like most of his kind, would ordinarily be forgotten, but a contemporary recorded his austere and selfless life, so we now know what sort of man he was, one who spent his life working for, and thinking only of, others. An epitaph is mounted above his stone with a worthy hope for the hereafter.

View from the south west

The C11th tympanum

It's a long way to the top

The chancel

Looking west along the nave

The north aisle and arcade

The font

Nave roof

Mural tablet

George III arms

The parish chest

From the north east

Stonton Wyville is a tiny hamlet of barely 20 souls in sparsely populated and scenic countryside in the south east of Leicestershire. In the past it was larger and south of the church there are the earthworks of the medieval deserted village. Despite its present day diminutive size Stonton Wyville still manages to support its parish church, and in the past it had a pub too. If its peace and quiet you want, this is the place for you, although you will need a few offshore accounts. The church, one of only six dedicated to the 3rd century saint and martyr St Denys (or Denis, derived from the original Dionysius) in Leicestershire, is externally unexceptional and modest, consisting of nave with western bellcote, chancel and south porch. There is also a clerestory which has different windows on the two sides, those on the south being small and quatrefoil-shaped, probably very early in origin, whilst those on the north are paired with trefoil heads. The building stone is a mixture of ironstone and limestone, with much patching and repairs. There is enough old fabric, particularly the chancel north wall and the blocked arcade to a demolished south aisle to suggest at least 13th century foundation. The arcade arches are just pointed, but would seem to date from shortly after the introduction of that form. The piers and capitals are round and plain, but the east respond capital has a form of narrow stiff-leaf carving, also an early indicator. Goddard of Leicester did a thorough restoration in 1869, which included the single-bell bellcote and south porch. Some of the medieval windows survived the remodelling, and a long lancet remains in the north wall. The priest's door in the chancel north wall may be 14th century. The interior has lots of atmosphere and contains several interesting items. Of particular note are the Brudenell memorials in the chancel, which include a fine altar tomb for Edmund Brudenell, who died in 1590. Next to his effigy on the top is a representation of his deceased infant child in swaddling clothes or chrysom robe. Two large mural tablets for other Brudenells are nearby, both ornate and showy. Outside on the south nave wall is another Brudenell memorial, to William (d. 1636). The Victorian pulpit is a fine example.

216

From the east

Porch and west end

William Brudenell memorial

Looking east along the nave

The blocked south arcade

The pulpit

Late medieval chair

Edmund Brudenell's tomb

……… and the effigies

Thomas Brudenell, d. 1661, and wife

Tho. Brudenell, d. 1705

Stiff leaf ornament on arcade respond

STOUGHTON ST MARY AND ALL SAINTS

From the north

Stoughton is perilously close to Leicester but has gallantly resisted being overwhelmed, and remains a village, situated in a west facing embayment of green country, while to the north and south housing development proceeds inexorably towards the east. St Mary is a fairly large, bold church, with the highlight being the splendid big windows. These, in part, are faithful reproductions or resettings of medieval antecedents, and are expressive and flamboyant, especially in the north aisle. The 14th century tower, which has a corbel table, trefoil frieze, modest battlements, gargoyles, pinnacles and a tall crocketted spire, is not far behind in impact, and can be seen from miles around. The tower and spire were rebuilt in 1861-2, to the same specifications as their predecessors. The builder, John Firn, also rebuilt the north aisle at the same time. An extension to the south aisle was built and the chancel rebuilt at the time of a later restoration by Dain and Smith in 1865-6. The latter also installed the clerestory and south porch. Thus, there is little remaining of St Mary's medieval structure except possibly the nave at the core of the building, but inside there are still significant survivals. Chief amongst these are the arcades, which show 13th century characteristics despite drastic recutting. The two westerly arches of the north arcade are round with stiff leaf carving on the respond, and are the oldest section, but elsewhere all the arcade pier capitals have nailhead ornament and there is again foliage carving on the responds. The large windows endow an invigorating sense of spaciousness and light, but, with two exceptions, the interior fittings are mostly unremarkable 19th century pieces, the exceptions being the exuberant font and a grand suite of memorials and monuments in the north aisle, mainly to members of the Beaumont family. Some of these are very fine, the highlight being the substantial table tomb of Sir Thomas Farnham (d. 1562) and his wife Helen (d. 1569). The Beaumont memorials include a large wall monument with obelisk and arms to Sir George Beaumont (d. 1737) and a wall tablet to Sir Thomas Beaumont and his wife Katherine, erected in 1631. In the churchyard is a well preserved medieval cross.

St Mary west end **Fine north aisle windows** **Churchyard cross**

Looking east from the nave, and west from the chancel

The font **Sir Tho. Beaumont, d. 1614** **Sir Geo. Beaumont, d. 1737** **Keck tablet, late C18th**

North aisle tomb and memorials **Sir Thomas Farnham tomb** **Hanoverian arms**

From the south

The site of the Battle of Bosworth has long exercised the minds of historians, but throughout there has been no doubt that Sutton Cheney lay at the heart of the action. More than any other church, St James's claim that Richard III heard his last Mass here, has the greatest credulity. And today, the Richard III Society maintains a connection with the church, and its annual activities commemorating the battle are focussed on this modest but historically significant building. A small display of appropriate items and a plaque is maintained in the nave. Suitably, the interior of St James is only lightly restored and has a real age-old look and feel; a palpable medieval atmosphere seeps from the ancient walls. The mostly 13th and 14th century building sits on a low hill and has a picturesque approach along a long path, with the building fully in view the whole way. The plan of the church is not exceptional in any way, and consists of tower, nave, south aisle and chancel, but the tower is unusual in that it possesses a brick-built upper stage and conical roof. The aisle is short, and doesn't extend onto the chancel, yet it has its own gabled roof. The main south doorway has a very weathered appearance, and is all the more appealing because of it. The priest's door into the chancel has lozenge ornament running along the outer chamfer of the arch both inside and out. The interior is worthy of a good exploration, starting with the four-bay south arcade that greets the visitor on entering. This is 13th century with one single-chamfer round arch to the east, and circular piers and capitals. The chancel arch is 14th century, the responds having leafy carving on the capitals. 18th century box pews adorn the nave, and the altar rails are of similar age. Much of interest can be found in the chancel, chiefly the memorials. There is one rather distressed but still impressive table tomb, of Sir William Roberts (d. 1633). Above him, carved on a separate mural tablet, are his two wives. On the opposite wall of the chancel is another fine mural tablet, commemorating Richard May (d. 1635), who kneels at a prie-dieu. Another tablet can be found above the priest's door, a simple one of words and two shields for Margaret Neale (d. 1567). The font is medieval and plain.

St James from the south

South doorway

Piscina and sedilia

Looking from the chancel to the west

Box pews in the nave

The Victorian pulpit

The font

Marg. Neale tablet

Richard May tablet

Sir William Roberts tomb

….. and the effigy

Sir William's wives

St George from the north west

The scattered village of Swannington lies in a confusing area which loosely equates to the now largely defunct coalfield of north west Leicestershire. There are many small roads and route finding can be a tricky business. Settlements large and small are dotted around and where they begin and end is often difficult to establish. The church explorer would naturally go to the main Swannington village in search of St George, but would be disappointed. Then, logically, he or she would deduce that it must therefore lie in New Swannington which is situated south east of the old village on the fringes of Whitwick. Not so. After a little head scratching and poring over the ordnance survey map they would spot a church marked adjacent to the A512 Loughborough Road in the dispersed settlement of Peggs Green, and at last St George is tracked down. It's not in Swannington, but never mind …Those fond of quirky church buildings will find interest here. The basic church was built of brick in 1825, and clear pointers to the architecture favoured at that time can be seen in the big, wooden-framed Y-tracery windows in the nave. But in the early years of the 20th century the architect George Fellowes Prynne was engaged to remodel the church and what resulted is decidedly odd by any standards. The work he did is concentrated at the east end where he lopped off one bay of the nave and perhaps a pre-existing chancel, and constructed a new chancel with vestry. The large south transept is also presumably his, but may be later. Recent additions at this east end have further confused the picture, but the overall effect is that things simply don't gel. The chancel is much higher than the 1825 nave and has a steeply pitched roof. It also is way off alignment with the nave. Prynne was also responsible for the substantial bellcote at the west end. The whole arrangement looks like its been transplanted from another church, and that is a clue to the probable reason for the incongruity. The work was almost certainly not finished and the old nave had to be retained, matching or not. Whatever the full truth of the matter, St George was left with plenty of character, and really should be seen.

St George from the south east and south west

Views from the south and north east   **East end and window**

Nave windows   **The bellcote**   **General interior view**

Where nave and chancel meet   **The pulpit and font**   **Distinctive headstone**

St Peter seen from the church gate

Normally a churchyard swept clear of gravestones is a rather dispiriting place, but here at Swepstone the sward of well-maintained grassland only serves to highlight the very satisfying shape of St Peter on its low hill, a view undisturbed by trees or other impediments. Those who favour the theory that many church sites were previously occupied by prehistoric pagan sites might find something for their imaginations here. Photographers will also be in their element, as St Peter can be easily and clearly pictured from all points of the compass. Like most churches, St Peter's fabric is a mixture of old and more recent. The present appearance owes much to Victorian remodellings, mainly by H. I. Stevens and A. W. Blomfield, although the aisles and nave with their bold battlements are 14th century. The clerestory dates from the 15th century. The tower is old at its core but in 1842 was clad in pale sandstone ashlar and doubtless the battlements and pinnacles date from this time also. It is interesting that early photographs show the tower as markedly white in comparison with the rest, but these days it has weathered into a good match for its church. The chancel was rebuilt in 1869 and the porch a year later. The whole building is of sandstone and structures within this rock have weathered out to give pretty sinuous patterns to many areas of stonework. Early Y- and intersecting tracery has survived in many of the windows, although it seems likely that everything was renewed at various times. Other windows follow Decorated patterns. Much deteriorated ogee forms can be seen above the blocked north aisle doorway and neighbouring windows. The interior is heavily Victorianised, conventional and unexceptional, and all the interest is concentrated in the south aisle, where there are two tomb chests. Neither has stood the test of time particularly well but nevertheless they are intriguing pieces. One is for William Humfrey and dates from 1591, his armoured effigy lies on top of the chest and he sports a natty pointed beard. The other never seems to have been identified, and always seems to have been the 'unknown lady'. Yet she must have been important to merit such a grand piece of monumental masonry. The plain font is old and often claimed to be Norman.

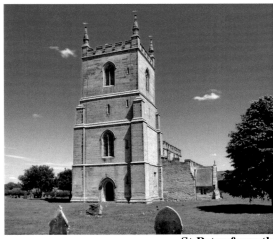
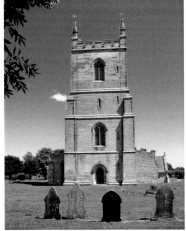
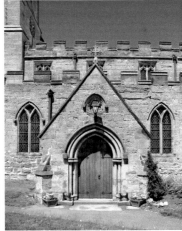

St Peter from the west **The handsome porch**

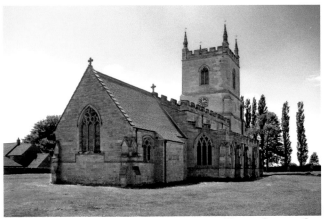

From the north east and north west

North aisle and clerestory **Resited quatrefoil tablets**

West and north doorways **Y- and intersecting tracery windows**

All Saints from Swinford High Street

Swinford is a neat, compact village in the deep south of Leicestershire. In its heart is the church of All Saints. The only disturbance to this rural idyll comes by way of sound from the huge M1/M6/A14 intersection barely a couple of kilometres away. All Saints is an individualistic church, both in construction and design. The battlemented tower is conventional enough, a 14th century model made with locally quarried sandstone and some rubble, but the rest of the church is largely built with water-worn cobbles collected locally from fields and river gravels. These are of various types and colours of stone, including quartzite, igneous rocks, ironstone, sandstone and some bricks. The end result is an engaging, homespun appearance. The church's origins were certainly in Norman times, or perhaps earlier. As is usual, the nave came first, and then the north wall was pierced to make an aisle in the 12th century. That was later rebuilt but retains a round Norman or Transitional pier and responds in the arcade with water leaf and primitive stiff leaf carving in the capitals. The south aisle followed in the 14th century, along with the tower, although they are not contemporary. At some stage early on, the nave was extended eastwards and the arcades lengthened. The east end has seen many incarnations from likely beginnings with a Norman apse, through a short semicircular battlemented apse built in 1778, to its present day enlarged version with a polygonal apse dating from 1894. Post-18th century additions include the porch, vestry and shallow organ chamber. The interior is quite plush, especially the east end which the Victorians endowed with several fine things, including a stone pulpit and matching low wall at the first set of steps into the chancel. The chancel is raised again by four more steps around the altar rail, thus there is an uplifting climb from the pulpit up into the panelled apse to the altar and its grand reredos. Organ pipes grace both sides of the chancel, adding to the effect. Medieval treasures include a unique red sandstone Norman font with round-arched arcading and curious non-matching pillars, a lovely nave roof and an ogee-headed piscina in the south aisle. The exuberant, painted, cast-iron Victorian lectern is a gem.

From Rugby Road to the south

The sunless north side

Porch and tower

Looking east and west along the nave

The Norman/Transitional part of the north arcade

Nave roof

The font

South aisle piscina

Benefactions board

Mural tablet (1817)

Cast iron lectern

Royal arms, 1798

SWITHLAND ST LEONARD

From the northern approach path

Swithland was the centre of the old slate industry which gave to Leicestershire and neighbouring counties the marvellous cornucopia of sculpture, gravestones and roofs that beautify so much of our county, its churches and churchyards. The slate is very fine-grained and hard, and ideal for carving. Its metamorphic texture also makes it extremely hard-wearing, so it is very suitable for external memorials. Even the very earliest gravestones from the 17th century can usually be read today. It also comes in several attractive shades from light grey through to purplish black. It is entirely appropriate that St Leonard should boast some of the finest and earliest examples of Swithland Slate carving, both inside and outside the church. In the churchyard is the superb chest tomb of Sir Joseph Danvers of 1745, by John Hind, with rural scenes on one face and military ones on the one opposite, all carved with consummate skill. It is alleged that part of the tomb is outside the churchyard so that Sir Joseph's dog could be buried with him on non-consecrated ground. Inside the church on the walls of the south aisle are several wonderful tablets, made from a particularly dark shade of Swithland Slate and all executed with amazing facility. The one for five children of Sir John Danvers with drapery, skull and cherubs is especially admirable. As for St Leonard itself, it is a compact, neat, much-cherished church with its origins in the 13th century, consisting of tower with battlements and very grand pinnacles, nave, south aisle with its own porch, chancel and north porch. Recently a new extension was built in the angle between the tower and aisle. The aisle was built in 1727 as a chapel for the influential Danvers family, but was remodelled in the 19th century. The arcade is much older, and clearly there was an earlier 13th century south aisle, also a north aisle, long gone, its blocked arcade still entombed in the wall. The nave walls have very rare and very early clerestory openings in the form of small portholes, only clearly seen in the south wall. Also look out for a few nice wall tablets, an elegant 18th century font, an 18th century pulpit with sounding board, a good 15th century remounted brass and an upgraded Snetzler organ of 1765.

The church from the east

Danvers tomb and early Swithland Slate headstones

Looking east along the nave

South arcade

Pulpit and sounding board

Two exquisite Swithland Slate tablets and two other fine wall memorials

Agnes Scott brass, C15th

Dainty font

Danvers arms

St Leonard's symbol

229

St Mary's north side

Sysonby is a deserted village site, although that is not immediately obvious, as there are lots of houses only a short distance from the church of St Mary. However, these are not the houses of old Sysonby, they represent the encroaching town of Melton Mowbray. Only the church and the neighbouring farm remain from the old village, the rest of the settlement lies buried beneath the greens and bunkers of the golf course to the west of the church. St Mary is a very likeable church, full of the charm associated with old ironstone buildings, but it very nearly didn't make it past the end of the 19th century. By then it was falling down, and it was only saved by a concerted effort led by Canon Blakeney, which enabled a virtual rebuilding in 1892. Thus it is hard to establish what is ancient and what is not, but it is clear that some of the fabric is crudely built in the style of the 13th century, especially the eastern portion of the north wall. The south wall, although partly rebuilt and with a date of 1915 on one of the buttresses, also retains some ancient-looking stonework and what must be the original doorway. The spindly tower with its transverse saddleback roof is hard to date but the stones of its fabric are well worn and it may be that they were reused when the tower was rebuilt; some parts, especially the lowermost levels and the tower arch, may be original. The extension to the north west is of 1925 and was built as a chapel for the philanthropic Dalgliesh family, and particularly Richard Dalgliesh, who helped and supported the church in many ways and is buried there. It is now a vestry but retains a plaque recording the achievements of said Richard. The nave, chancel and sanctuary are all contained within a single space, very nicely laid out recently with chairs obtained locally, and sensitively lit. The delicate 18th century font came from St Mary at Melton. The altar rails would seem to be 18th century in date, as well. There are very few mural tablets and none of any historical interest, but there are three well-preserved and tended floor memorials in front of the altar rails. The sole window in the south wall boasts a beautiful rural design in stained glass of 1934, in memory of Norah Stirling, who lived at Sysonby Lodge.

From the churchyard to the west

The tower

Looking east and west along the church

East end of the church

Tower arch

Norah Stirling window (1934)

The font

Dalgliesh plaque

Main doorway

Swithland Slate roof

SYSTON ST PETER AND ST PAUL

From the south east

St Peter and St Paul has a presence that comes from its size, noble lines and dignified Perpendicular styling. It is one of Leicestershire's more imposing churches, with a particularly fine tower enhanced by the limestone ashlar top stage and proud pinnacles. These are accompanied by the usual battlements and frieze. Apart from the tower, most of the exterior of the church is not genuine Perpendicular, it was very heavily remodelled by Ordish during a 10 year restoration between 1870 and 1880. Despite that, the architect's realisation of the Gothic church he had in his mind is largely successful, but perhaps not with church purists. Amongst many other things, Ordish remade the south aisle but retained a 14th century recess on the outside, which is a prominent object near the equally old south porch. The north aisle is very similar to the south. Ornament was applied liberally everywhere in the form of battlements, friezes, corbel tables, large and small pinnacles, parapets, etc. There are heads of men and beasts everywhere, on headstops, corbels and gargoyles. One of the oddest is a group of three heads, said to be a man and two women, on the south west buttress of the tower near the top, leaning out accusingly at passers-by. The interior is stately and imposing, and has many fine things. One of the first to attract attention is the nave roof, beautifully restored and repainted in 1985. The timbers are adorned with a cornucopia of motifs, figures and heads, full of character and vivacity. That is not all, on the wall posts are 12 large angels, fallen in 10 cases because their wings have been removed. The two by the chancel arch are Victorian recreations of the fully winged originals. All hold shields bearing various emblems, and sit on grotesque corbels; these, like the angels, are full of life and expression. The 14th century arcades also demand attention, their design is rare in Leicestershire; they are panelled. Not only that, but the tower arch is similarly treated, and the jambs of the clerestory windows. The 13th century 10-sided font with its faint blank shields has survived through until the present day, as has the resited 13th century sedilia and piscina in the sanctuary. Certain of the Victorian fittings are opulent, especially the magnificent pulpit.

The tower from the west

C14th recess, south aisle

The infamous trio

From nave to chancel and vice-versa

The lady chapel (south aisle)

Nave roof

Nave wall plate figures

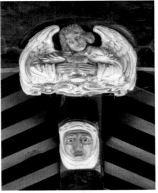

Nave roof bosses

The pulpit

The font

Piscina and sedilia

THEDDINGWORTH ALL SAINTS

From the north

Theddingworth is strung out along the A4304 and is very close to the Northamptonshire border in south Leicestershire. In the past the village enjoyed a tranquil existence, but these days traffic on the road has increased exponentially and crossing it requires nimble feet. The increase in traffic was bad news for All Saints too, as it is situated just a few metres from the road. Despite the usual 19th century restorations and changes, All Saints still generates a genuine frisson of the deep past on entering. Some of this is due to the rather decrepit state of the interior, but the sepulchral gloom is also a major factor. The interior is one of the most eerie and cold in the county, and only when the lights are turned on can the many attractions of the church be appreciated. The building is dominated by a lovely tall tower/spire which looks down imperiously on the aisled nave, chancel and two porches, which appear almost insignificant in comparison. Both aisles have chapels at the east end, the southern one small, pleasant and open, the northern (Hothorpe) one large, dark and containing a great Snetzler organ of 1754 which obscures the two grand memorials therein. The detailed and sophisticated chancel with its steep pitched roof stands higher than the nave and is almost entirely the work of G. G. Scott in 1857-8; the ambitious, though sadly deteriorated, painted scheme at the east end is by Clayton and Bell. Externally, All Saints appears mostly Perpendicular, but inside its true origins are revealed in the shape of a bold late Norman round-arched north arcade which has differently carved capitals for each of the four piers. The arch from the chancel to the north chapel is contemporary with the arcade. The south arcade is also round-arched but slightly later, with two chamfers. The plain Norman font is surmounted by a fantastic cover of 1893 by Bodley. There are three memorials of note. Of the two large and showy ones in the north chapel, the first is Elizabethan and is two tiered, with the husband above; the other of 1656 shows a couple from bust upwards in medallions with their 17 children kneeling beneath. The third in the south aisle is a flowing classical piece from 1772 depicting the life-sized figures of the Rev'd Slaughter Clark and his wife.

From the south east

Nature lays claim to the south porch

Looking east along the nave

View from the chancel westwards

Font and north arcade

South arcade through the chancel arch

Sanctuary and altar

Mural above the east window

Bathurst (1656) and Clark memorials

Davies tablet

Elizabethan memorial and organ

Ancient parish chest

Rood loft doorway

North arcade capital

Fine Victorian pulpit

Chancel screen, a low marble wall

Two snapshots of St Peter

From Main Street in Thornton, passing travellers have little inkling that St Peter lies nearby, unless they glimpse the top of the spire or catch sight of the Church Lane street sign. This is because the church lies away down a slope that ultimately ends in Thornton Reservoir, built in 1854 and now a picturesque beauty spot open to the public. Also, like rather too many churches, St Peter hides behind a screen of tall mature trees, which circumscribe any attempt to photograph the building as a whole, and turn the site into a gloomy glade on dull days. But this is a church that really should be sought out, as it belongs in the category of 'buildings with a wonderful atmosphere'. The church has its roots in the 13th century and the nave would probably be of this time, with the granite aisles following around 1300. The north aisle was restructured around 1450. The sandstone tower and spire are 15th century Perpendicular, as is the clerestory. The chancel is of 1864. The south aisle has features such as an early piscina and plinth for a statue that indicate its use as a chapel from the 14th century. The atmosphere inside St Peter owes a lot to a relatively light 19th century restoration, which was concentrated mainly on the chancel. Left untouched were an impressive set of medieval benches in the nave, as were several other interesting old fittings. The ancient feel is reinforced by brick floors and a large medieval south door with a fine array of original ironwork. Other survivals include some semi-complete scenes in 14th century medieval glass in the south aisle east window and a couple of panels from the old chancel screen. These, inexplicably, are fixed for display in the south aisle one behind the other with the painted sides facing the wall. The font is a slightly odd piece, probably of the 15th century, and has two bands of ornament on the bowl, the lower of which contains quatrefoils. The curious 'flattened triangle' west window in the north aisle was only discovered and reinstated in the 19th century and is undoubtedly early in date. There are few wall memorials, but on the internal tower wall are three 18th century lead tablets salvaged during roof repairs. High in the nave roof partly hidden behind wooden struts that support the leaning nave walls are four handsome boards of 1820 containing the Lord's Prayer, Decalogue and Creed.

From the east

The porch on the north side

Looking west along the nave

The leaning south arcade

The nave looking east

Lord's prayer, decalogue, creed boards

George IV arms

The font

Medieval benches

Medieval glass

C18th lead plates from the roof

THORPE ARNOLD ST MARY THE VIRGIN

St Mary from the north approach path

Thorpe Arnold sits a little nervously atop a hill just beyond the eastern fringes of Melton Mowbray, looking down on the ever-encroaching larger town. It is to be hoped that the remaining green belt between them is maintained. The village's hilltop site has long been recognised for its strategic importance, for there are ancient earthworks here, although no-one is quite sure of the date of the oldest ones, which may be prehistoric. Later it seems a moated manor stood here, to the south west of the church. Doubtless the church of St Mary the Virgin also occupies an important ancient site, although the present building, founded in the 13th century, is almost certainly not the first ecclesiastical building to be erected here. It is a likeable, welcoming church, neat and trim on the outside and comfortable and attractive inside. Recent upgrading has seen carpets and other modern comforts installed, yet the legacy of the past has not been compromised. Despite the well aged appearance, most of the St Mary today is the result of extensive rebuilding and restoration in the period 1860 to 1880, most of it masterminded by R. W. Johnson. At that time, almost the whole church was rebuilt and refitted, although much of the old fabric seems to have been reused, and the old layout adhered to. Not surprisingly given the location, ironstone was extensively used as the main building stone, but the north aisle and clerestory in particular are mostly of limestone. The plan is standard, with west tower with pyramid roof, aisled nave, raised in the 15th century to accommodate a clerestory, chancel and south porch. Curious narrow extensions abut the tower to the north and south, maybe surviving from the pre-1860 church. The interior has no great monuments or grand architecture, but there are several more than interesting items. Pride of place must go to the stunning font, which may be Saxon, with its vivacious carvings of St Michael battling many-headed dragons. There is a fine show of ancient grotesque corbels in the nave, some of a decidedly rude nature! Another lively carving adorns the south aisle east respond, consisting of a man's head flanked by grinning lions. A medieval grave slab sees service as a chancel window sill.

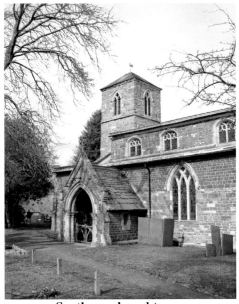

The church from the east

South porch and tower

Looking east and west along the nave

Chancel and sanctuary

The font, one of Leicestershire's finest

Grotesque (and rude!) corbel figures

East respond, south aisle

South aisle piscina

Chancel wall tablet

Early grave slab, now a window sill

St Leonard basks in Spring sunshine

Thorpe Langton is a small, rather exclusive village set in attractive countryside in south west Leicestershire. Its church of St Leonard, one of only four dedicated to that saint in the county, stands alone south west of the main village, but it seems likely that it was once a lot more central to the medieval village, whose houses have now gone. It is a nicely balanced building, but its appearance is much changed from its 13th century origins. The attractive tower with its pinnacles and corbel table, also the broach spire, are from that time, as are scattered parts of the fabric, but the nave and chancel reside now under one roof due to the unusual configuration of the 15th century clerestory. This has been extended over the chancel so that nave and chancel are contained within one neat high-sided rectangle. This imparts an imposing air to the church, and especially the chancel, which has no arch. The relatively short and low aisles sit almost apologetically beneath these tall walls. A north porch and vestry complete the plan, both built in the 19th century. Inside, the impression is of space and antiquity, and the eyes are drawn upwards to a very fine nave roof. The early 14th century arcades have quatrefoil piers, embellished with ballflower ornament in the capitals of the east pier and east respond in the north arcade. At the base of the arcade piers are remnants of walling, which may be remnants of the original aisleless nave walls. Corbel heads abound in both nave and aisles, some now parted from their arches or wall plates and resited. Some of these corbels are thought to be from around 1200. The human heads are easily distinguished, but several other beasts are harder to identify, although one seems to be an ape and others domestic animals. The wine-glass pulpit is a nice piece, of indeterminate date, but incorporating panels from a 15th or 16th century predecessor. The font is prominently located near the north door and is a particularly impressive 15th century example, raised up on a bold two-step base. The bowl and stem are ornamented with tracery designs. The screen is Victorian but is strongly medieval in form, and may incorporate parts of a medieval original. An interesting rood loft opening with moulded surround and steps survives.

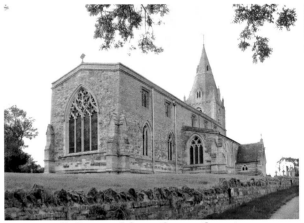
St Leonard from the north east

From the west

Nave roof

Looking west through the screen

View east along the nave

Piscina and sedilia in the chancel

Rood opening

Corbel heads

Elegant pulpit

The font on its imposing base

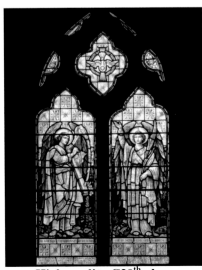
High quality C20th glass

Donations box

241

THORPE SATCHVILLE ST MICHAEL & ALL ANGELS D3, SK 732 117

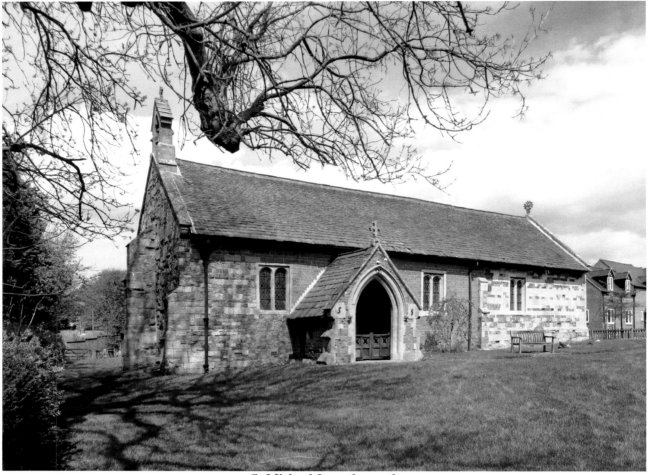

St Michael from the south

A large part of north east Leicestershire is broken up by a series of north west to south east ridges, which give the area much scenic appeal. Thorpe Satchville sits astride one of these ridges, with Ashby Folville and Gaddesby strung out along it to the west. The village is small and linear, and lacks a focal point. Often in such settings it is the church that provides the central heartbeat of a community, but here at Thorpe Satchville St Michael is tucked away west of the main street, hiding shyly behind recent housing. It is altogether a very modest and unprepossessing building surrounded by a rolling lawn, lacking grand architecture. But it is neat and tidy, and still clearly holds a place in the village's affections. The plan is simple, a long central block housing both nave and chancel, plus a south porch and north east transept. On the west gable sits a small one-bell bellcote. A substantial buttress in a central position supports the west wall, but it seems highly unlikely that there was ever a tower. The fabric is a patchwork of ironstone blocks, regularly coursed squared ironstone 'bricks', and cream limestone. Today's appearance is a result of much restoration, remodelling and renovation over many years, which lends the church a homely, rustic air. Nothing about the architecture allows a tight constraint on age, but we are told that St Michael is basically a 15th century building, with periods of major remodelling in the 19th century. These restorations were headed by Goddard in 1861 when the east window and new fittings were installed, and Johnson in 1869 who built (or rebuilt) the north transept and added the porch and bellcote. The chancel was apparently restored earlier in the 19th century. Most windows are in the 'Tudor' or late Perpendicular style, but the east window and transept north window have flowing Decorated-type tracery. The south doorway is original 15th century work but has a restored hood mould. The interior is rather uninspiring and what 'feel' there is, is Victorian. All the fittings are Victorian too, and they include a decent pulpit, late Perpendicular-style octagonal font, low chancel screen and pews with poppyheads. The Leicestershire Round long-distance footpath crosses the churchyard.

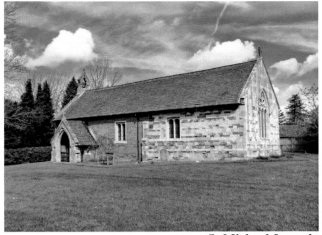

St Michael from the south and north west

The west end

East window

Transept window head stop

The bellcote

South doorway

The porch

Swithland Slate roof on porch

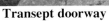

Transept doorway

Ornate hinge

St Andrew from the north west

Thringstone is a large village that makes no concession to grandeur, it grew in the 19th and 20th centuries largely to provide housing for local workers, particularly coalminers and factory workers in the nearby Coalville coalfield. Today, coal is no longer mined underground here and the environment is cleaner, thus Thringstone's star has risen and it has become a desirable place to live. At the height of the village's expansion in the middle of the 19th century the need was clearly felt for a church large enough to accommodate the burgeoning population, and St Andrew is the result. Another influence on its genesis was the Rev'd Francis Merewether, who wanted to counteract what he saw as a Catholic revival in the area begun when the nearby Mount St Bernard Abbey was built between 1837 and 1844. St Andrew was built 18 years later in 1862 to the designs of one of the best known of Victorian architects, the impressively named James Piers St Aubyn (1815-1895). His plan was imaginative, and for this he chose an Early English style, with a nod to the Normans in the use of apses for the chancel and vestry, and transepts off the north and south sides. The result was a very distinctive cruciform church, whose solidarity and self-assurance is reinforced by the use of local hard and durable Charnwood igneous rock for the fabric. There is no tower, only an almost apologetic little bellcote on the nave roof. The windows are almost all single lancets, except for a single round one in the west wall and two in the transepts, which have a sort of very early Decorated styling. The south porch has much merit, and features a bold Early English type doorway flanked by buttresses, with four orders in the arch and hood mould. A pretty lancet window sits above in the steeply angled gable. The vestry lies in the north east corner of the building, so that the church's two apses are next to each other. The interior has clean, austere lines and has been upgraded in recent years, this work included a new kitchen. All the fittings are 19th century and include a plain drum font. In the churchyard is the grave of Charles Booth (1840-1916), renowned for his work amongst the poor, particularly in London. His work led ultimately to the provision of old age pensions.

View from the north

The bellcote

St Andrew south side

The two apses

West wall

West end and south porch

Charles Booth's grave

THRUSSINGTON HOLY TRINITY

Holy Trinity south east aspect

Once again at Thrussington we have the familiar story of a church that finds itself on the margins of its settlement probably due to the migration of the houses. In Thrussington's case the village has shifted to the north west, leaving Holy Trinity on the south east edge facing open country. However, that is not of great importance here, as the church is still within easy reach from all parts of the small nucleated village. Holy Trinity is compact and attractive, and is one of the furthest west of the county's ironstone churches. It is a typical, though extensively restored, example, with narrow west tower with oversized battlements, pinnacles and gargoyles, aisled nave, chancel and south porch. There is the customary Perpendicular clerestory. Despite the far-reaching restoration of 1877 by Goddard and Paget, many original features remain from the 13th-15th century church. Also, there are tantalising glimpses of an earlier (perhaps the original) unaisled church, seen in the walls of the nave externally and internally. The tower is unusual, though by no means unique, in that it is largely built within the last bay of the nave. That occurred when the present structure was tacked onto a pre-existing bellcote. The chancel, though certainly tidied up, is 13th century work and the style of the restored windows is of that time. All, or nearly all, of the rest were put in during the 19th century restoration. The church is entered through a 13th century south doorway; the arcades are 13th century too or a little later, but are unexceptional. The north aisle impinges into the nave, leaving the interior rather unbalanced. There are several nice things to see inside. In the chancel is a pretty double piscina with a central pier with stiff leaf ornament in the capital. Sadly the head stops are damaged and thick layers of whitewash obscure detail. Another simpler and later piscina resides in the south aisle, accompanied by a single sedile. The bowl of the font is octagonal and thought to be 14th century, the rest is 19th century. A single ancient head is mounted incongruously in one of the panels, it probably came from elsewhere. There aren't many mural tablets, but three of them are interesting, though fairly modest. It is understood that internal changes are planned.

Views from the east and south

Looking east to the chancel

Looking west from the chancel

Chancel piscina

The south arcade

South aisle sedile

The font

Three fine mural tablets

Chancel wagon roof

THURCASTON ALL SAINTS

The approach from the south east

Thurcaston was originally a small nucleated village clustered around the church, but has paid the price for being close to Leicester. Over the last 100 years or so, a tentacle of ribbon housing has extended along Leicester Road towards the city. This has recently leapt over the A46 ring road and an estate is now established even nearer; it seems likely this will grow considerably and merge with the housing spreading inexorably the other way from the city, and the absorption of Thurcaston by its big neighbour will be complete. Hopefully that event will be delayed for many years. Around All Saints is a different setting, the oldest of the village housing is here and a less urban feel. And All Saints has much to recommend it, for a start it is the church most associated with local churchman Hugh Latimer, a martyr who was burnt at the stake in 1555 for his religious views, which clashed with those of the Catholic monarch Mary. There is a memorial to him in All Saints, by Broadbent, created in 1843. As befits a church on the fringe of Charnwood Forest, the local hard igneous rock was used in the construction, with slate from nearby Swithland for the roofs and to a small extent in the fabric, with sandstone for the battlements and facings. The plan is a familiar one, short, broad tower, nave with north aisle, chancel of similar length to the nave, chancel chapel and south porch. Work from the 12th to the 19th century can be found within the structure and amongst the fittings, but, like most Leicestershire churches, much of the church is 13th to 14th century in date, with some later remodelling in Perpendicular times to include a clerestory and top to the tower. However, there are some earlier features, the south doorway has zigzag ornament and is Norman, and on the tower arch one capital has upright leaves, while the other has a vine trail emerging from the mouths of two 'green men'. This work may be 12th century. Spanning the tower arch is a medieval screen and nearby is an old chest and the unusual Perpendicular font. There are many excellent memorials, some are very early Swithland Slate tablets and others large wall tablets from various dates. The east window contains some pieces of 15th century glass, and there is a 13th century grave slab.

The church from the south

South doorway arch

Latimer head stop

Nave and north aisle from the chancel

Looking east

Tower arch and screen

Tower arch capital with Green men

Old Swithland Slate tablet

Green Man corbel

Stained glass

Grave slab

Latimer memorial

The font

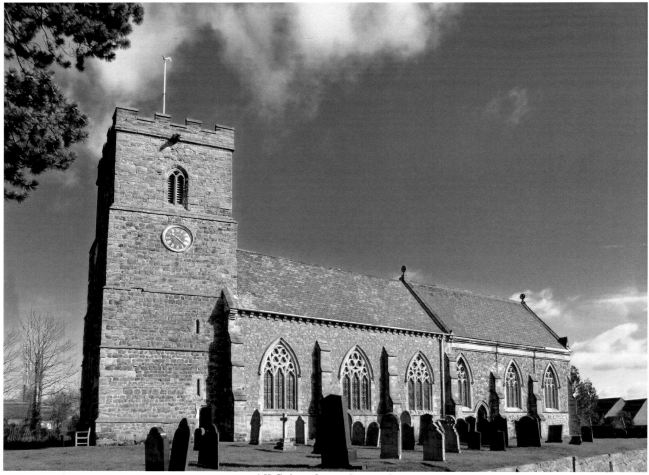

All Saints from the south

Thurlaston before 1900 was very small, and its heart was around All Saints. The village remains small but has now grown to the east and west to accommodate commuter housing, and the rest has seen much infill, so that the village atmosphere is now diluted with a more 20th century urban feel. Even around All Saints, only a very few old houses remain, but the church rises above all that and is a fine, bold building, raised slightly above the village in its elevated churchyard. Little of what we see externally today is old. The tower is the oldest part, with the basal parts probably early 13th century and the rest 15th century. The body of the church was largely remodelled in the late 18th and 19th centuries during a series of restorations that saw a south aisle removed and the nave redesigned, the north aisle renovated and the chancel rebuilt. All the windows were renewed during the later phases of the upgrading programme. The chancel almost matches the nave in size. The north aisle has its own separate gabled roof. Inside All Saints the look and feel are of an older time. The visitor is immediately struck by the impressive arcade to the north aisle, with its thick piers and carved capitals. The motifs have a Romanesque look and include leaves and crockets, and the whole probably dates from the early 13th century. A pair of corbel heads at the west end of the arcade are probably from the same time. A double sedilia was retained from the earlier church but was displaced during the restorations, it now resides in the vestry. With the exception of the monuments in the north aisle, almost all the other fittings are 19th century. The pulpit incorporates linenfold panels from an older structure, possibly a screen. The north aisle houses what was in the middle ages the Turville Chantry, a chapel dedicated to that prominent local family, and it contains a rather neglected group of memorials, remnants of a much larger set. Amongst these is a once grand 16th century tomb chest surmounted by the effigies of Sir Edward Turville and his wife. In a niche is a battered 14th century effigy and nearby are the effigies of a lady where only the bust and feet are seen, and a man praying. Two striking 17th century wall memorials also reside in the chapel.

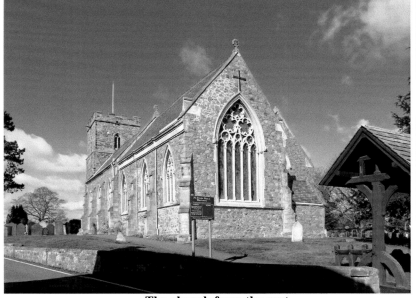

The church from the east

View through the lych gate

The north aisle

Looking east along the nave

Looking west from the chancel

The arcade

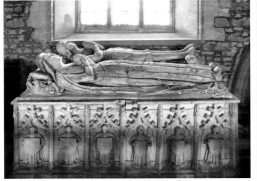

Turville chest tomb

More Turville effigies

One of the wall memorials

The pulpit

Blocked rood loft opening

Corbel head

St Michael from Melton Road in Thurmaston

Thurmaston once boasted two churches, or more properly, two chapels. St Michael and All Angels is clearly alive and well, but St John in north Thurmaston went out of use probably in the 16th century and all that remains is a portion of the west wall. St Michael was a chapelry of St Peter, Belgrave until 1841 when it became a fully fledged parish church. It is ironic that St Peter now stands empty and forlorn, while its once daughter church marches confidently into the 21st century. Like a number of churches, at the dawn of the 19th century St Michael was in a poor state of repair and as a result was extensively renovated and remodelled in 1848-9 by a familiar name, H. I Stevens. The old church had a clerestory and west gallery, with a short nave and longer chancel, but none of this survived. Stevens retained the 14th century tower, which is very much a typical Leicestershire example, but everything else, at least externally, was thoroughly renewed. His major achievement was to introduce a massive all-over roof to cover the nave and both the aisles, necessitating a timber arcade to be constructed to extend the nave walls upwards to connect with the new (and rather striking) hammerbeam roof. The overall roof gives the church a very distinctive outline. The chancel and aisles are not exceptional, and Stevens chose a Perpendicular style for the fenestration. There is an organ chamber of 1890 to the north but, oddly, no porches. The internal furniture and fittings still exude a very Victorian air, but some modern comforts like carpets have been introduced. The major exception to the 19th century stylings are the two arcades, which were retained from the old church. These 13th century structures feature both quatrefoil and octagonal piers. The western bays are lower and narrower than the others, and were constructed at the same time as the tower, in order to connect the existing church to the new structure. All is neat and tidy, but the interior generally lacks impact, as there are few imposing fittings. Nearly everything is Victorian, although the font is probably older. There aren't many noteworthy memorials, but two good ones can be found in the base of the tower, to members of the Simons family.

From the main approach to the church

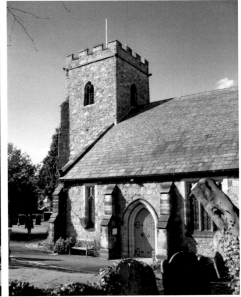

Main entrance and tower

From the churchyard to the west

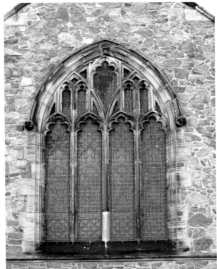

The east window

Tower gargoyle

St Michael from the east

Swithland Slate gravestones

THURNBY ST LUKE

St Luke enjoys a fine situation in Thurnby village

St Luke is an unusual church, both in plan and outline. For a start, Leicestershire has very few central towered churches, and St Luke's is a fine example of that type. The outline shows that the church is broader than it is long; which is due to the width of the large aisles, which rival the nave in size. Another unusual feature is the variety of stone used in the fabric, the tower lower stage is ironstone and this stone also crops up in some of the buttresses. However, the top stage is limestone ashlar, and an even greater contrast is provided by the granite used for the rest of the building. To complete the broad palette of stone, some buttresses use a friable sandstone. The plan is derived from an original Romanesque building erected in the 12th century at the end of, or shortly after, the Norman period of architecture. The Normans favoured central towers and at Thurnby we can still see the original, though much restored, massive piers that support the tower. A small section of original scallop carving survives on the north east pier. Very little of the original church survived a comprehensive rebuilding in 1870-3 by Slater and Carpenter, but they were keen to retain the spirit of the original and reused materials where they could. In the porch is a fragment of a Norman arch with chevrons. The 13th century arcades are from the early church and some ancient corbel heads can still be seen in the nave (and the porch). The font on its shaft of clustered columns is thought to be 13th century, the piscina and sedilia in the south aisle may also be 13th or perhaps 14th century. Part of the 19th century restoration was a completely new chancel, replacing one taken down at the end of the 18th century. This is a grand piece of work, with many typical neo-Gothic fittings, like the intricate mock sedilia and angels in the roof. There are so few old wall tablets that it seems certain that most were disposed of during the restoration. Only one is of any note, to the Rev'd Allinson, but that only dates from 1819. The best of the stained glass is the so-called Bradgate window in the south aisle, dedicated to local philanthropist Charles Bennion, who bought and then donated Bradgate Park to the city of Leicester. Many features of the Park can be seen in the design.

Views from the east and south

Resited Norman chevron work

Looking east and west along the nave

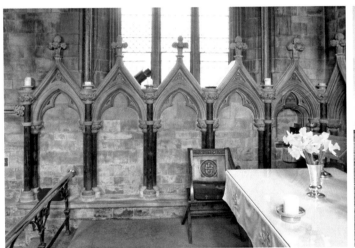

The Victorian arcading in the chancel

Heads, mural tablets and chancel angel

Piscina, sedilia and old chest in the south aisle

Font and Norman pier

'Old John' in stained glass

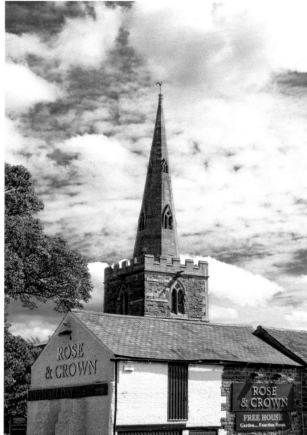

St Peter is one of the best of Leicestershire's village churches

St Peter is an admirable church both to see and to visit. It enjoys a favoured position in the heart of Tilton at the intersection of important roads, and stands at a height approaching 215 metres (700 ft) above sea level, making it one of the highest churches in the county. Like most east Leicestershire churches it has an ironstone fabric complemented with cream limestone facings and adornments. What takes it beyond the ordinary is the lovely setting, and the harmonious and pleasing outline. The large, intricately traceried windows, especially those of the Perpendicular clerestory, add stateliness and distinction. The plan is standard, with tower and limestone spire, aisled nave, chancel and south porch; the churchyard is beautifully kept and peaceful. St Peter's origins go far back in time to the 12th century, evidenced by the base of the tower with its fine arch to the nave, and the round-arched priest's doorway in the chancel south wall. Many changes and remodellings took place in the ensuing centuries, and many of these were promoted by the patronage of powerful and rich families in the area, especially in the 14th and 15th centuries; families like the Digbys, who enjoyed much influence for several centuries. The beautifully airy and light interior lives up to the promise of the exterior, if anything it is more exciting, for there are many fine things here. One of the first things to impress the observer is the very obvious non-alignment of the tower and nave. The north arcade runs directly to the tower arch north respond, necessitating the provision of complex stonework to facilitate the junction. Several very fine tombs grace the building, beginning with two that lie beneath the arches of the south arcade, to Sir John Digby (d. 1269) and his wife. In the south aisle is a well-preserved tomb chest for Sir Everard Digby (d. 1509), and in the chancel is a large 17th century chest without effigy. Also in the chancel is a lovely 16th century hanging monument. The nave arcades boast a redoubtable collection of 15th century stone heads, more reside high up as wooden roof bosses. A pier in the north arcade has a veritable menagerie of beasts chasing around the capitals, while another has angels. The font looks for all the world like a Norman capital, and is indeed 12th century. Fine old piscinae and sedilia can be found in the south aisle and chancel. There is much more to delight the senses.

C12ᵗʰ doorway

Mellow beauty of south aisle, porch and clerestory

C12ᵗʰ font

Looking east along the nave

… and west

Chancel piscina and sedilia

St Peter's four tombs

Stone heads, angels and a wolf

Stone heads, a lion and a fox carrying a goose

Roof bosses and screenwork

Nichols wall monument

St Thomas from the southern approach

Substantial Norman elements are distinctly rare in Leicestershire churches, so when something as significant as a tower still exists, it's a cause of considerable interest. For many years it was even believed that parts of Tugby's low, squat tower, were Saxon, but now the consensus is that the oldest parts are late 11th century, post-Conquest. It is unlikely that the tower's appearance today is as built, and the round arched windows in the west and south walls may have been resited. The rather nice two-light window with bold arch and central pier with chevron ornament in the south wall of the second stage almost certainly was, and probably post-dates the typically Norman belfry windows above it in the last stage. These latter have lost their central piers. At the top is a good corbel table. Elsewhere in St Thomas there are a few more Norman remains, in particular the round-arched south doorway and a similar smaller one forming an entrance into the chancel aisle. Both of these look as though they have been retooled and the latter was certainly resited. Whilst a good-looking church in most respects, there is little else structurally of interest in St Thomas, which consists of a short nave and south aisle, plus chancel with its own south aisle/chapel, and south porch with 19th century Norman details. Inside, the far-reaching Victorian restoration of 1858 eradicated almost everything of interest, with one major exception. That was the retention of a fine array of impressive wall monuments, which lift the interior above the mundane. Many of these are substantial and important pieces, none more so than the one to Richard Neell of 1574, which dominates the nave from its position on the north wall. This is a bold yet restrained Elizabethan memorial with Corinthian columns and lots of script, but, oddly, no figures. Also distinctly on the large side is the dark monolith of c. 1588 to Henry Skipwith mounted high on the west wall. Sadly this is showing its age and little of the text can be discerned. In the chancel is another enormous wall tablet for Thomas Wilson, this one in a light stone and dating from around 1720, featuring a bold pediment supported by two Doric pilasters. Several less magnificent, but still fine, mural tablets adorn the walls. Some windows have fine 19th century glass.

The tower, south face

Tower west doorway and window

South doorway

Looking towards the altar

View west from the chancel

South arcade

Nave north wall

Three scenes from Matthew 25: 35-36

Neell memorial

Three memorials to: Thomas Wilson, Henry Skipwith and the Peppin family

Font, thought to be C14th

259

St Andrew southern aspect

Tur Langton is in most respects a typical east Leicestershire village, small, charming and rural. Which is why it is a surprise to find a church like St Andrew right in the middle of it. It is, quite simply, a church of the town or city, far more likely to be encountered lurking amongst terraced streets than in deepest Leicestershire. That aside, it is actually very rewarding to find it here, where its true merit can be appreciated in a setting where it is afforded space and can be viewed all around. For make no mistake, this is a very fine building and a marvellous example of a classic Victorian church, built at the zenith of the era in 1865-6, when confidence and certainty in the 'British way' were unchallenged. What's more, it is almost entirely unchanged from when built, retaining all its original fittings, affording a very rare opportunity to experience an authentic mid-19th century church. The Early English inspired design by Joseph Goddard is creative and intriguing, mostly realised in brick but with lovely limestone counterpoint in the windows. Liberal use is made of different coloured and shaped bricks, patterned to promote a lively feeling of movement, there is nothing dull or oppressive here, so often a fault with Victorian churches. The tower is unusually positioned in the north west corner of the building and is an assertive structure, the chancel is apsidal and there is an exuberant mini north transept for the organ. A less endearing lean-to vestry runs off the chancel south wall. A set of five commanding and matching windows pierce the nave south wall; these admit lots of light, thereby avoiding another Victorian bete noir, the gloomy interior. The north side has a narrow aisle which precludes big windows, but that is compensated for by a pretty clerestory above it. The apse is the main feature inside with its beautifully designed roof, but the arcade is also very fine and busy brickwork everywhere catches the eye. Around the curving east wall are set boards with texts and there is some excellent stained glass in the east and west windows. The font is square and quintessentially Victorian, with nice marble legs. There is good ironwork in the altar rail and some tasteful wood carving in the pulpit and choir stalls.

The tower **Apsidal chancel and organ chamber** **Nave south windows**

Views looking east and west along the church **Chancel roof** **The font**

Nave windows **Accomplished stained glass** **The arcade**

Altar rail ironwork **Finely carved pulpit** **Detail of the choir stalls**

Chancel doorway **Altar, Lords Prayer, Decalogue and Creed boards** **Original iron railing of 1866**

261

TWYCROSS ST JAMES

From the A444 road

St James has a number of excellent features and is well worth a visit. One of these features is of far more than parochial interest, but it is worthwhile to look first at the mostly 14th and 15th century building itself. The sharp-eyed will soon spot that there is no obvious chancel, east of the typical Leicestershire tower there is a single long building under one roof. Closer inspection reveals some interesting facets in the fabric, it will be seen that the eastern part is constructed of roughly tooled sandstone cobbles, rather crudely laid, while the rest further west is built of more regular blocks. The block walling has been extended along and above the cruder cobbles, thus signalling that the cobble walling pre-dates the regular walling. Also the two windows in the eastern section are of quite different type to the others. All that indicates that the eastern end is the oldest part and was always designated as a discrete area, i.e. a chancel, even though it is not a clearly defined structural unit externally. The interest here extends to the interior too, because in the nave south wall there is a section of old stairway clearly associated with a higher doorway, all part of the old rood loft access. But the stairs and doorway are now in the nave, indicating that the chancel was moved further east at some point. These are rather esoteric aspects, but St James possesses a much greater claim to fame which extends far beyond Leicestershire's borders. This is a collection of some of the earliest stained glass in the country, of a quality and rarity not equalled elsewhere. It is assembled, not altogether satisfactorily, in the east window, together with a rag-bag of other medieval fragments. The fine glass is of 12th and 13th century date and is French, mostly from the churches of Saint-Denis and Sainte-Chapelle in Paris, which reached these parts by a circuitous route which at one point involved William IV. It was removed from Paris for safe-keeping. The scenes vary in completeness, but are all marvellously evocative of their time and the colours are still vivid. Elsewhere inside is a nice set of box pews for the local gentry, complete with fireplace, an old pulpit, a west gallery with most of its original furniture which is extended across the north aisle and a decent 14th century font.

From the western approach path

The chancel

Looking west and east along the nave

The north aisle and box pews

Old pulpit

The font

Chancel piscina

Mural tablet

Stained glass from Sainte-Chapelle

… and from Saint-Denis

The lovely contrast between the tower and the body of the church is a feature of St Andrew

It's hard to miss St Andrew in Twyford, it occupies pride of place in the centre of the village opposite that other essential village facility, the pub. And a lovely sight it is too, a nicely balanced building of individuality, whose eye-catching white/cream ashlar limestone tower contrasts most effectively with the golden ironstone fabric of the rest. The south frontage has three large, transomed Perpendicular nave windows, which give an imposing air and add to the attractive whole. The nave also has prominent battlements. St Andrew is the product of many centuries of change and modification, beginning way back in the 12th century, with remodellings in all the subsequent centuries, culminating with the inevitable Victorian makeover in 1849. To the west is a tower with battlements, pinnacles, corner gargoyles, narrow corbel table and an understated frieze of shields, crosses and heraldic symbols. The south face of the second stage has an odd carving of St Andrew flanked by shields. The building is completed by a short high nave, north aisle, a chancel with only one window (east), a porch, vestry and organ chamber. The latter two are 19th century additions. There's a decent area of churchyard to the south, but very little to the north. Inside there is one outstanding feature, the arcade. This is late Norman, with round arches and a very unexpected set of piers. Normally, a high quality Corinthian capital would not be encountered in a small rural church, or similarly finely carved respond capitals. This work at Twyford is clearly the product of master masons, and it has been compared with high status carving in Oakham Castle, although why Twyford was the recipient of such embellishment isn't clear, unless these were trial pieces or surplus. The substantial square font is also late Norman and has rode out the centuries, although not without some damage. Only one side is carved, with a fancy foliate cross. At the corners is heavy nailhead decoration. The pleasing nave roof is restored 15th century and retains original bosses and wall plates with corbels. At least one wooden corbel survives in the aisle. The east window contains most attractive stained glass of 1962, effected in a crisp, modern style by Harry Harvey.

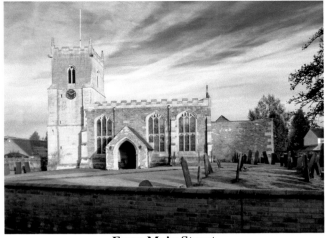

From Main Street

A frosty winter's morning at Twyford

Views east and west along the church, and the arcade

The Corinthian pier

Arcade east respond

The font

Wooden corbel

Nave roof and otherworldly bosses

The pulpit

The east window, by Harvey

265

WALTHAM on the WOLDS ST MARY MAGDALENE E2, SK 803 250

St Mary seen from the west

St Mary at Waltham is one of Leicestershire's larger village churches and is widely admired for its position, size and distinctive outline. It is constructed of the local Lincolnshire Limestone which first begins to show at the surface up in this far north east corner of the county. This handsome stone is of a most attractive creamy yellow hue, best appreciated when the sun shines. St Mary's origins go way back into Norman times, and the core cruciform plan of central tower, nave to the west of it and chancel to the east, plus transepts, undoubtedly had its genesis courtesy of the Norman designers in the 12th century. Since then the fabric and structure have been renewed and remodelled many times, so that very few 12th century features survived, but the cruciform outline remains and there are three doorways that still have Norman features. One is the main south entrance and there are two others on the north side. None of these is particularly flamboyant but all have the typical round arch, much restored in each case. Later additions to the cruciform plan were two aisles for the nave, a south porch and a much later vestry running off the chancel north wall. The impressive tower and graceful spire are Perpendicular, apart from the lowest section. The windows are a mixed array of styles, some with intricate tracery, but most if not all appear to be renewed. The Perpendicular clerestory has large windows which imbue the interior with an airy lightness. In common with many parishes in the mid to late 19th century, Waltham was host to a particularly zealous and rich vicar, Gabriel Gillet, who was responsible, together with G. G. Scott in 1850, for a sweeping internal restoration, which resulted in an ambitious Victorian furnishing and decorative scheme, including a fairly opulently furnished chancel with excellent reredos. Some medieval elements were retained, including the octagonal Norman font with its arches and unusual foliate ornament, the sedilia and piscina in the chancel and a much eroded 14th century incised slab. Two grand 18th century chandeliers hang in the nave and crossing. An earthquake in early 2008 resulted in serious damage to the spire and the church had to be closed. Happily, all is now restored.

St Mary from the east, south and south west

Chancel with transomed windows

East end details

A fearsome gargoyle

South doorway arch

Three doorways - two Norman, one Early English

South porch

Two headstops and a gargoyle

WALTON ON THE WOLDS ST MARY

St Mary from the south

St Mary is an unprepossessing building, cheaply finished in red brick with a traditional church design of little architectural merit, but it is very much of its time and as a result has some historical interest, despite later restorations. The church on the site which preceded St Mary, dedicated to St Bartholomew, had deteriorated so badly by the 1720s/30s that it was no longer fit for use and was deemed a danger to its congregation. Rather than embarking on restoration, the decision was taken to pull down the old church and build a new one. Money was perhaps an issue because the new building, started in 1736, was undertaken by local craftsmen (lead plaque in the tower) and the incumbent John Bainbrigge. It seems that there was no external professional input. The tower appears to have been left unfinished, as the top stage truncates suddenly after a few courses of brick. The original appearance of this late 1730's building was later overprinted and largely lost when two major Victorian rebuilding programmes were deemed necessary, presumably due to early decay of the (poorly constructed?) Georgian building. In 1856 the chancel and vestry were rebuilt and in 1877 it was the turn of the nave, so it seems that the whole edifice with the exception of the tower was rebuilt. The style adopted was a mundane version of Gothic. All the church body fenestration is clearly Victorian, but the openings in the tower retain their Georgian aspect, particularly the round windows. However, the west doorway looks suspiciously like a Victorian replacement. The churchyard has some reminders of the earlier church in the shape of a reasonably complete medieval cross, which only lacks the greater portion of its shaft. There is also a good group of old Swithland Slate gravestones and, lurking against the west wall of the tower, a 13th or 14th century grave slab with Maltese cross design. Immediately to the north of the church is the 18th century rectory, a grand building illustrating well that Walton was a rich living at one time. This is now, like most older rectories, a private house. Inside all is Victorian, with lots of stained glass and some wall memorials. The carved organ stool is a fine item and was originally a choir stall in Peterborough Cathedral.

The tower

The ancient cross

View from the west

Chancel window

West doorway and oculus window

Nave windows and the cross

C13th/14th grave slab

Old slate headstones

The best view of Our Lady, from the south west

Within living memory, Wanlip was an isolated, secluded hamlet, in a sequestered spot by the river Soar, but during the last half of the 20th century into the 21st, it became a village under siege, as a baleful coalition of estate houses and intensively used trunk roads encroached upon it. Nearby Birstall pushed out estates from the south, while the A46, A6 and A607 roads that grip Wanlip in a stranglehold were developed into super highways carrying a mass of traffic that never ceases. But an initiative that began in the late 20th century came to Wanlip's rescue, when local authorities cooperated to turn a string of old sand and gravel workings that ran immediately to the east of Wanlip into a country park, named Watermead. This has developed very successfully and now incorporates bird reserves. Wanlip thus has a lovely green and watery oasis on its doorstep and further urban development in the immediate area has ceased. All that was good news for Wanlip's church, which was allowed to retain its pleasant environment and rural atmosphere. Our Lady and St Nicholas is a simple, appealing building constructed mostly of local granite but also incorporating other rock types, mainly varieties of sandstone. The plan is of modest tower with large battlements, nave and chancel contained within one long building, again with oversize battlements (and gargoyles), and a bijou south aisle. Despite thorough restorations in the 19th century it still has many old features, including a good early Perpendicular window in the chancel south wall, with a small, simple low-side window next to it. Most of the fabric dates from the late 14th century, an unusual time for church building, in the aftermath of the Black Death. The south aisle is of 1904 and contains the main entrance, also an unusual arrangement of three sentry box-like buttresses on the west wall, rising in size and containing two windows and a door. A round window sits above the largest 'box'. Inside is a fine brass of 1393 with the earliest known prose inscription in English, recording that the lady depicted built the church. The arcade is the original 14th century one despite the much later aisle. There are several good mural tablets and a fine marble font of 1796.

270

Nave and south aisle

The tower from the west

Niche above south doorway

Late C14th chancel window

Low-side chancel window

The east window

Old Swithland Slate headstones and carving

St Michael from the south

Wartnaby is a small, secluded and peaceful hamlet in the wolds country about three miles north west of Melton Mowbray. If time has stood still anywhere in Leicestershire, it must be here, and the church of St Michael exudes the same sense of unhurried calm from its pretty position to the west of the main village. It is reached across a field path. Ironstone was previously quarried around the village and of course the church is constructed of this useful stone. The exterior is unremarkable except for the thin tower at the west end which is capped by a substantial bellcote in more or less original 13th century condition with two large openings to the east and west and two blocked belfry windows to the north and south. Much of the fabric of the rest of the church is 13th century but a major restoration in 1868-9 saw most windows replaced with narrow faux Early English lancets and the chancel substantially remodelled. One original (internally only) window survives in the tower west wall. St Michael has a south aisle with porch and a clerestory on the south side only with plain square windows. In the nave north wall is a blocked, unrestored Norman doorway with round arch and imposts. Inside, St Michael boasts a lovely 13th century arcade with round arches and carvings on certain capitals, that has somehow retained an original very early painting scheme. This is quite expansive in content with many different motifs, mostly floral in derivation. Concern has been expressed about the deteriorating condition of this important feature and it is to be hoped that more conservation work will be sanctioned and funded. The walls were apparently all scraped during the 19th century restoration, and it is a reasonable guess that much more painting was originally applied to them. The plain cylindrical font is also probably part of the original 13th century furnishings. The story of St Michael in its later centuries is one of support and administration by a number of rich local families and several memorials to them can be found on the walls. Appropriately, some of these are for members of the Wartnaby family, whilst others are to Binghams and Cants. Two sets of 15th century bench ends sit by the altar rail, made up into stalls with more recent parts.

The church from the south east and north east

Norman north doorway   **Tower and bellcote**   **Looking east along the nave**

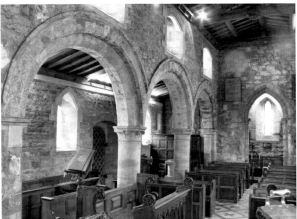

Looking west along the nave   **The arcade**   **Painting detail**

Arcade details and the font   **Two mural tablets**   **C15th bench end**

St Bartholomew from the south east

There are several isolated churches in Leicestershire, and others sited some little way from their settlements, but the small church of St Bartholomew located about a couple of miles north west of the centre of Melton Mowbray is quite alone. It once had a village for company but enclosures mostly in the 18th century to house a far more profitable sheep population, saw the villagers evicted and the settlement's demise. All that remains is a series of humps and hollows in neighbouring fields to show where the village once lay. On a bleak winters day, as the church comes into view from the narrow and little used Welby Lane, it is hard to imagine that a large business park and old ironworks lie nearby. Its survival and continued use today by a travelling congregation is quite remarkable. The church's origins go back at least to the 13th century and the narrow tower with its bellcote and saddleback roof is the best surviving representative of that time. The west lancet in the lower stage indicates an Early English assignment. The foundation of the church is traditionally associated with the powerful figure of Roger de Mowbray, who died around 1188, and indeed he is known to have supported many religious foundations and causes. The plan is simple, consisting of the aforesaid tower with its Swithland Slate roof and small belfry openings, a nave and chancel under one (Welsh slate) roof and a south porch. The windows are a bit of a mixed bag and look to date from the 19th century, the east one is the most ambitious and features Perpendicular-style tracery. The churchyard is small, neat and well maintained by obviously dedicated supporters. Inside there is an ogee-headed piscina and a presumed aumbry in walls either side of the altar and a plain octagonal 17th century font, but the best features are a commanding pulpit and reading desk made out of pretty Jacobean panels. Repairs were undertaken in the 17th century and the Victorian restoration (by Johnson) in 1860-2 removed most medieval features, but the interior retains a strong tang of the past. Further repairs have become necessary recently and the church is attempting to raise the considerable sum of £150,000 to fund these.

St Bartholomew from the north east and south west

The saddleback tower

The way in

Tower from the south

Tower west lancet

Tower from the north

WELHAM ST ANDREW

From the northern gate

One hesitates to call any medieval church unattractive, but the view from the north of St Andrew is unappealing. The 15th century limestone ashlar tower is quite fine but the north wall of the ironstone nave is obscured and overpowered by an ugly stucco'ed box, the Edwards mausoleum of 1810. The irony is that the imposing monument inside the mausoleum is one of the best things in the church, albeit rather neglected. A large evergreen tree, though handsome in its own right, has taken over the churchyard and is supported by a number of other overgrown trees which together hide the church and imbue the scene with a gloomy, unkempt atmosphere. On the other hand, the south side presents a more satisfactory picture. From here the chancel of 1870 can be better appreciated with its fine gabled buttresses, with heads. The original chancel was medieval but was pulled down around 1720 during a renovation sponsored by Francis Edwards. Thus for 150 years St Andrew lacked a dedicated chancel building. The restoration of 1870 by Goddard remedied that and the new chancel conformed to a classic Victorian Gothic structural and furnishing plan, which remains virtually untouched to this day and is well worth a look. Francis Edwards was an important man in St Andrew's history, and indeed, Welham's, for he built many houses in the village and was very munificent in his refitting of the church. Apparently, his scheme left St Andrew with a typical Classical Georgian imprint, but this was swept away by Goddard in 1870. It is Francis Edwards for whom the vast memorial of 1728 in the mausoleum was made, by his daughter; it was originally in the churchyard. Its deterioration led to the family commissioning the mausoleum to house it in 1809. Inside, apart from the marble Edwards monument with its steps, urns, obelisk and big tomb chest with corner volutes, a neat and nicely preserved 15th century pulpit still stands proudly in its accustomed place. The plain ribbed font is pre-Victorian but hard to date and a very faded George III arms and benefactions board of 1804 are tucked away in the tower room. A plain mural tablet is dated 1652, but only two others, both 19th century and uninspiring, adorn the interior walls.

The tower from the north

West entrance through the tower

Chancel angle buttress

Looking east along the nave

…. and west

The Edwards tomb

Urn in Edwards mausoleum

Two mural tablets – 1652 and 1829

The pulpit

The font

George III arms

Benefactions board

WHETSTONE ST PETER

St Peter from the south east

Whetstone is another old village that has suffered due to its proximity to Leicester and it was an early casualty of the latter's demand for commuter housing. These days it is little more than an amorphous expanse of estates, barely separated from its neighbour Blaby, also a victim of Leicester's expansion. But St Peter has managed to retain a relatively undeveloped area around it, and something of the old village feel. Indeed the approach from High Street along Church Lane is most attractive and reveals the church's best asset, its tall tower and spire combination. Unfortunately the promise of this vista is not fulfilled by the rest of the church, which is a rather unappealing mixture of elements with little harmony, the whole too low and squat to balance the height of the tower. The history of the building follows a familiar pattern for Leicestershire with a 13th century (or earlier) foundation, remodelling in the next century to include a south aisle and the tower and spire, and later modifications culminating in the inevitable 19th century makeovers. These were by Parsons and Dain in 1856 and Goddard and Paget in 1895-7, the latter after the top of the spire fell into the church. Much is made of a date of 1335 carved in a buttress east of the north porch, but there is no context to help with deciphering its importance or whether it refers to a major rebuilding at that time. There is no significant structural distinction between nave and chancel and both are housed under one long roof. Internally it can be seen that the chancel is quite lengthy, often a sign of early foundation. It may be the oldest part of the church. In place of a full chancel arch there are only the two piers, the arch element either wasn't built or was removed at some stage. The capitals of the piers feature amusing and enigmatic carvings including the familiar image of a man with his tongue out, another holding his neighbour's head and robed clerics depicted horizontally. In the chancel is a set of particularly fine 13th century sedilia, accompanied by a damaged piscina. Another old piscina resides in the south aisle, indicating the former presence of a chapel. The lovely pulpit survives from an 18th or early 19th century refit. The roof has some remaining medieval woodwork, including good bosses. Most of the other fittings are Victorian or later.

From Church Lane

Looking east along the nave

The arcade

Sedilia and piscina in the chancel

South aisle piscina

The pulpit

Medieval elements of the roof

Font of 1856

East window by Morris and Co., 1935

Details of the chancel arch pier capitals

Remains of a low side window

St Peter, 1902

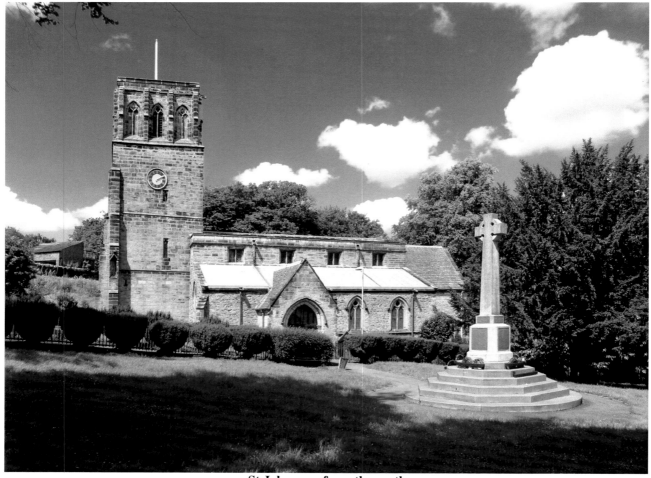

St John seen from the south

The situation of St John at Whitwick is somewhat unusual, as instead of standing on a high point like many churches, it is tucked into the hillside in a small dell and the visitor must descend from North Street to the main south door. Despite the proximity of good tough Charnwood rock, the majority of stone used for St John is local sandstone, sometimes as cobbles or rough blocks, sometimes as ashlar, as in the sturdy, assertive tower. However, there is some Charnwood stone in the fabric. In the tower south west buttress are two niches, which once housed statues of St John and probably the Virgin Mary. A small fragment of a Saxon cross incorporated into the chancel wall indicates that an early church stood on this site, but the oldest of the fabric seen today is 13th century. The tower may be from early in that century, also probably parts of the nave and chancel, with the majority of the rest following in the 14th century. Most of the church is Decorated in style. The south doorway is an attractive 13th century design with two orders of shafts and tiers of mouldings in the arch. The clerestory was added at a relatively late date, around 1620. The Victorian restoration by J. P. St Aubyn in 1848-50 was particularly rigorous, during which the nave and north aisle were extended east by one bay and the chancel arch resited. There were more changes in 1898 with the result that the interior has a pronounced Victorian feel, but the neo-Gothic edges of the 19th century have been smoothed away by later refurnishing and the interior today is rather characterless and, with a few exceptions, lacks items of interest. One of the best features is the tomb effigy of Sir John Talbot (d. 1365) in the north aisle. A tomb recess in the external south wall of the south aisle may once have housed this effigy. The octagonal font with its panels showing shields and blank tracery is 14th century. Two stained glass windows are worthy of attention. The first is the east window in the south aisle of around 1889, and this depicts the returning of the tithes to Whitwick in 1235; various prominent people involved in that event are featured. The other is the east window of the north aisle of 1914, which is a memorial to local miners and quarrymen who died at their work.

From the west

Top stage of the C13th tower

North aisle east window

South porch

External tomb recess

Head stops

North aisle doorway

THE CHURCHES OF WIGSTON MAGNA

ALL SAINTS, Moat Street
 C4, SP 604 100

From Moat Street

Wigston embodies much of the ugliness of urban sprawl, having been overwhelmed by Leicester, and is tarnished by dreary dormitory estates, corporate shops of no distinction and seemingly endless traffic seething through. A belated attempt to salvage something of the old village came in 1977 with the implementation of a conservation area around All Saints church, which itself continues to offer an uplifting vista to the passing world. It is a grand medieval church, large and ambitious, consisting of stately sandstone ashlar tower and limestone spire, battlemented nave with north and south aisles and an imposing chancel. Two porches (the south now an oratory), organ chamber and sacristy complete an impressive layout. Most of the body of the church is completed in hard local granite blocks. The tower sits within the west end of the church, and has arches into it on three sides. In the north wall near the porch is a 13th century recess and internally in the north aisle near it is another one, roughly contemporary. The priest's doorway into the chancel also looks 13th – 14th century in date. Most of the fenestration is Victorian, but some windows probably follow medieval antecedants. The earliest fabric is from the 13th century, but the structure of the building has been several times modified in ensuing centuries, culminating in a big 19th century overhaul by Kirk in 1863-4 which left an overarching Victorian atmosphere and internal appearance. The Anglo-Catholic leanings of All Saints, dating from 1912, have resulted in a more ornate and showy interior than seen in most Leicestershire Anglican churches and there are no less than four altars, with appropriate Catholic influenced settings. There are a large number of interesting features and fittings, too many to list here, but the beautifully restored and colourful nave roof, fine (restored) 15th century screen, south arcade capital carvings, dainty 18th century font, some excellent mural tablets, piscinas (3) and sedilia, and the high quality 19th century seating and pulpit, must be seen.

All Saints from the south

Tomb recess, north side

Priest's doorway

Nave and screen

A corbel and south arcade capital carvings

Tomb recess, north aisle

C18th font

Elegant wall memorial

Piscina and sedilia, chancel

Pews with linenfold carving

Nave roof

ST WISTAN, Bull Head Street

From the north east

Tower from the south east

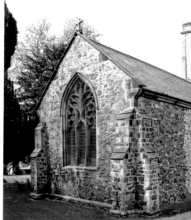
Chancel and east window

St Wistan has had a very chequered career from its medieval beginnings. The most credible history states that it was founded as a shrine to St Wistan in the 9th century and was a place of pilgrimage, later expanded to form a chapel. This was in use as a religious centre until the Reformation, after which it lost its raison d'etre when pilgrimages were discouraged. In subsequent centuries it hung on in a very delapidated condition, but continued to be used as a schoolroom, mortuary and barn, amongst other things. In the 18th century part of it had been converted into almshouses. By the middle of the 19th century it was ruinous, but as a result of the revival in church going and belief it was deemed worthy of restoration. The body of the church was dismantled and only the 13th/14th century tower and spire were retained, to which was added a simple rectangular building to house both chancel and nave. A south porch was added. The result of the restoration was a plain, functional church with no frills or treasures. Nothing survives from its early days and the interior is quite stark. The only concession to flamboyance is the Decorated-inspired east window.

ST THOMAS THE APOSTLE, St Thomas Road (South Wigston)

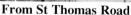
From St Thomas Road

From the east

From the south

St Thomas is a strange, red-brick, very late Victorian concoction which defies categorisation. What can be said is that it is a powerful presence, courtesy of the amazing tower and gargantuan nave. There is a chancel, but no aisles. Many details are Early English, but other stylings are just odd. It was built in 1892-3 by local architect Stockdale Harrison and the tower was tacked on in 1901 in the south west corner, presumably as a road impinged to the west. The fascinating interior is vast and there are many intriguing features, particularly the neo-Jacobean pulpit and stained glass.

WIGSTON PARVA ST MARY THE VIRGIN

From the south west and south

From the west   **Romanesque north doorway**   **Medieval south wall lancet**

The tiny cluster of houses that constitutes Wigston Parva has no connection with the far larger Wigston Magna on the southern edge of Leicester, and in fact the hamlet lies about 12 miles to the south west of its totally contrasting namesake. The church of St Mary is equally diminuitive, although it is possibly not the smallest Anglican church in the county, that honour may lie with Drayton. The building is very simply constituted, just a single rectangular box to contain nave and chancel. There are windows at the east and west ends and three lancets in the south wall. On the west gable sits (rather precariously) a wooden openwork bellcote, with one bell. Despite its small size St Mary is of some importance due to its early origin, certain features such as the round-headed north doorway and a lancet opening indicate 11th century beginnings, which is about as old as extant churches get in Leicestershire. St Mary was restored in 1845 and again circa 1900. Inside are a small suite of fittings, some sourced from other establishments. The font was acquired from Hemingford church in Huntingdonshire, and the altar was donated by Thurmaston parish in 1909. There are commandment and Creed boards, an openwork pulpit and the roof is 16th century. Seating is with chairs, the pews long gone. One oddity is that the building is situated in the midst of a vegetable garden owned by a villager, the church itself only owns the land on which it stands.

From the north east

Sandstone tower

Thankfully, Willoughby Waterleys has largely escaped the late 20th century and 21st century plague of intrusive infilling and dormitory estates that has blighted so many villages. There is some new building, but it is on a manageable scale, and Willoughby remains a pleasant, secluded place with an old time atmosphere. It also possesses many fine old houses. The church of St Mary is not quite in the same league as the important secular buildings, but is nevertheless an attractive building in a good setting, although rather hemmed in and over-endowed with trees that obscure vistas of the church. Particularly nice is the approach from the west along the narrow lane that threads its way from Main Street. The building is of a typical type for Leicestershire, mostly constructed in the 13th and 14th centuries with a battlemented tower of local greenish sandstone, nave, north aisle, chancel, organ chamber and north porch. The porch and organ chamber probably date from 1875. Much of the body of the church is constructed of local cobbles. Smith's refit of 1875 was an aggressive affair during which the interior was sanitised and a new chancel built. A 14th century window with ballflower in the surround survived the onslaught and can be found in the nave south wall. The interior now has few medieval fittings, but notable exceptions are the large number of corbel heads and roof bosses of human form that fill the nave and its roof. Whoever were responsible for their creation must have been gloomy souls because almost all these characters are depicted with malign, deformed or downright miserable faces. That's not to say they are not a great deal of fun, they are, and much enjoyment can be gained from tracking them all down. The one significant exception to the misery is the battered but unbowed bust of a bishop who sits proudly at the west end of the roof, gazing down on the congregation below. Although the chancel is of 1875, the medieval piscina and sedilia, though restored, have survived and there is also an old font, located in the south aisle near the main entrance. This is quite plain and said to be 13th century, but the base is modern. The Victorian fittings are mostly realised in an insipid Gothic style, but are nice quality, especially the wooden reredos with its carved figures, and the pulpit. A nave window has Kempe glass of 1910.

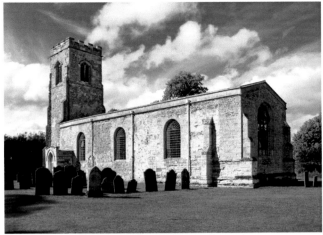
St Wistan from the south east

East end with characteristic C18th window

The C12th doorway

Looking west along the church

The east end and sanctuary

North side of the interior showing box pews

Richard Halford tomb

Charles Halford memorial

William Halford tablet

For Elizabeth and Henry Halford

George III arms and organ pipes

St Peter from the south   **South side turret**

Witherley is right on the border with Warwickshire, which lies just a few metres from the village's western edge along the course of the river Anker and to the south along the A5. Many industrial estates lie along the seething A5 and Witherley has a large, ugly one on its doorstep a short distance to the west. That might suggest that this is anything but a sequestered place, but Witherley has its pleasant corners, and as is so often the case, the church is at the heart of a conservation area, with the river Anker at the bottom of the churchyard and green spaces beyond. St Peter's highlight is the striking 15th century tower and tall, slender spire, a grand sight for miles around. The rest of the church consists of nave with north aisle, chancel and south porch. The nave, aisle and porch are 14th century, but the chancel is a Victorian creation of 1858 by Robert Jennings of neighbouring Atherstone. Its mundane design doesn't match the rest of the building at all. It was built with different stone, has an incongruous steep pitched roof and is higher than the nave. The tower and spire have many interesting details, the spire is octagonal and has delicate crockets, while at the top of the tower are pinnacles and attractive traceried panels on the battlemented parapet. The panel design is echoed on the 15th century octagonal font inside. In the lowest stage of the tower is a bold west door with flattened triangular head, above which is a large window with Perpendicular tracery and above that is an unusual opening flanked by blank shields. The south porch has a very large doorway and age-old patina, the quatrefoil openings with their ancient stone surrounds and arrow sharpening grooves are a distinctive feature. An odd turret on the south side is Victorian and is used as a vestry. Inside are some good things, especially the wall tablets. The best is one for Richard Farmer and his wife of c. 1768, consisting of a pedimented plaque with arms, and scrolls to the side. There are several good 19th century tablets to members of the Roberts family. The best of several 15th century glass fragments is an excellent Madonna and Child. The nave and aisle roofs are (restored) 15th/16th century, with wooden corbels and bosses. Sedilia and piscina in the aisle are from the 14th century, and indicate a former chapel. There is a George IV arms board.

From the south east **From the south west** **Tower west doorway**

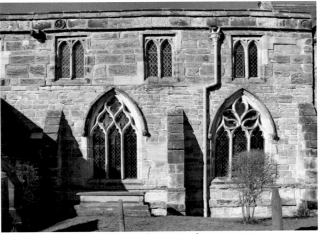

Nave fenestration **North aisle and railed tomb**

The porch **Blocked north doorway** **Tower gargoyle**

Porch window (interior) **Curious old tomb in the churchyard**

The church from School Lane, and the striking tower from the west

Woodhouse enjoys a favoured position on the edge of Charnwood Forest and is very much sought after as a place to live. Like its village, St Mary-in-the-Elms is attractive and well looked after. The name is unique, but Ipswich has a St Mary-at-the-Elms. Visitors are greeted by a pleasantly intimate atmosphere and there is a lived-in and welcoming feel inside that must be the envy of many other churches. All is spick and span. Some of that may be due to a laudable scheme whereby a local Catholic congregation also has use of the building for its services. On first sight the age of the building is hard to establish, which is a facet of Charnwood stone churches, they simply don't weather, but there are indications of a 15th century origin and there is a row of seven lovely 17th century rectangular mullioned windows in the nave south wall. Most of what is seen today is the result of major Victorian overhauls which included a new north aisle, porch and south transept. The tower was also rebuilt and the interior radically remodelled. The layout shows several quirky architectural features. The narrow tower has a pyramid roof, tall and shallow two storey extension off the north wall and a prominent chimney/exhaust flue. The nave and chancel are in one and are only demarcated inside. The north aisle is an otherwise conventional structure but has a central gable, presumably built to house the large stained glass window that resides there. Running off the south wall of the tower is an unexpectedly large transept. To add to the irregular plan, very recently a new extension was built into the angle between the aisle and the tower, to house modern facilities. The interior is a pleasure to experience, and while it lacks outstanding features and is almost entirely Victorian, there are several excellent items and the fittings are of good quality. One of the oldest fittings is a pulpit of 1615, with fine carving of ornament and text. The font with its cusped panels containing blank shields may also be old, and there are some pieces of 15th century glass in the chancel. Several extravagant alabaster wall tablets adorn the walls, nearly all 19th century, but one plain black one is much older. The nice linenfold panelling in the sanctuary is partly 16th/17th century, as are some pieces of woodwork incorporated into the aisle screen.

St Mary seen from the east and north east

Looking west and east along the nave　　　　　**The font**

Pulpit of 1615　　　**The oldest mural tablet**　　　**C18th tablet**

Flamboyant Victorian tablets　　　　　**The panelled sanctuary**

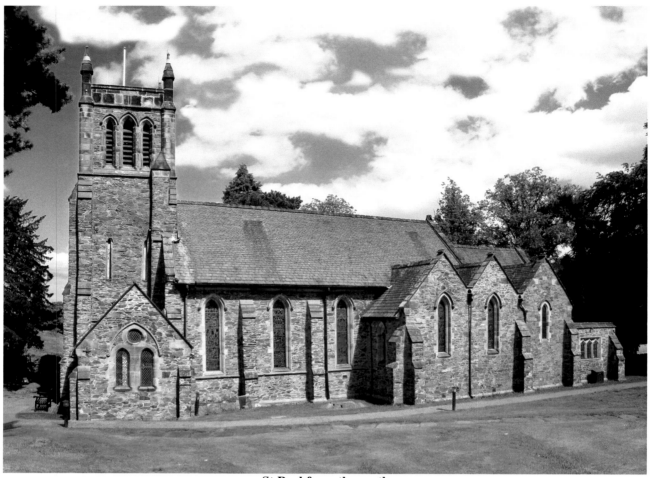

St Paul from the south

Woodhouse Eaves, like Woodhouse, enjoys an enviable position in the craggy Charnwood Forest, but is even more scenically set than its namesake. St Paul stands on a high point near to an old slate quarry and has a relatively short, but interesting history. It was consecrated in 1837 and the architect was William Railton, who in the 1830's undertook several projects in Leicestershire, including the almost exactly contemporary church at Copt Oak. He also built Groby St Philip and St James a few years later and then Thorpe Acre All Saints in 1845. His best known work is Nelson's Column in London. Unsurprisingly, his two churches at Woodhouse Eaves and Copt Oak have much in common. Both are constructed of tough Charnwood stone, have sharply angular and rather unforgiving Early English lancet style designs and lack aisles. Originally, both churches would have looked closely similar, but in 1880 St Paul was further developed by the addition of transepts, in fact the church bristles with them. There is one off the tower south wall, north and south double-gabled transepts off the east end of the nave and a further two off the chancel south wall. One of the latter is gabled while the other is flat-roofed. The transepts have been utilised as vestries, chapels and an organ chamber. The architect responsible for the 1880 expansion was Ewan Christian. The chancel was enlarged slightly earlier, in 1871. Originally, the windows were filled with plain glass, but beginning with the east window in 1871, the glazing was progressively replaced with stained glass, much of it fitted during the 1880 building programme, with more later. The inevitable outcome of that policy is that the interior of St Paul is very gloomy, especially as the church lacks a clerestory. The first building had a west gallery, but that had a short life, being removed in 1880. Internally, everything dates from the 19th or 20th centuries, the font is a typical Victorian model. Like all churches, the building has continued to evolve to meet the needs of its congregation and has seen the familiar intensification of that process as the 20th century passed into the present one. Recent changes have seen improved auditory facilities and the tower transept adapted as a toilet.

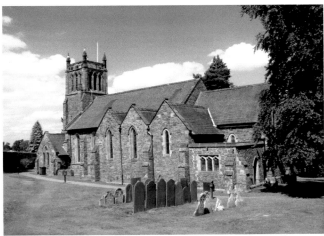

Views from the south east and north east

Chancel east end

From the approach path

Commemorating the 1880 changes

Lancet window

The 'postcard view' of the church and war memorial

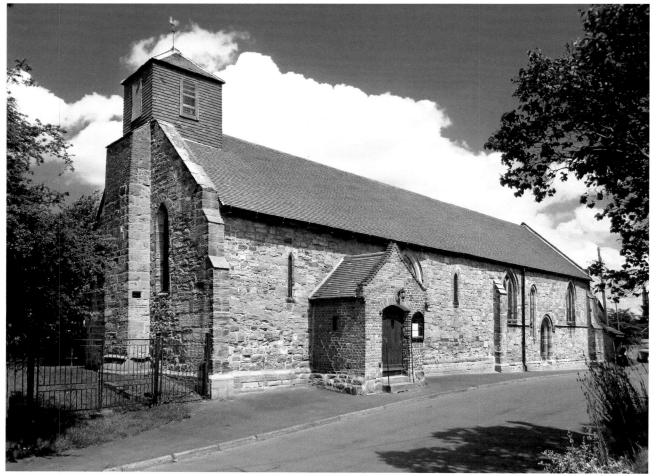

From the south west

Some Leicestershire churches are characterised by their very ancient appearance and atmosphere, with origins deep in the mists of time. Later restorations and changes have done little to dispel this 'feel'. Worthington St Matthew is a case in point, it is a remarkable little church, time-worn and bearing many reminders of its distant beginnings in Norman times. From the round-headed doorways and bowed nave walls to the deeply splayed lancet windows, it is clear that this is a very old church. The plan has changed little since the 12th century, the original rectangular outline remains unaltered except for an eastward expansion in the 13th century, and it houses both nave and chancel. The fashion for adding towers and aisles didn't reach this little visited part of the county, or maybe there were insufficient funds. A modest wooden bellcote was added at some stage and, much later, a quaint, rustic, brick-built south porch (bearing a much-eroded and almost indecipherable date plaque of 1781). This porch rests on a plinth of stone coursing, indicating the presence of an earlier version. A medieval sepulcral gloom envelopes the interior, thanks to the dominance of narrow lancet fenestration. In the chancel area larger 13th century windows admit a little more light. An uninspired restoration took place in 1890-1, at which time the walls were scraped clear of plaster. Usually this practice does little for a church interior, but in this case it had the effect of revealing the most remarkable stonework. The stone is local sandstone, probably Triassic in age, but it may have been sourced from Coal Measures beds. Whatever its origin, it has beautiful colouration in a variety of reddish and buff tones, streaked with cross-bedding and other sedimentary structures. There are no great treasures in the church, most of the fittings date from the restoration and are dull, but the pulpit has an interesting openwork structure. The 18th century altar rails consist of budget range thin planks. The font, probably dating from the 12th century church, has been mutilated by lopping off the top section. This has left the original quatrefoil ornamentation pruned of its topmost lobe. In the quatrefoils are shields. The original piscina and aumbry survive in the sanctuary.

From the south east

Two Romanesque doorways, one in use, one clearly not

Looking east and west along the nave

The east end

Pulpit and screen

Altar rail and aumbry

Well-used old chair

Lancet window

The piscina

The font

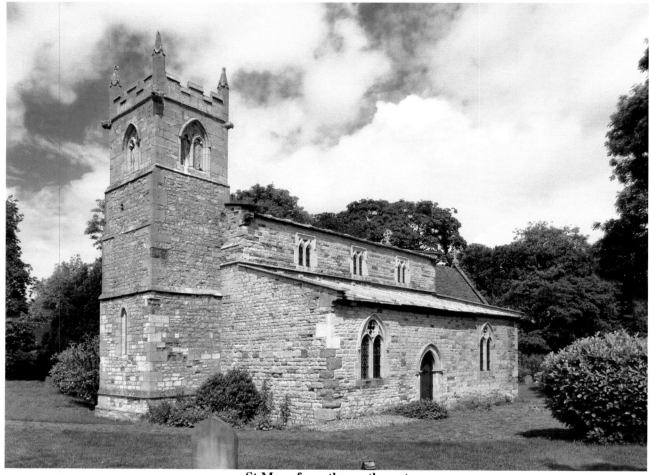

St Mary from the south west

Wyfordby is a tiny, secluded backwater to the east of Melton Mowbray, just a handful of houses set in the valley of the River Eye. A little used single track road passes through and winds its way eastwards to the equally miniscule settlement of Stapleford. To the west lies the slightly larger, but equally rural village of Brentingby. The remarkable thing is that each of these three hamlets boasts a church, the wonder is that there was ever sufficient patronage to keep them viable, but it wasn't until the middle of the 20th century that Brentingby and Stapleford were declared redundant. The former is now converted to a dwelling but retains its 14th century tower, which is under the care of the Churches Conservation Trust. Stapleford, a regionally important 18th century Grade 1 listed building, has fared better and is maintained in good order, also by the CCT. That leaves just Wyfordby as a fully commissioned, functioning church, and a particularly attractive one it is too, built largely of the handsome cream Lincolnshire Limestone stone, with some patches of ironstone. Though quite small, St Mary has an expansive plan with three-stage tower, nave with two aisles and chancel. The oldest sections are 13th century and include the tower (the battlements and pinnacles are 14th or 15th century Perpendicular) and the south arcade. The main Victorian restoration came in 1869 and was comprehensive, involving almost complete refenestration and interior refitting. The result, unfortunately, was to render the inside of the church perfectly ordered but ultimately dull and sterile. Almost all medieval fittings were swept away, leaving only the structurally fixed features such as the arcades, tower and chancel arches, piscinas and aumbrys. Of these latter there are three and two respectively. Each aisle has a piscina, also the chancel, and all are different, highlighting the different ages of the chancel and each aisle, but all seem to be 13th or 14th century. As is so often the case, the medieval font was retained and it is a decent example, with traceried panels. One attractive feature dating from the Victorian restoration is the (restored) hanging lamps in the nave. The pulpit too is pleasing, with an unusual panelled design.

St Mary seen from the south east and west

Looking east and west along the nave   **Victorian glass**

The three piscinas – north aisle, chancel, south aisle

The aumbrys   **The pulpit**   **The font**   **Hanging lamp**

A sight to stir the senses, St Mary from the south west

First of all, St Mary is a noble building of largely 14th and 15th century origin, sited in the centre of Wymeswold and unmissable by all passing through, but it also has a broader claim to fame. Augustus Welmore Pugin (1812–52) was the Crown Prince of Victorian Gothic-inspired architects, celebrated in his own day and perhaps even more now as the fashion for Victoriana undergoes a revival. His work for the new Palace of Westminster in London stands as his greatest achievement, rightly recognised as a pinnacle of High Victoriana, known all over the world. Pugin was a prolific worker, but he did little in Leicestershire – St Mary is a notable exception. It was Henry Alford, the incumbent at Wymeswold from 1835-53 and himself a larger than life figure, who commissioned Pugin to come to Leicestershire. Alford was dismayed on finding his new charge at Wymeswold to be in a poor state of repair, so he asked Pugin, who may well have been known to him, to undertake a comprehensive restoration, which he did in 1844-6. Thus, St Mary stands as a rare local example of Pugin's grandeloquent style, although it has to be said that his work at St Mary doesn't rank amongst his best or most inspired. Despite that, Pugin enthusiasts make regular pilgrimages to Wymeswold. The restoration touched every part of the church and the ambitious two-storey north porch, the south porch and the aisle windows all belong to it. Inside, the overhaul was even more extensive, almost all the furnishings were replaced, including the font, pulpit, screen, lectern, seating, sedilia and roofs, but it is perhaps the little touches that most characterise the architect, like the specially designed candle sconces, chandeliers and the delightful angel corbels supporting the nave roof. A few medieval items were retained, but only as souvenirs of the old church, such as the fragments of the old Perpendicular screen mounted on the walls near the font and the bombastic late 17th century wall memorial for William Leeke, which was banished from the chancel to a place under the tower. There are good examples of 19th century stained glass in the windows, and it is to be applauded that very little of Pugin's vision for Wymeswold has been altered in subsequent years.

St Mary from the south

Tower doorway and window

Looking east and west along the nave

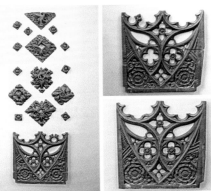

C15th screen fragments

Leeke memorial

The pulpit

Nave roof angel

Chancel piscina and sedilia

Chancel roof

The font

WYMONDHAM ST PETER

Two views of St Peter from the south and south west

Wymondham is one of Leicestershire's old market villages, its glory days long gone, but an atmosphere of that time still pervades the place, in much the same way as it does at Hallaton, and also like Hallaton it remains a picturesque and sought-after village in which to live. Being in the east of the county close to the Rutland border, the church is unsurprisingly built chiefly of local ironstone, but the proximity of outcrops of Lincolnshire Limestone means that fine stone also occurs widely in the fabric, particularly the topmost stage of the tower and the spire. Both are made entirely of this stone. St Peter's plan is quite elaborate and impressive, as well as the usual tower/spire, nave and chancel, there are two aisles and two transepts, as well as a south porch and vestry. The clerestory is particularly fine, with large bold Perpendicular windows almost filling the wall space. The oldest fabric is early 13th century, for example the bottom stage of the tower and the chancel. The ensuing two centuries also saw additions and improvements, before a long lull was broken by a string of Victorian restorations between 1864 and 1875 during which both the nave and chancel were refitted. The interior is one of the county's more interesting ones, with lots of good things dating from medieval to 18th century. A lot of these are gathered together in the south transept, which seems to have been laid out as a modest museum. The oldest thing on show is the late 13th century cross-legged effigy of Sir John Hamelin on the floor, which is in a fair state of preservation. Next to it is a floor brass from 1521, for Sir Morys Berkeley and his wife. Hers is the only brasswork surviving. A chest tomb with incised cover for Sir Thomas Berkley and his wife stands nearby, dated 1488, with shields on the side. Also in the south transept is a large early 18th century cupboard and other ornate woodwork. A squint here allows a view of the altar. In the chancel is a handsome 13th century triple sedilia, with piscina to its left. Many grimacing and grotesque stone heads can be found in the nave and aisles, and several arcade pier capitals are stylishly embellished with musical angels, animals, ballflower, etc. The font is 15th century but appears to be recut.

The box-like south transept

Ogee-headed blocked north doorway

C13th effigy

Looking east and west along the body of the church

Rood doorway

South arcade capital carving

C16th brass

Effigy and chest tomb

Piscina and sedilia

Characters

Treasures of the south transept, and squint

References and Select Bibliography

The literature pertaining to churches in general is voluminous and to list every book would require several large tomes. Even Leicestershire churches, which are less visited and studied than most, have a long list of titles dedicated or referring to them. The following list is therefore selective, but nevertheless covers most of the relevant literature. The best source of information is guides and leaflets that were written for specific churches, they can usually be found in the churches concerned. However, these go in and out of print rapidly and often 'run out'. Of the books, just a small number are actually of importance in Leicestershire church research, many of the others merely repeat the information found in the main sources. Of these, the 2003 printing of Pevsner's Buildings of England: Leicestershire volume, with important additions by Brandwood and Williamson, is indispensable and I freely acknowledge the large part it played in the writing of this book. It also contains much useful information on churches generally and a good glossary. For information about church architecture, history and furnishings there are many books available, and some recent publications are excellent; clearly and concisely written in easy-to-follow, enthusiastic style, for example Taylor (2003), Fewins (2005) and McNamara and Tilney (2011). And don't underestimate the small and easily obtainable 'Observers' book on English churches by Jones (1965), one of the best and most comprehensible introductions to English churches. John Betjeman, one of the greatest champions of English churches, wrote several books on them and all are worth reading. Specifically for Leicestershire, the work by Geoff Brandwood in the 1980's embodied in three splendid and carefully researched booklets (1984, 1987, 2002) was also constantly to hand. Five slim volumes published in 2000 by Leicestershire County Council for the local Historic Churches Trust were useful for the relatively few churches they covered. To a much lesser extent, Cantor (2000), Hoskins (1970, 1972) and Mee (1948) were helpful. The other chief sources of information were provided by the internet, by several excellent sites. However, the most informative by far was British Listed Buildings, at www.britishlistedbuildings.co.uk, which includes the data from the national Statutory Buildings Register. An online version of the incomplete Victoria County History for Leicestershire, at www.british-history.ac.uk, also proved invaluable for the 40-odd churches it covers. Several other sites provided information for specific churches, and the 'online guide', a digital version of the old paper church guide, is becoming more common on individual church sites. Other sites concentrate more on the photographic side, and Leicestershire & Rutland Churches: a Photographic Journal, at www.leicestershirechurches.co.uk, contains excellent photographs of many Leicestershire churches presented in a modern enhanced style.

Books

Brandwood, G. K. 1984. The Anglican Churches of Leicester. Leicestershire Museums Publication No. 51. Leicestershire Museums, Art Galleries and Records Service, Leicester.

Brandwood, G. K. 1987. Ancient and Modern, Churches and Chapels around Market Harborough. Leicestershire Museums Publication No. 91. Leicestershire Museums, Art Galleries and Records Service, Leicester.

Brandwood, G. K. 2002. Bringing them to their knees: church building and restoration in Leicestershire and Rutland 1800-1914. Leicestershire Archaeological and Historical Society, Leicester.

Cantor, L. 2000. The Historic Parish Churches of Leicestershire and Rutland. Kairos Press, Newtown Linford, Leicester.

Fewins, C. 2005. The church explorers handbook. Canterbury Press, Norwich.

Firth, J. B. 1926. Highways and Byways in Leicestershire illustrated by Griggs, F. L. Macmillan & Co., Ltd., London.

Harvey, A. and Crowther-Beynon, V. B. 1912. Leicestershire and Rutland. Little Guides series. Metheuen & Co. Ltd., London.

Hoskins, W. G. 1970. A Shell Guide. Leicestershire. Faber & Faber, London.

Hoskins, W. G. 1972. The Heritage of Leicestershire. City of Leicester Publicity Department, Leicester.

Jones, L. E. 1965. The Observer's book of old English churches. Warne, London.

McNamara, D. R. and Tilney, H. 2011. How to read churches: a crash course in ecclesiastical architecture. A. and C. Black (Publishers), London.

Mee, A. 1948. The King's England. Leicestershire and Rutland. Hodder & Stoughton, London.

Pevsner, N. 2003. The Buildings of England, Leicestershire and Rutland. Revised by Williamson, E. Yale University Press, New Haven.

Taylor, R. 2003. How to read a church: a guide to images, symbols and meanings in churches and cathedrals. Rider, London.

Trubshaw, B. 2004. Good Gargoyle Guide. Medieval carvings in Leicestershire and Rutland. Heart of Albion Press, Wymeswold, Loughborough.

Valentine, D. C. 1975. Church Brasses of Leicestershire. Vaughan Paper No. 20, Vaughan Archaeological and Historical Society. University of Leicester.

Whitelaw, J. W. 1996. Hidden Leicestershire and Rutland. Countryside Books, Newbury.

Church Guide Books

Allchin, M. U. 1968. St Edwards Parish Church, Castle Donington. A Guide and History to this Ancient Church. Reprinted 2011.

Anon. undated. A brief history of St. John the Baptist Church and the Village of Muston.

Anon. undated. A guide to All Saints' Church, Nailstone. Diocese of Leicester.

Anon. undated. A short guide to Thornton Parish Church. The British Publishing Company Limited, Gloucester.

Anon. undated. All Saints Church, Cossington. A guide.

Anon. undated. All Saints' Church, Gilmorton. Statement of significance – All Saints' Church Gilmorton (Grade II*).

Anon. undated. Melton Mowbray Parish Church. The British Publishing Company Limited, Gloucester.

Anon. undated. Saint Bartholomew's Church, Foston, Leicestershire.

Anon. undated. St. James the Great, Birstall. Parish of Birstall and Wanlip.

Anon. undated. St. John the Baptist, Grimston, Leicestershire.

Anon. undated. St Mary & St John, Rothley Parish Church, for the curious visitor.

Anon. undated. St. Nicholas Lockington. A brief guide.

Anon. undated. The Church of St Thomas of Canterbury, Frisby on the Wreake.

Anon. undated. The History of the Church of St. Mary, Barkby, Leicestershire.

Anon. undated. Welcome to St Michael & All Angels, Eastwell. A Framland Trail Church.

Anon. 1993. St John the Baptist Church, Billesdon.

Anon. 1994. The Church of Saint Peter, Saltby. A History of the Parish and Description of the Church.

Anon. 1996. St. Peter Brooke. A History & Guide.

Anon. 1999. Wistow through the ages. St. Wistan's Church, Wistow.

Anon. 2004. All Saints Church, Theddingworth. 4th edition.

Anon. 2005. A History of All Saints Lubenham. Whiteoakpress Ltd.

Anon. 2005. The Parish and Collegiate Church of St Mary de Castro, Leicester. History & guide, fully revised and updated. Terry Doughty, Leicester.

Anon. 2009. A walk around Hathern Parish Church.

Anon. 2009. St Nicholas. Leicester's Oldest Place of Worship. Guide Book.

Anon. 2010. St Peter's Church, Thornton. Leicestershire. The Friends of St Peter's, Thornton, Leicestershire.

Anthony, V. 2009. Church of St Peter, Allexton, Leicestershire. The Churches Conservation Trust, London.

Armson, A. 1938. Ibstock. The story of a Leicestershire village.

Armson, J. M. 1991. St. Mary de Castro, Leicester. A brief account. 6th edition.

Banner, J. W. 1985. St. Denys Parish Church, Evington, Leicester.

Banner, R. 2010. A walk around Ratby Church. 3rd edition.

Barker, S. 1984. A History of the Parish Church of St Andrew Welham.

Battell, M. and Liggins, O. undated. A history of the Ancient Parish Church of All Saints, Narborough.

Bilney, K. 2000. St Peter's Church, Leire. Leire Village History Group.

Bloor, L. 1979. A commentary on All Saints' Church, Dunton Bassett.

Brandwood, G. K. 1991. Leicester All Saints. Redundant Churches Fund, London.

Brandwood, G. K. 2003. St Michael & All Angels Church, Edmonthorpe, Leicestershire. Series 4, No. 192. The Churches Conservation Trust, London.

Brandwood, G. K. 2006. All Saints' Church, Highcross Street, Leicester. The Churches Conservation Trust, London.

Brandwood, G. K. 2010. Church of St Mary, Garthorpe, Leicestershire. The Churches Conservation Trust, London.

Brandwood, G. K. and Davies, J. C. 2009. A brief history of the Church of St Dionysius, Market Harborough and The Old Grammar School. Russ Newlands Publishing, Folkestone.

Broughton, J. 1999. 'Ad Majorem Dei Gloriam', A Guide to the Architecture and Furnishings of All Saints Church, Wigston Magna. Broughton Publishing, Wigston Magna, Leicestershire.

Broughton J. 1999. All Saints, Wigston Magna. A History of the Parish Church. Broughton Publishing, Wigston Magna, Leicestershire.

Broughton, J. 2000. 'The Old Church', A History of St Wistan's Church, Wigston Magna. Broughton Publishing, Wigston Magna, Leicestershire.

Brushe, J. 1992. St. John the Baptist, King's Norton, Leicestershire. A guide.

Bullows, M. E. 2007. Saint Thomas Becket Church, Tugby. Monumental Inscriptions.

Caswell, P. J. 1984. The Parish Church of Lutterworth in Leicestershire where John Wycliffe was Rector 1374-1384.

Caswell, P. J. 1984. The Parish Church of Lutterworth in Leicestershire where John Wycliffe was Rector 1734-1384. A guide to Lutterworth Church. Revised edition.

Cherry, S. 2003. Time's Thumb Mark. A guide to All Saints Parish Church, Loughborough. All Saints with Holy Trinity Parochial Church Council, Loughborough.

Chinnery, A. 1983. The Church of St. John the Baptist, Hungarton. Sycamore Press, Wymondham, Leicestershire.

Cocks, T. 1990. Past and Present. A Brief History and Description of the Church of St. Mary Magdalen, Knighton, Leicester. Third Edition.

Collett, A. J. 1996. St. Margaret's Church, Stoke Golding. Jones-Sands Publishing, Coventry.

Cooper, A. 2003. A History of St. Bartholomew's Church, Quorn, Leicestershire. Quorn United Church Council.

D. A. B. 1966. The Parish Church of St. Peter, Tilton-on-the-Hill, Leicestershire. Brief History of the Church.

Dare, M. P. 1955. The Church of St. Mary the Virgin, Bottesford, Leics. and its Monuments. 5th edition. The British Publishing Company Limited, Gloucester.

Day, J. 1999. All Saints' Church, Peatling Magna.

De Lisle, M. R. and Heselton, K. Y. 1991. A walk-round guide to St Peter's Church, Stockerston.

Dixon, H. 2007. A Church Guide and History, The Parish Church of St Mary-the-Virgin, Burrough-on-the-Hill, Leicestershire.

Dunham, A. undated. A walk around Hallaton Church.

Fox, D. 2001. The history of the Church and Parish of Kirkby Mallory. 2nd edition.

Friends of St Peter's. 2010. St Peter's Church, Thornton. Leicestershire. A short history & description. The Friends of St Peter's.

Greiff, M. 2008. Dr. Elias Travers D. D., Rector of Thurcaston cum Cropston, Leics. 1621-1641. Thurcaston & Cropston Local History Society, Village History Series, No. 1.

Haddelsey, S. 2010. Syston Parish Church, a short history and guide.

Hawker, K. 2003. The Church of St. Peter, Thornton, Leics. A short guide & history. Friends of St Peter's, Thornton, Leicestershire.

Heselton, K. Y. 2003. The Church of St Nicholas, Bringhurst.

Heselton, K. Y. 2005. St. Andrew's Church, Great Easton. 2nd edition.

Hooper, B. E. 2009. Parish Affairs, The Financial Dealings of Thurcaston Parish from the Distant Past to the Present. Thurcaston & Cropston Local History Society, Village History Series, No. 2.

Ireland, D. 2000. History of Holy Rood Church, Packington. The Packington Village History Group.

Jeffries, B. 2005. Wartnaby Parish and Church of St. Michael and All Angels. A history of the church and village.

Jones, G. undated. St Margaret, Leicester. History and fabric of the Prebendal Church.

Jones, N. 2007. All Saints Church, Sheepy Magna.

Jones, R. 2011. View from a (Ratcliffe) pew. The Sheepy Group Gazette. Volume 13, Issue 5.

Lacey, J. 2008. St. Nicholas Church, Mowsley. The Mowsley Heritage Society.

Leicestershire Historic Churches Preservation Trust. 2000. Historic Churches. No. 1 North Leicestershire, No. 2 South Leicestershire, No. 3 East Leicestershire, No. 4 West Leicestershire, No. 5 Leicester. Leicestershire County Council.

Lynam, J. E. 1976. Welcome to Stonesby "The Village by the Tree Stump".

Mack, H. 1947. Shepshed Parish Church. A short history of the Church of St. Botolph, Shepshed (Regis) and matters of ecclesiastical interest connected therewith.

M. B. and J. P. undated. The Story of Skeffington. A short history of Skeffington. Skeffington Church. Skeffington Hall. Skeffington Village.

Meredith, R. 2005. A little history of Cold Overton and its Church. The Church of St. John the Baptist, Cold Overton, Leicestershire.

Morris, E. undated. The Prebendal Church of St. Margaret, Leicester. A short historical and descriptive account. The Church Publishers, Kent.

Ockenden, M. 2009. Holy Trinity Church, Ashby de la Zouch. A brief guide.

Owens, J-A. 2001. The Church of St. Botolph and St. John the Baptist, Croxton Kerrial. Guide book.

Phillips, K. C. and P. R. 1974. A Guide to Thurnby Parish Church. Thurnby Parochial Church Council.

Rampton, R. 2009. Parish Church of St. Peter, Whetstone.

Reed, A. 1999. Some historical notes on Twycross Church.

Rees, G. undated. St Nicholas Church, Mowsley. A short history.

Revill, D. 2007. A History of the Church of St John the Baptist, Old Dalby. 2nd edition.

Reynolds, R. E. undated. A short guide to Fenny Drayton church and village.

Robinson, N. undated. A brief guide to St Peter's Church, Market Bosworth.

Scott, J. E. 1982. Ellistown from 1140 to 1982. The story of "The Town that Ellis Built". St Christopher's Church, Ellistown, Leicester.

Smith, E. D. 1968. The Parish Church of St. Luke, Gaddesby.

Smith, G. 2004. St. Andrew's Church, Aylestone. A short history. St. Andrew's Parochial Church Council, Aylestone.

Smith-Carington, J. H. 1990. Guide to St Mary's Church, Ashby Folville. Reprinted 2009.

St. Mary's District Church Council. 1992. St. Mary's Church, Melton Mowbray, Leicestershire. A walk round guide.

Taylor, K. 2002. St Michael & All Angels' Church, Cosby. A short history.

Taylor, R. 2010. St. Denys' Church Goadby Marwood, Leicestershire. A history and guide. 2nd reprint edn.

Taylor, R. P. 1976. St. Peter's Church, Wymondham, Leicestershire. A history and description.

Templeman, S. undated. St Bartholomew's Church. Visitor's guide. (Quorn)

Tyldesley, D. W. 1981. A History of the Parish Church of All Saints, Sapcote, Leicestershire. Rev'd Tyldesley, Sapcote Rectory, Leicestershire.

Tyler, V. 2005. The Parish of the Six Saints circa Holt. The Church of St Giles, Medbourne.

Wessel, C. 1989. St Martin's Church, Desford. An illustrated guide. Desford & District Local History Group.

White, P. 1998. Prestwold and its church. Reprint, Loughborough.

Wilcox, P. 2000. Holy Trinity Church, Thrussington.

Williams, B. undated. All Saints' Church Long Whatton.

Williams, B. C. J. 1996. The story of St. Mary and St. Hardulph Church, Breedon on the Hill. A history guide.

Leaflets

A brief guide to St. Guthlac's Church, Stathern, Leicestershire.

A brief history of St. Mary the Virgin, Bottesford.

A history guide to St. Luke's Church, Gaddesby.

All Saints Church, Asfordby, Leicestershire.

All Saints Church, Hoby. Parish of the Upper Wreake.

All Saints' Church, Somerby, Leicestershire. A guide.

Appleby Magna Parish Church. A short guide.

Brief history of St Mary Magdalen Church in Knighton.

Brief notes on the history of St. Leonard's Church, Swithland, Leicestershire.

BGS. 2011. All Saints Church Husbands Bosworth. A brief history.

Bradgate Sewing Circle. 2001. The Rothley Heritage. The story of Rothley sewn into a tapestry in 1999 & displayed in the parish church.

Framland Church Trail. Leicestershire County Council.

Parish Church of St. Mary the Virgin, Osgathorpe.

St. Andrew's Church, Twyford, Leicestershire.

St Botolph's Church, Shepshed in the Diocese of Leicester. A brief introduction to the many historical features now visible to visitors.

St. James, Little Dalby. Church, hall and people.

St Nicholas' Church, South Kilworth.

St Thomas Becket Church, Tugby, Leicestershire.

The Church of Saint Helen, Plungar.

The History of Elmesthorpe Church.

The Parish Church of St Mary, Sileby, Leicestershire.

The Parish Church of St. Michael and All Angels, Markfield.

The Parish of Saint John the Baptist Church, Hungarton.

Thurlaston Church – a brief history. Revised 2010.

Welcome to All Saints' Church, Cadeby.

Welcome to our Village and St. Peter's Church, Shackerstone.

Welcome to St. Mary's Church, Melton Mowbray.

Welcome to St. Peter's Church, Oadby.

A last word - the top twenty five

Just a little indulgence before I sign off. The following is a purely subjective and personal list of what I consider to be the twenty five churches that simply have to be seen in Leicestershire, in completely random order:

Kirkby Mallory, Bottesford, Breedon on the Hill, Thornton, Gaddesby, Lockington, Peatling Magna, Croxton Kerrial, Leicester St Mary de Castro, Orton on the Hill, Prestwold, Aylestone, Shepshed, Melton Mowbray, Tur Langton, Sutton Cheney, Tilton on the Hill, Peckleton, Ashby de la Zouch St Helens, Barkby, Lubenham, Hallaton, Theddingworth, Ashby Folville and Claybrooke.

I wish you many happy days in them, and in all Leicestershire's parish churches. And don't forget that all our churches need financial support, please leave a donation after your visit.

Andrew Swift, Easter 2013